The HIGHLANDS

CALUM MACLEAN INTERVIEWING ANGUS MACNEILL AT SMEARISARRY

The HIGHLANDS

Calum I. Maclean

FOREWORD BY
Sorley Maclean

WITH PHOTOGRAPHS BY
Cailean Maclean

MAINSTREAM
PUBLISHING

The Publisher acknowledges subsidy of the Scottish Arts Council
in the production of this volume.

This edition published in Great Britain in 1990 by
MAINSTREAM PUBLISHING COMPANY (EDINBURGH) LTD
7 Albany Street
Edinburgh EH1 3UG
ISBN 1 85158 365 3 (cloth)

Jacket photographs by Cailean Maclean:
Loch Garry looking west in winter and summer.

British Library Cataloguing in Publication Data
Maclean, Calum
The highlands.
1. Scottish culture: highlands culture, history
I. Title
941.15

ISBN 1-85158-365-3

Design and Finished Artwork by James Hutcheson and Paul Keir
Typeset in 10/12 Goudy by Novatext Graphix Limited, Edinburgh
Printed in Great Britain by Butler and Tanner, Frome, Somerset

Tha an saoghal fhathast àlainn

Acknowledgments

The family of Calum Maclean acknowledge the help of the following in the preparation of this edition of *The Highlands*: Bill Campbell, Peter MacKenzie and all the staff of Mainstream Publishing Co.; Seán Ó Súilleabháin, for giving permission to reprint his "Memoir"; Peter MacLeod, for giving permission to reprint his later brother John's elegy "Do Chalum Iain MacGhill Eathain"; Donald A. MacDonald for his translations; and to Frank Thompson, whose excellent work on the second edition of this book greatly facilitated the production of the third.

CONTENTS

GLEN FINNAN: "THE PRINCE'S MONUMENT STANDS AS A SILENT, GAUNT REMINDER OF THE DAY, 19 AUGUST 1745, WHEN THE STANDARD WAS RAISED TO STRIKE A LAST BLOW FOR THE STEWARTS."

FOREWORD

BY SORLEY MACLEAN

IT IS right that one of my brother Alasdair's sons should have done so much for this book, for no one did more than Alasdair and his wife Rena for Calum, especially when he needed it most, during his last illness. The book hardly needs an introduction by me or anyone else when it contains such a noble Memoir by Seán Ó Súilleabháin, who quotes generously from the "noble tribute" Basil Megaw paid to Calum in *Scottish Studies 1960*, fifteen years before Ó Súilleabháin's Memoir in the 1975 Club Leabhar edition of the book. Such tributes I find especially moving when I think of the affectionate words Calum so often used of Megaw and Ó Súilleabháin to myself, words of the warmest affection and admiration. Ó Súilleabháin says that Calum, "a full-time collector, though coming on the scene almost a century later, when traditions had thinned out a great deal, was destined to surpass, in both extent and quality these early pioneers". These pioneers included John Francis Campbell of Islay, Hector MacLean, Hector Urquhart, John Dewar and Alexander Carmichael. In 1962 Professor Nicolaisean, Professor of English and Folklore at the State University of New York at Binghampton and 1961 President of the American Folklore Society, wrote for *Fabula* of Calum, "He was always conscious of being a successor to those great collectors who had gone before him: John Francis Campbell of Islay . . . Hector MacLean, Alexander Carmichael, Ewan Maclachlan and others; and he excelled them all."

The admiration and affection that Calum evoked in colleagues and other scholars and writers was almost universal. One has only to look at *Tocher* (Number 39), edited by Alan Bruford, Donald Archie MacDonald and Cathie Scott, to realise that; and I am certain that there were many more, some people I myself knew well and many that I never saw or read or even heard of.

In that *Tocher*, the great first article is by Dr Hamish Henderson. There are also articles by Francis Collinson, who wrote the Pibroch "Lament for Calum MacLean"; by the present Director of the School of Scottish Studies, Donald Archie MacDonald; by Alan Bruford; by Miss Ann Munro; by Miss Jemima Sutherland; and by Donia Etherington. Dr John Macinnes is quoted as saying that Calum was "a master of Gaelic prose", and I myself quote Dr Stewart Sanderson's opinion that Calum was the bravest man he had ever known. Roger Leitch notes a very cordial opinion of Calum by John Macinnes (Iain Pheadair) and a very cordial one from Donald John MacDonald of Peninerine, son of the famous Duncan.

In other places I have heard or seen references to Calum's friendliness, kindness, devotion to Scotland and to his work and to his fellow Highlanders and to his "immense courage" from all kinds of people, too numerous to mention, but they include George Campbell Hay, Iain Crichton Smith, Professor Strömbäck, Professor Oke Campbell, David Murison, Hector McIver, Louis MacNeice, David Thomson, Alan Lomax, the Lewis poet Norman MacLeod, Gordon MacLennan, and Irish men and women such as Nessa Ní Shé, Seán MacRéamoinn, Professor de Bhaldraithe and many more. I was greatly moved by the Irish scholar, the late Dr Tom Wall, asking me to be allowed to keep a book of Calum's, and by the words of Ó Ceileacher, the Irish poet, when I was one of the four Scots, with Morag Montgomery, Angus MacDonald and William MacDonald, reading and singing and piping at Clonmel. Ó Ceileacher said that if it had been known that I was a brother of Calum's, the great crowd present would have been quintupled. A few years ago, Sandy Russell of Newtonmore, Convener of the Highland Region, said that knowing Calum was by far the best thing that Edinburgh University had given him.

The famous "Jake" MacDonald said that Calum was the "greatest personality" he had ever known, and that fine and humorous Uistman, John MacLeod, wrote the moving elegy in this book. Lesley Scott Moncrieff and Professor de Bhaldraithe called sons after Calum.

It was in 1958 that Calum finished *The Highlands* and in 1959 it was first published by Batsford and sold out very soon, but it was not reprinted until 1975, by Club Leabhar. For that reprint, which added three elegies and Seán Ó Súilleabháin's great Memoir, my brother John and I were greatly indebted to the generous representations of Dr John Lorne Campbell of Canna, and of course, to Frank Thompson of Club Leabhar.

The Highlands have changed much since the book was written. For instance, Calum's beloved Lochaber has been industrialised and largely de-industrialised since 1958, and I doubt if Calum's ardent Jacobitism would have remained so very strong after the researches of so many brilliant new historians, but I am certain that his Scottish Nationalism would have become even stronger than it was in 1958. The Prince, Charles Edward Stuart, of course, was the only Prince to so many of Calum's most beloved helpers, such as the bard John MacDonald of Lochaber, and Calum was so fond of men like John MacDonald and the MacKenzies of Strathglass that his own feelings could not fail to be strongly affected by theirs. But it is invidious to mention some and not others; and there were many more, and many of those were not specially Jacobite or Nationalist or Catholic, for the chapters include Morar, Arisaig and Moidart; Ardgour, Ardnamurchan and Morvern; Badenoch; Urquhart and Glenmoriston; Strathglass, Easter Ross and Inverness; Sutherland and Wester Ross; Lorn and West Perthshire. He praised tradition-bearers in Free Church and Free Presbyterian areas even more than those in Catholic and Episcopalian and Church of Scotland areas, for the former had greater obstacles. Nevertheless, there was much in Calum of the "noble ingénu", of which I saw very much in George Campbell Hay. The book does not deal with the Islands nor with Shetland and the Borders.

Calum was famous for his dealings with old people, the tradition-bearers, but there was one occasion when he was helped by an act of kindness by our father many years before he met the recipient. Sometimes Calum was inclined to play down those of his own MacLean name, for he mentions as Dundee's followers at Killiecrankie, MacDonalds, Camerons and Stewarts. I have gathered from history that there were more MacLeans than Stewarts at Killiecrankie. When he mentions Skye misbehaviour in Glenmoriston after Culloden, he says that only the "dregs" of Skye would have been Hanoverians. Perhaps he was right if he remembered that those "dregs" were probably only one or two with power, floating on the top. Of course, Calum was dealing in this book only with the Highland mainland. Probably his favourite place of all was South Uist (he had not collected in North Uist, Harris or Lewis), but I know he was bowled over by Mull. He was hardly in Tiree or Islay, and in Barra he had the greatest of friends, such as James MacKinnon, Donald Joseph Mackinnon and Calum Johnston. His great friends in Uist were innumerable, so much so that it would be invidious to mention any in particular. In Edinburgh there was one than whom no one was better to him. I speak of Stuart MacGregor.

I know Calum loved the people of every district in Scotland in which he worked and that he was loved in all, not only in the Highlands and Western Isles but in Shetland, Ireland, Sweden and Norway as well. He combined zeal, unworldliness and great humour and friendliness; and this book reflects that. It was a Lewisman who, hearing of his death, said in four words: "*Calum, an gille glan.*" I think that this book too is *Leabhar glan*.

MEMOIR

BY SEÁN Ó SÚILLEABHÁIN

THE first time that I laid eyes on Calum Maclean was one autumn day in 1939. The offices of the Irish Folklore Commission where I worked were on the top floor of University College, Dublin, and, as I was passing through the crowded hallway on the ground floor, I noticed the usual group of students standing, between lectures, around the notice-board of An Cumann Gaelach (The Irish Language Society). There was something unusual about the group that day, however, for in their midst was a young man who wore a Scottish kilt. He was low-sized and sturdy, and seemed, from the laughter of the group, to be the life and soul of the party. I passed on, not knowing that he was Calum Maclean, or that, within a short while, he would become a colleague of mine and a very dear friend.

Calum was born on the island of Raasay, between Skye and the mainland of Scotland, on 6 September 1915. He was the third son of Calum Maclean, a tailor, and his wife, Curstaidh Nicolson, of Braes in Skye. Two of Calum's brothers became doctors, and two others, headmasters of secondary schools; Somhairle, now headmaster at Plockton, is acknowledged as being one of the finest Scots-Gaelic poets of recent centuries. From Portree Secondary School, Calum went to study the Celtic languages at the University of Edinburgh, from 1935 to 1937, under Professor W. J. Watson, and graduated with First Class Honours, under J. Carmichael Watson, in 1939. He also won the McCaig and Macpherson Scholarships, which enabled him to go to University College, Dublin, to study Early Irish under Professor Osborn Bergin and Medieval and Modern Welsh under Professor J. Lloyd-Jones.

When war broke out in 1939, Calum's scholarships came to an end, and he looked around for some means of livelihood in Ireland. He found work in a factory in Clonmel, Co. Tipperary, which unfortunately came to an end when shortage of materials forced the factory to suspend operations. While in Clonmel, Calum became a Catholic.

He was attracted to Connemara and stayed with the Dillon family at Indreabhán, west of Galway city, where Irish was generally spoken. He grew interested in the local traditions and contacted the Irish Folklore Commission, which took him on as a part-time collector and paid him some money for what he was able to collect. Aided by his knowledge of his native tongue, Scots-Gaelic, he quickly acquired a knowledge of the local dialect of Irish, and from August 1942 to February 1945 he sent to the Commission a large body of South Connemara lore, which is now bound in six volumes, amounting to over 2,300 manuscript pages, written in minuscule hand, the letters of the words separated as they would be in print; that was Calum's style of handwriting.

Calum's main informant in Indreabhán was Maitiú Mór Ó Tuathail, aged eighty-two, from whom he recorded a large number of tales, some of the international variety, others derived from the heroic Gaelic world, still others belonging to the realm of local *seanchas* (traditional lore).

A singer himself, it was to be expected that Calum would have a quick ear for local songs, and this led to his special interest in the poetic compositions of his friend, Pádhraic (Larry) Ó Fínneadha, a native of the district in which he was collecting. He set about writing down the songs of this poet which were in local currency; there was no scarcity of them, as Pádhraic was very productive and could turn out a long song about any local event which caught his fancy. Having collected as many of the songs as he could discover, Calum edited them, with a fine introduction and explanatory notes, and submitted his work as a thesis for a Master of Arts Degree at University College, Dublin. In this he was successful.

Having been brought up in the Gaelic tradition of his native Scotland and later having savoured the same tradition, with only minor shades of difference, in Connemara, Calum was able to make the following perceptive remarks about local poets in his introduction. I translate:

> There still are, in the Gaelic-speaking areas of both Ireland and Scotland, local poets about whom very little is known in the outside world. They compose poems and songs which are rarely, if ever, written down. The people of the district learn them by heart, however, and sing them by the fireside, and thus they become known throughout the district. It is seldom that they spread beyond the local confines, because they are of interest mainly to the poet's neighbours. The compositions of such poets may not win much acclaim as poetry; still, their works are of interest and even importance since they give us an insight not only into the mind of the poets themselves but also into that of the local people and into their way of life. The Poet of Lochán (Ó Fínneadha) needs no apology or introduction as his poems and songs are already part of the lore of his neighbours. They are sung by the firesides in Cois Fharraige (South Connemara), and they would live on even if they were never written down. Pádhraic Ó Fínneadha was born at a time when history was being made in Ireland (Land War years of the late nineteenth century); that is why even people outside of Cois Fharraige will be interested in his songs, since his outlook was wider than is normally the case with local poets.

It may be apposite here to state that some of Ó Fínneadha's poems, with Calum's notes, were published in *Ar Aghaidh*, an Irish monthly, by the editor, An t-Athair P. E. Mac Fhinn, from January 1961 onwards; the thesis otherwise remains unpublished.

As the name Colm (Calum) is quite common in Connemara, the Indreabhán people silently decided to refer to the visitor from Scotland as Colm Albanach, to indicate the land of his origin. His Dublin friends often spoke of him as Colm Beag, since he was low-sized. All had a deep personal affection for him.

In April 1945, he was appointed a member of the indoor staff of the Irish Folklore Commission, and I had the pleasurable duty of training him as a cataloguer of folklore. I myself had been trained at Uppsala ten years previously and had adapted the Swedish system for use in Ireland. Calum quickly learned the craft. He was very intelligent, I need hardly say, very assiduous in his work, and an extremely pleasant companion.

He set about excerpting some printed collections of Scottish folklore as a start: *Waifs and Strays of Celtic Tradition* (1889), edited by Lord Archibald Campbell; *Sia Sgialachdan*, a collection of tales made and edited by John Lorne Campbell of Canna; and *The White Wife* (1865), by Cuthbert Bede. He went on to make thousands of card-references to the contents of the first three (out of four) volumes of John Francis Campbell's *Popular Tales of the West Highlands* (1860-2). As an extension of this excerpting from printed sources, he began to make card-references to the contents of 364 manuscript pages of folklore collected in Eriskay in 1933 by Donald MacDonald, a native of that island, who was then a student at Glasgow University. This fine collection of Scots-Gaelic lore from beyond the Sea of Moyle was the first acquired by Professor Delargy for the Irish Folklore Institute (which preceded the Commission). It consisted of many folktales and scores of riddles, some recorded from Archibald MacInnes of Eriskay, whom MacDonald mentioned as being "one of the few who supplied Mrs Kennedy Fraser with most of her songs when she was collecting in Eriskay in 1905".

On 19 December 1945, Calum set out for Scotland on a preliminary expedition as collector on behalf of the Irish Folklore Commission. I translate from his diary, written two days later:

> I, Calum I. Maclean, began two days ago to collect the oral tradition of the island of Raasay. I was born and reared on this island. When I was young there were many people here who had tales and songs which had never been written down, and which never will be, since the old

people are now dead, and all that they knew is with them in the grave. There are still some people alive who remember some of the songs and traditions of their forefathers, and as it seemed to me that there were more songs than anything else available, I decided to write down those which I could find. I realise that we are sixty years late in beginning this work of collection, but we may be able to save at least some of the traditional lore before it dies out. I must express my pleasure at meeting those whose names I shall mention in my notebook. It is they who have remembered what others have forgotten, and it is they who deserve thanks for what I hope to be able to save.

He collected in Raasay until February 1946, from his father, Calum, his mother, Curstaidh, his brother, Somhairle, his aunt, Peggy Maclean, and his uncle, Angus Nicolson. The material recorded was mainly songs and associated lore, 390 pages in all. In a final note, Calum remarked: "I have now finished my first collection of Scots-Gaelic lore. There are many other songs still to be recorded. All of those which I have written down have associated airs, save one, and all of the tunes are different from one another. It is a great 'sin' that I was not born thirty years earlier, as the best of the lore has gone into the grave with those who had it. There is a terrible gale blowing here today."

Calum returned to continue his cataloguing work in the Dublin archives until June. As there was still no central folklore institute in Scotland in 1946, the Director of the Commission decided to ask Calum to work in his native land and to transmit what he could collect to Dublin. While very anxious to help in the preservation of the lore of Scotland, Calum was lonely at leaving Ireland. I translate from his diary:

> June 22, 1946. At six o'clock this evening, I boarded a ship in Dublin on my way to Scotland. Although the weather was beautiful, I was very lonely to leave Ireland. I bade farewell to her and gave her my blessing. I love everything in Ireland: the men and the women, the boys and the children, the active youths and the beautiful girls. Ireland, the delightful and lovely! I remained on the upper deck until the mountains of Wicklow faded from sight. Then I went to bed.

He first re-visited his home in Raasay and kept a diary for each day's work, mentioning the weather and the local happenings. This he continued to do for the subsequent four-and-a-half years while he still worked in Scotland for the Irish Folklore Commission. For that time, his diaries alone fill five bound volumes (over 2,000 pages), and the lore which he collected is bound in nineteen volumes, comprising over 9,000 manuscript pages. The Commission had supplied him with an Ediphone recording machine, similar to those used by the collectors in Ireland, as well as wax cylinders, which he regularly transmitted to Dublin together with the transcriptions. He was in constant touch by letter and telephone with the Dublin office, to which he returned occasionally to report progress and receive fresh instructions.

From Raasay he went to Eigg and on to Canna, where he received a warm welcome and generous help from John Lorne Campbell. He then crossed the sea to South Uist and Benbecula in April 1947. So rich was the vein of folktales in these two islands, that he spent almost a year-and-a-half recording from storytellers there, but especially from two, to be mentioned later: Angus (Barrach) MacMillan of Griminish, Benbecula, and Duncan Macdonald of Peninerine, South Uist. Those two fine storytellers died in 1954, by which time Calum has succeeded in saving much of their extensive repertoire of tales.

It may truthfully be said that, with his discovery of the folklore riches of these two islands and his devotion in recording them, Calum's real life-work had begun. He was ideally suited for the task; he was a native speaker of Scots-Gaelic and had already some experience of collecting in both Ireland and Scotland. He was in good health, though partly deaf, and had the ability to endure and survive the rigours of field-work under adverse conditions. But, above all else, his personal qualities stood him in good stead and opened all doors and hearts to him in his homeland, as in Ireland. He had kindness, generosity, open-heartedness, candour and firmness of opinion; he was good-humoured and light of heart. He was unselfishly devoted to his task. He loved country people best of all perhaps, and his ability to sing or lilt or play music or tell stories ensured that he was quickly accepted into the company of strangers.

Easy acceptance of a collector of folklore by a strange community is by no means automatic. Country people in general are conservative and reserved by nature and rather suspicious of one who comes among them from outside, especially if he is equipped with pen, notebook, or recording machine. I still remember with amusement a cartoon in *Punch* of a middle-aged folklore collector, wearing knickerbockers, seated on a chair in the centre of the floor of a country tavern, pen and notebook at the ready to record folklore, while the locals, standing along the bar, all look at him as if he were some exotic specimen which had escaped from a zoo! Good collectors, such as Calum, do not approach their task in this manner. They make enquiries before entering a new area about the most likely informants to be found there and are introduced to one or two of them quietly by some local person of their acquaintance, such as a teacher. The confidence of a new informant can never be won by a lofty approach; he must be told news and stories from outside by the visitor and gradually given to understand that he has a great deal to tell which nobody else can do equally well. Once such an approach has been made, personal contact and understanding are quickly established, and mutual trust and friendship follow. Calum was the ideal collector in this way. People liked him from their first meeting, and he gave almost as much as he got in the course of his work.

Apart from his diaries, Calum has left us, in an article entitled "Hebridean Traditions" (*Gwerin*,1., 1956), an invaluable account of his work as collector in the Hebrides during the four-and-a-half years 1946-50, when he was on the staff of the Irish Folklore Commission, and the succeeding years as a member of the School of Scottish Studies in Edinburgh. In that article, he devoted some introductory paragraphs to the Hebridean landscape, to the influence of the Vikings on local place-names, to the systems of landholding and the general economy of the islands in recent centuries, to the disappearance of the "black house" and the old ways of agriculture, as well as to the state of the vernacular Gaelic language. He found that piping and traditional dancing still flourished, and some fine Gaelic singers were still alive.

Two deservedly famous part-time collectors had preceded Calum in the Hebrides. The first of these was John Francis Campbell of Islay (1822-85), who was urged by G. W. Dasent (translator of the folk-tales collected by Asbjørnsen and Moe in Norway, under the title, *Popular Tales from the Norse*) to visit the Outer Hebrides — just as the Irish poet, W. B. Yeats, was later to advise the playwright, John Millington Synge, to turn his back on Paris and go to the Aran Islands. Campbell's *Popular Tales of the West Highlands*, already mentioned, resulted. Edited, with a fine introduction by Campbell, the tales were garnered with the aid of many collectors, notably Hector Maclean, an Islay schoolmaster, Hector Urquhart, a gamekeeper from Ross-shire, and John Dewar of Arrochar. The four volumes contain about one thousand tales, mainly from South Uist and Barra. Describing his visit to the Hebrides in 1859, Campbell wrote:

> Men and women of all ages could and did tell me stories, children of all ages listened to them; and it was self-evident that the people generally knew and enjoyed them. Elsewhere I had been told that thirty or forty years ago men used to congregate and tell stories; here I was told that they now spend whole winter nights about the fire listening to these old world tales; in every cluster of houses is some old man famed as 'good at *sgeulachdan*', whose house is a winter

evening's resort. I visited these and listened, often with wonder, at the extraordinary power of memory shown by untaught old men.

The other collector arrived in the Hebrides about 1865. He was Alexander Carmichael (1823-1912), whose five volumes of chàrms, incantations, and folk prayers are an outstanding thesaurus of that type of religious and semi-religious poetic lore. Carmichael also noted, as Calum has stated, much valuable information about beliefs and festival customs, grazing and tillage customs, agricultural methods, field monuments, legends and tales, as well as items about storytellers of the latter half of the nineteenth century.

It is not to be wondered at that Calum Maclean, a full-time collector, though coming on the scene almost a century later when traditions had thinned out a great deal, was destined to surpass, in both extent and quality, the work done by these early pioneers.

Calum, during his fourteen years as collector in Scotland, recorded from some hundreds of persons. Of these, he has told how four especially made a strong impression on him by their rich repertoire of tales and other traditional lore. He had been but a few months working in the Outer Hebrides when he was told about a famous storyteller, still alive in Barra at that time. His name was Seumas MacKinnon, who lived near the road to Northbay on the island's eastern shore. He was a shoemaker and was busy at his work when Calum called to meet him for the first time. "For any folklore collector," Calum wrote, "the crucial time is when contact is first made with the tradition-bearer. To Seumas MacKinnon I was a complete stranger, and much depended on the outcome of our first meeting. Every folklore collector must be prepared to efface himself and approach even the most humble tradition-bearer with the deference due to the high and exalted." How true! Calum spoke to Seumas in Gaelic, and the old man, then aged eighty, was immediately pleased. "I noticed that he was very tall," wrote Calum. "His face was weather-beaten and his features were beautifully chiselled. He wore the blue-peaked cap of fishermen and blue dungarees. The life of eighty years had been spent as much on sea as on land. At eighty he was still a very handsome old man. He was the first practised storyteller I had heard in Scotland. His diction was crisp, concise and clear. Every sentence was short and perfectly balanced. His style was that of the traditional Gaelic storyteller. His voice was beautifully clear and pleasing. He stamped his own personality on every story he told, and his lively sense of humour enhanced his story-telling considerably. His aim was to delight and entertain, and he certainly did both."

MacKinnon had learned his tales sixty years previously from an old bed-ridden man named Roderick Macdonald who lived in a "black house" in Earsary on the eastern coast of Barra. When Seumas and some young men came to old Roderick's house each winter evening, the mattress on which the old man was lying was taken from the sleeping quarters and placed beside the fire, which was in the centre of the floor. When Roderick had been propped up into a comfortable position, he started to tell his stories; these were the tales which Calum recorded from Seumas sixty years later. Such is the occasional tenacity of folk memory! MacKinnon had never been to school, could neither read nor write, and knew little, if any, English. Calum spent five months recording some of his tales, and his repertoire was far from being exhausted at the end. He was eighty-eight when Calum last visited him in March 1956, "resting after a day's work planting potatoes".

One summer in the late 40s, Calum invited me to visit him in Scotland; it was my second visit to that country. We travelled together by train from Glasgow through the beautiful countryside by Glenfinnan to Morar, where we spent two days. On Sunday afternoon we went on a sea-excursion to Isle Oronsay, and next day crossed by steamer to Lochboisdale in South

Uist. After spending a week in Barra, we returned via Eriskay to Benbecula, and stayed together at the house of Angus Maclellan, where Calum usually resided when collecting on that island.

Next day he took me to meet a man whom he described as the greatest storyteller he had met thus far, Angus (Barrach) MacMillan of Griminish. Two years previously, Calum had heard of Angus' prowess as a narrator of tales and had already recorded a large number of them from him when I met him. For myself, going to meet such a man was like making a pilgrimage. Angus was seventy-two years of age at that time; powerfully-built and over six feet tall, he was wearing a blue "gansey" as he sat by the fire. As I had only a smattering of Scots-Gaelic, as spoken, I had difficulty in understanding the long tale which Calum recorded from him for my benefit. When the narration was over, Calum, as was his wont, replayed on the Ediphone machine the concluding sentences of the tale in order to check the clarity of the recording, and Angus, having heard his own voice again, gave his usual verdict (as Calum later told me) by uttering the only word of English which he knew: "Perfection".

In eighteen months, Calum recorded from Angus MacMillan such a large collection of tales that they occupy almost 5,000 large manuscript pages, bound in volumes in the folklore archives in Dublin. He later spent a similar period recording from Angus for the School of Scottish Studies. The storyteller had learned the tales from his father, who had died in 1917. "Angus maintains," Calum wrote, "that he has not even a third of the tales his father had." Like Seumas MacKinnon, Angus could neither read nor write. He was endowed, however, with a prodigious memory, and some of his longer romantic tales took from seven to nine hours to narrate (this would be abnormal in more recent Irish storytelling). One bound manuscript volume in Dublin contains almost 300 large manuscript pages of autobiography, as dictated by Angus to Calum. He was a truly remarkable man. He died in May 1954.

Calum's next great storyteller, Duncan MacDonald of Peninerine in South Uist, died three weeks later. His ancestors had been hereditary bards to the MacDonalds of Skye, and his people had been poets and storytellers for generations. Duncan had taught himself to read and write Gaelic, and was himself a poet. Calum regarded him as the greatest stylist among the storytellers whom he had met in Scotland: "He tells stories perpetually and is now (1956) a master of the art. His command of language is magnificent, and some of his tales are highly ornamented."

A fourth prolific narrator of tales, whom Calum discovered, also deserves a special mention. He was John Macdonald (the Bard), a roadman of Lochaber, from whom he recorded a total of 524 tales, some of them short and part of local *seanachas*, during his first five months with the School of Scottish Studies in 1951. Calum described MacDonald as having a wonderful fund of local historical lore: "He seems to know everything that ever took place in Lochaber. He can give the date of almost every battle and clan fight as far back as the fifteenth century, almost to the exact day and month of the year."

Calum has also left us a good summary of the protocol associated with storytelling:

> There are strict rules of etiquette regarding the telling of tales. When a stranger visits a house, the goodman tells the first tale. The stranger has then to continue for the rest of the night. No son tells a tale to the company in the presence of his father, and no younger brother in the presence of an elder brother. Men as a rule are the story-tellers, but here were quite a number of women story-tellers too. Several of these are still remembered in Benbecula and in other islands. In two houses in Benbecula fifty years ago old women told tales to regular visitors. Several men have recorded tales heard from old women. In a family of tradition-bearers the men have the tales, the women the songs.

16

Calum transferred on loan from the Irish Folklore Commission to the new School of Scottish Studies on New Year's Day 1951. The Commission gave the School a microfilm copy of all its Scottish folklore manuscripts. Mr Basil Megaw, Director of the School, paid a noble tribute (*Scottish Studies* 1960) to Calum's devoted work during the nine-and-a-half years when he was based in Edinburgh, both as collector and as archivist: "He gave himself unsparingly to the great work of recording the traditional tales, customs and beliefs of his own countrymen. It has been estimated that the enormous Gaelic collection he made during that time amounts to nearly a hundred miles of tape; but his constant warning was that this was very far from being enough." Calum also made recordings in Shetland and in the Borders. Mr Megaw continued:

> The full significance and range of the oral material preserved as a result of Calum Maclean's work in Scotland will only become apparent after years of study, but already Scandinavian and other scholars who have had access to it have expressed their admiration for the skill and care displayed in the recording, no less than the intrinsic value of the material. The unique combination of his inherited gifts, training and experience, lends particular weight to his own final conclusion that, for richness in oral tradition, no area in these islands — not excepting even the west of Ireland — can compare with South Uist.

Although Calum spent so much time collecting in the field, often in the depths of winter, and transcribing the material, he still found time, after studying under Professor Dag Strömbäck in Uppsala, to set up an index-system for Scottish folklore based on the Swedish one (as had been done in Ireland). He contributed many articles to folklore journals, reviewed several books, contributed to BBC programmes, and, just a year before he died, had the pleasure of seeing published his great book, *The Highlands* (1959), to this reprint of which I am honoured to contribute this personal tribute to my friend, the author.

In 1957 Calum lost his left arm in an operation. By that time too, his hearing had become still more impaired, but he bore these afflictions with stoic courage, and even his sense of humour survived. He wrote to me in the summer of 1958 to say that he wished to come to Dublin to see the All-Ireland Hurling final at Croke Park. We went to the game together, and he spent a week with me, renewing old acquaintances, still gay and laughing as had been his wont. One of his favourite stories described how, on a night of howling gale and raging sea the previous winter, he had set out on the steamer *Loch Mór* for Lochboisdale, and had met on board another man, very tipsy, who had also lost an arm. As the ship pitched and rolled, the stranger had taught Calum how to tie his shoelaces with his remaining hand. "He was the best teacher I have ever had the good luck to meet!" said Calum.

Calum never sought honours or the limelight. His delight in, and devotion to, his work were his main reward. A few weeks before he died, news reached him that the University of St Francis Xavier in Antigonish, Nova Scotia, had decided to confer on him the degree of LL.D., *honoris causa*, in recognition of his great work for Scotland. I feel, knowing his nature and his humility, that he would willingly have transferred that great honour, were it possible, to each of the storytellers with whom he had worked for so long.

Bidding farewell to his colleagues at the School of Scottish Studies, as he was about to leave for the hospital in South Uist where he was soon to die (16 August 1960), he begged them not to inscribe the word "scholar" on his tombstone. Thus spoke the humble Calum Maclean whom we all loved.

LOCH SUNART FROM ARDSLIGNISH, ARDNAMURCHAN: "...THE NORTHERN SHORE OF LOCH SUNART IS CLAD WITH BIRCH-WOOD.
THE SUN BROKE THROUGH THE CLOUDS MOMENTARILY AND WE SAW THE COUNTRYSIDE AT ITS LOVELIEST."

Calum Iain Maclean

Tune: *The Lament for the Children*

Beloved Calum, since you died
saddened and heavy are we after you:
short was your span, short your life,
long-lasting the wound that smote your kindred.

You were the gay one, witty, light-hearted,
fervid, fair, humorous, human,
enduring, brave, fighting disease
without fear or flinching at point of death.

Scholar without blemish, judicious, expert,
who collected our tunes, gathered every tale:
you won fame over in Ireland,
and here in Scotland there was much need of you.

Warm was your heart, liberal, genial,
gentle, good, kindly, generous,
but cold and damp tonight, cheerless, gloomy
the bed of deep sleep from which you will not wake.

(Translated by Donald A. MacDonald)

Calum Iain MacGhill Eathain

Air fonn *Cumha na Cloinne* (Hedre heì hedre hea)

CHALUIM, A GHAOIL, on do dh'eug thu
's airtnealach trom ás do dhéidh sinn;
geàrr bha do réis, geàrr do shaoghal,
buan an creuchd bheum do dhaoine.

'S tusa bha mear eirmseach aotrom
dealasach ceart éibhinn daonda,
fulangach treun gleac ri eucail,
gun fhiamh gun ghealt ri uchd éig thu.

Sgoilear gun mheang tuigseach gleusda
thionail ar fuinn thruis gach sgeulachd;
choisinn thu cliù thall an Eirinn,
's bhos an Albainn mór bha dh' fheum ort.

Blàth bha do chrìdhe fialaidh mùirneach
macanta còir coibhneil fiùghant,
ach 's fuaraidh an nochd aognaidh ùdlaidh
leaba na suain ás nach dùisg thu.

SHORE AT BETTYHILL, SUTHERLAND

OLD CHURCH, LAIDE, WESTER ROSS

Elegy
for Calum I. Maclean

I

The world is still beautiful
though you are not in it,
Gaelic is eloquent in Uist
though you are in Hallin Hill
your mouth without speech.

I can hardly think
that a Gael lives
and that you are not somewhere to be found
between Grimsay and the Sound,
kindling ancient memory
with kindness and fun,

that you are in Hallin Hill
and though the company is generous —
as generous as is to be found in any place —
that there is not heard the breaking of laughter
or clang on a golden string.

If you were in Clachan
or on Cnoc an Ra,
you would be among half your kin,
among the straight generous people;
choice Macleans and MacLeods.
The dust is not weak.

If you were in Sròn Dhiùirinis
you would be in a good place,
among the other half of your kin,
among your mother's Nicolsons,
among the big generous men of Braes.
The dust is not weak.

If you were in the other Clachan
that is over here in Lochalsh,
that brave man of your ancestors,
Ruairi Beag of the glittering helmet,
would be proud to move
to let you to his shoulder —
if you were to come over.

Cumha
Chaluim Iain MhicGill-Eain

I

THA AN SAOGHAL fhathast àlainn
ged nach eil thu ann,
is labhar an Uibhist a' Ghàidhlig
ged tha thusa an Cnoc Hàllainn
is do bhial gun chainnt.

'S gann as urrainn dhomh smaointinn
gu bheil Gàidheal beò
's nach eil thu 'n àiteigin ri t' fhaotainn
eadar Grimeasaidh 's an Caolas
a' beothachadh na cuimhne aosda
le coibhneas is le spòrs,

gu bheil thusa an Cnoc Hàllainn
's ged tha an còmhlan còir —
cho còir 's a gheibhear an àite —
nach cluinnear ann am bristeadh gàire
no gliong air teud an òir.

Nan robh thu anns a' Chlachan
no air Cnoc an Rà
bhiodh tu a-miosg leth do chàirdean
a-miosg nan daoine dìreach còire,
brod na Leathanaich 's na Leòdaich.
Chan eil an duslach lag.

Nan robh thu an Sròn Dhiùirinis
bhiodh tu an àite math
miosg an leth eile dhe do chàirdean
miosg Clann Mhic Neacail do mhàthar,
miosg fir mhóra chòir' a' Bhràighe.
Chan eil an duslach lag.

Nan robh thu anns a' Chlachan eile
tha bhos ann an Loch Aills
bhiodh am fear treun ud dhe do shinnsre,
Ruairi Beag a' chlogaid dhrìlsich,
moit ei l 's e deanamh gluasaid
gu do leigeil-sa ri ghualainn —
nan tigeadh tu a nall.

25

I am not acquainted with Hallin Hill
but you are there,
and though there were with you only the Eosag,
the company would be rare and noble —
but that is not scarce.

Since you are not in Clachan
or on Cnoc an Ra,
among the Macleans and MacLeods,
we left you among Clan Donald.
There is no better place.

Among the brave generous people
you are in the dust;
since we always liked Clan Donald
we gave them the most generous gift
when we put you in their dust.

To them that have will be given
even nobleness itself:
We gave you to Uist,
and it was your own choice;
We gave you to Uist,
and it was not the worse of your clay.

II
There is many a poor man in Scotland
whose spirit and name you raised;
you lifted the humble
whom our age put aside.
They gave you more
than they would give to others
since you gave them the zeal
that was a fire beneath your kindness.
They sensed the vehemence
that was gentle in your ways,
they understood the heavy depths of your humanity
when your fun was at its lightest.

Chan eil mi eòlach an Cnoc Hàllainn
ach tha thusa ann,
's ged nach robh cuide riut ach an Eòsag,
b'ainneamh is uasal an còmhlan —
ach chan eil sin gann.

On nach eil thu anns a' Chlachan
no air Cnoc an Rà
miosg nan Leathanach 's nan Leòdach,
dh'fhàg sinn thu a-miosg Chlann Dòmhnaill.
Chan eil aìte 's fheàrr.

Miosg nan daoine treuna còire
tha thu anns an ùir:
on bu thoigh leinn riamh Clann Dòmhnaill
thug sinn dhaibh a' ghibht bu chòire
nuair chuir sinn thu 'nan ùir.

Dhaibhsan aig a bheil 's ann bheirear
eadhon an uaisle fhéin;
thug sinn thusa do dh' Uibhist,
's gum b'e do raghainn fhéin;
 thug sinn thusa do dh' Uibhist,
's cha mhisde i do chré.

II
That iomadh duine bochd an Albainn
dh' an tug thu togail agus cliù;
's ann a thog thu 'n t-iriosal
a chuir ar linn air chùl.
Thug iad dhutsa barrachd
na bheireadh iad do chàch
on thug thu dhaibh an dùrachd
bu ghrìosach fo do bhàigh.
Mhothaich iadsan an dealas
a bha socair 'na do dhòigh,
thuig iad doimhne throm do dhaondachd
nuair a b'aotroime do spòrs.

You are talked of in Cois Fhairrge
over in Ireland:
Between Cararoe and Spideal
you left many a knot.
You were to the Gaels of Ireland
as one of themselves and of their people.
They knew in you the humanity
that the sea did not tear,
that a thousand years did not spoil;
the quality of the Gael permanent.

You proved in Shetland
and in Sweden
and in Norway
that there is no bitterness in the sea:
that the "malice" is only a word
that chokes lasting truth.
Since you were a favourite with the Gael
you were a favourite with the Gall.
Since you cared for the man
and did not know guile
or sleekitness or fawning for place,
you made Gaels of the Galls.

Many of your friends are gone,
many of the great ones of the Gaels:

Duncan of Peninerine,
and Donald Roy of Paisley,
and she who gave you the two marvels,
MacCormick's wife from Haclait;
but there is another in Lionacro
for whom you are still alive,
she who did not keep you from the treasure
that was in Trotternish, her home.

Four called Angus have gone:
MacMillan and the two MacLellans,
and one of the Nicolsons —
Uistman, Benbecula men, and a Skyeman.
The Skyeman is in Sròn Dhiùirinis,
one near to you in kinship,
eye of wisdom, mouth of music,
the generous, gentle, strong Angus.

Tha sgeul ort an Cois-Fhairge
ann an Eirinn thall:
eadar an Ceathramh Ruadh is Spideal
dh' fhàg thu iomadh snaim.
Bha thu aig Gàidheil Eirinn
mar fhear dhiubh fhéin 's de 'n dream.
Dh' aithnich iad annad-sa an fhéile
nach do reub an cuan,
nach do mhill mìle bliadhna:
buaidh a' Ghàidheil buan.

Dhearbh thu ann an Sealtainn
agus anns an t-Suain
agus ann an Lochlann
nach eil seirbhe anns a' chuan;
nach eil 'sa' ghamhlas ach facal
a thachdas fìrinn bhuan.
On bu mhùirnean thu do 'n Ghàidheal
bu mhùirnean thu do 'n Ghall.
On bha t' ùidh anns an duine
's nach b'aithne dhut an fhoill
no sliomaireachd no sodal stàite,
rinn thu Gàidheil dhe na Goill.

Dh' fhalbh mòran dhe do chàirdean,
móran de dh'uaislean nan Gàidheal.

Dh' fhalbh Donnchadh Peigh'nn an Aoirein
agus Dòmhnall Ruadh Phàislig,
's an té o'n d' fhuair thu an dà mhìorbhail,
bean Mhic Carmaig á Hàclait:
ach tha téile 'n Lìonacro
dh' am bheil thu fhathast an làthair,
té nach do chùm bhuat an stòras
bha an Tròndairnis a h-àrach.

Dh' fhalbh ceathrar air robh Aonghas:
Mac Mhaoilein 's an dà MhacGill-Fialain
agus fear de Chloinn MhicNeacail —
Uibhisteach, Baodhlaich, agus Sgitheanach.
Tha 'n Sgitheanach an Sròn Dhiùirinis,
fear bu dlùth dhut ann an càirdeas,
sùil na tuigse, bial a' chiùil,
Aonghas còir ciùin làidir.

William Maclean is gone,
from whom you got the summit prize,
great pupil of MacPherson,
heir of MacKay and MacCrimmon,
prince in the music of the pipes.

There is the grey-haired one in Drimbuie,
over here in Lochalsh
who will not forget your talk
and who would not grudge tale or rhyme:
Calum as lasting in his life
as Iain Mac Mhurchaidh of the Cro.

There is a grey-haired one in Barra,
another Calum, mouth of grace,
key of music, and finger of art,
the wide generous warm heart,
head that holds the treasure of our lore,
jewel of Clan Neil and Clan Donald.

You were in Spean Bridge
like the best of the MacDonalds,
in Morar and in Arisaig
and in Glen Roy.

In the Glens of the Grants,
between Ceannchnoc and Corriemony
you gave and got the kindness
that grew happily about your steps.
You were in the Ross of Mull
like an unyielding Maclean,
like lame Hector come home
with his wounds from Inverkeithing.

III
You took the retreat,
little one of the big heart,
you took your refuge behind the wall
where the bent grass of Gaelic is sweetest,
little one of the great heroism.

Dh' fhalbh Uilleam MacGill-Eain,
fear o 'n d' fhuair thu bàrr na prìse,
oileanach mór Mhic-a-Phearsain,
tàinistear MhicAidh 's MhicCruimein,
prìomhair ann an ceòl na pìoba.

Tha fear liath air an Druim Bhuidhe
a bhos ann an Loch Aills
nach cuir air dhìochain do bhruidheann
's nach sòradh sgeul no rann:
Calum cho maireann dha ri bheò
ri Iain Mac Mhurchaidh anns a' Chrò.

'S tha fear liath eile 'm Barraidh,
Calum eile, bial an àigh,
iuchair a' chiùil, is miar na h-ealain,
an cridhe farsaing fialaidh blàth,
ceann 'sna thaisgeadh leug ar n-eòlais,
àilleagan Chlann Nèill 's Chlann Dòmhnaill.

Bha thu an Drochaid Aonachain
mar Dhòmhnallach nam buadh,
am Mórair is an Árasaig
agus an Gleann Ruaidh.

Ann an glinn nan Granndach,
eadar Ceannachnoc 's Coire Monaidh
fhuair is thug thu 'n coibhneas
a dh' fhàs mu d' cheum le sonas
Bha thu san Ros Mhuileach
mar Leathanach nach tréigeadh,
mar Eachann Bacach air tigh'nn dhachaidh
l' a leòin á Inbhir-Chéitein.

III
Ghabh thu an ràtreuta,
fhir bhig a' chridhe mhóir,
ghabh thu do dhìon air cùl a' ghàrraidh
far 's mìlse muran na Gàidhlig,
fhir bhig an treuntais mhóir.

31

You took the retreat
to the western edge,
you who did not take the breaking,
who were never broken,
who reached the mouth of the grave
with your spirit always the victor.

Often do I ask
of my own heart
if it was the creed of Rome
or rare hardihood in your kind
that put your heroism to its height,
as it were without effort.

You dearly bought the pride
that we bought in your death:
for four years without hauteur
you hid from your kin your certainty
that death was so near.

We dearly bought the pride
that increased with your death:
that your heroism was a marvel
hidden in your fun;
that seldom was seen your like
in such an extremity.

You dearly bought the fishing
when the pain was in your flesh,
when your net was taking in
the gleaming white-bellied salmon, a store:
with the net of your four years of agony
you gave us a pride beyond store.

IV
You were often in Uist,
the island of your barley without stint,
lifting as without effort
the crop that fell to your hand,
your toil hidden in your kindness,
the joyful stooks of your fun.

Ghabh thu an ràtreuta
gus an iomall shiair,
thusa nach do ghabh am bristeadh,
nach do bhristeadh riamh,
a ràinig bial na h-uaghach
is do spiorad sìor bhuadhach.

'S tric a bhios mi foighneachd
dhe mo chridhe fhìn
an e creideamh na Ròimhe
no cruadal annasach 'nad sheòrsa
a chuir do threuntas g' a aìrde,
mar gum b'ann gun strì.

Is daor a cheannaich thusa 'n t-uabhar
a cheannaich sinne 'nad bhàs:
fad cheithir bliadhna gun àrdan
chleith thu do chinnt air do chàirdean
cho faisg 's bha do bhàs.

Is daor a cheannaich sinne 'n t-uabhar
a mhiadaich le do bhàs:
gu robh do threuntas 'na mhìorbhail
air falach 'na do spòrs;
gur tearc a chunnacas do leithid
ann a leithid de chàs.

Is daor a cheannaich thusa 'n t-iasgach
nuair bha am pianadh 'nad fheòil,
nuair thug do lion a-stigh na bradain
thàrr-gheala lìomhach 'nan stòr:
le lìon do cheithir bliadhna ciùrraidh
thug thu cliù dhuinn thar gach stòir.

IV
'S tric a bha thu 'n Uibhist,
eilean t' eòrna nach bu ghann,
's tu togail mar gun shaothair
am bàrr a thuit gu d' làimh,
do shaothair air falach anns a' choibhneas,
adagan aoibhneach do spòrs.

33

But another Spring came
and you went over the Sea of Skye:
did you not go to Uist
with your body at your struggle's end,
did you go home to Uist
to wait for the very end?

I went up Dun Cana
on the Friday before your death,
my eye was only on Uist —
not as it used to be —
I forgot the Cuillin
looking at Ben More,
at Hecla and Staolaval,
they all grew big.

On the Tuesday after
Peter came with the tale,
with news I saw in his face,
that your brave spirit had gone.
I knew that you went unbroken,
that your victory was without flaw.

On the Friday after
you were carried in concord,
a Campbell and two MacDonalds
leading your course.
Your body was taken to Hallin Hill
under the shade and cover of their music.

Since he was worth their music
they took the Maclean to his Cro,
MacDonald, Campbell, MacCrimmon;
he got a great pomp in Uist.

And the white sand of Hallin Hill
lies lightly on the bones
of him whose great spirit
misfortune did not beat down, though his trial
was for four years beyond telling,
and he at grips with the work of his devotion.

And though he is not in Clachan
in Raasay of the MacLeods,
he is quite as well in Uist.
His debt was great to Clan Donald.

Sorley Maclean

Ach thàinig earrach eile
is chaidh thu thar Chuan Sgìthe:
saoil an deachaidh tu a dh' Uibhist
le d' chorp an ceann do shtrìthe,
an deach thu dhachaidh a dh' Uibhist
a dh' fheitheamh ceann na crìche?

Dhìrich mi Dùn Cana
Di-haoine roimh do bhàs,
cha robh mo shùil ach air Uibhist —
cha b'ionann 's mar a b' à'ist —
dhìochainich mi 'n Cuilithionn
's mo shùil air a' Bheinn Mhóir,
air Teacal is air Staolabhal,
's ann dh' fhàs iad uile mór.

'N Di-màirt sin as a dheaghaidh
thàinig Pàdraig leis an sgeul,
le naidheachd a chunnaic mi' na aodann
gun d' fhalbh do spiorad treun.
Bha fhios a'm gun d' fhalbh thu gun bhristeadh,
gu robh do bhuaidh gun bheud.

Air an ath Dhi-haoine
bha 'n t-aonadh mu do ghiùlan,
Caimbeulach 's dà Dhòmhnallach
a' treòrachadh do chùrsa.
Thugadh do chorp a Chnoc Hàllainn
fo bhrat is sgàil an ciùil-san.

On a b'fhiach e an ceòl
thug iad an Leathanach d' a Chrò,
Dòmhnallach, Caimbeulach, MacCruimein;
fhuair e greadhnachas an Uibhist.
Agus tha gainmheach gheal Cnoc Hàllainn
'na laighe gu h-aotrom air cnàmhan
an fhir sin nach do chlaoidh an t-ànradh
a spiorad mór, ged bha a dhìachainn
fad cheithir bliadhna thar innse
's e 'n sàs an obair a dhìlse.

'S ged nach eil e anns a' Chlachan
ann an Ratharsair nan Leòdach
tha e ceart cho math an Uibhist.
Bu mhór a chomain air Clann Dòmhnaill.

GAELIC SLOGAN, LOCHAILORT

CAMUS NAN GEALL, LOCH SUNART, ARDNAMURCHAN

To Calum I. Maclean

We got news yesterday
which pierced our hearts with sharp arrows,
and the whole land
was overcast from that time;
for we heard you lay dead,
Calum, strengthless on boards,
and never again will the land
be the same as before it lost you.

That was a body always well-controlled,
cheerful and noble was your face,
your bearing was without arrogance,
you were modest, courteous, and gentle;
and in gatherings of people
you made many an impact, won much fame —
how much poorer are we now
that we cannot hear the sound of your music!

Famous indeed
what was ours to relate and acclaim
that you were no fool
and were not acquainted with rage or deceit:
old and young
with pride would mention your name,
you were the maker of fun
who made sorrow and sadness wither away.

A wealth of learning
filled your mind from your earliest years,
you proved it time upon time
in the great places in which you spoke:
you got a talent from God
and you gave good measure and more
and you never denied
your duties to your God and to your own standards.

To the young generation
you gave new knowledge
of manners and a way of life
and music, our own ancient heritage
which would soon have been lost
if you had not cherished them so —
who else in our time
loved our language so well?

Do Chalum Iain MacGhill Eathain

FHUAIR SINN NAIDHEACHD an dé
chuir saigheadan geur 'nar crìdh,
's gun robh 'n dùthaich gu léir
fo phràmh ann an déidh na tim,
o na chualas mu d' bhàs,
a Chaluim, air clàr gun chlì,
's cha bhi 'n dùthaich gu bràth
mar bhà i is tu 'ga dìth

Sud a' cholann bha stuam',
bha aoibhneas is uails' 'nad ghnùis,
bha do ghiùlan gun uaill,
bha thu iriosal, suairc, is ciùin,
's aig cruinneachadh sluaigh
thug thu iomadach buaidh is cliù,
's bochd dhuinne san uair
nach cluinn sinne fuaim do chiùil.

O 's cliùiteach gu dearbh
na bh'againn ri luaidh 's ri sheirm,
gun robh thu gun chearb,
's cha b' aithne dhut fearg no ceilg!
Bhitheadh sean agus òg
a' labhairt le pròis mu d'ainm,
bu tu fhéin am fear spòrs
chuireadh tùrs' agus bròn gu searg.

Gun robh foghlum nach gann
'nad cheann agus t'aois glé òg,
's thug thu dearbhadh gach àm
le d' chainnt an ionadan mór,
fhuair thu tàlant bho Dhia
's thug thu riarachadh seachad is còrr,
's cha do dh' àicheidh thu riamh
do dhleasndas do d' Dhia 's do d'chòir.

Do 'n ghinealach òg
gun tug thusa eòlas ùr
air cleachdadh 's air dòigh
's air ceòl a bh'againn o thùs
bha thuar dhol air chall
mur b'e gun do chuir thu ann ùidh —
có eile san àm
d' ar cainnt thug urad de rùn?

How happy the young
who savoured the sweetness of your talk
and tasted the bards
through your devoted hard work!
You put down on record
many a story and beautiful tune,
and we, now you have left us,
will go on praising you in your grave.

And though you strove
hard against death,
your body gave out
under the weight of an outrageous disease:
but you found your health
in a place where pain is not felt,
and your soul for ever will be
in blessed Paradise with God.

It was a high example
you set your kinsfolk always,
to each brother and sister
you abundantly showed your love:
there was witness for all
while you were being lowered into the grave
how much love and affection
your dear Uist bestowed on you!

As for her who bore you —
no wonder her sorrow is great,
thinking every day
how soon you were laid in the ground
and she was bereft of the supporter
who will never return as long as she lives;
it will break her heart,
and our feelings will always go with her.

Though I went on for ever,
there would always be something more to tell and to praise,
and words cannot recount
every beauty of this precious jewel:
we shall miss every day
a prince who belonged to the North —
peace be with you, Calum,
in the glory of Heaven above.

(Translated by Donald A. MacDonald)

O 's buidhe do'n àl
fhuair blasad de d' mhànran maoth,
's a bhlais air na bàird
troimh 'n spàirn a thug thu le d' ghaol;
gun chuir thu air clàr
iomadh eachdraidh is aìlleachd chiùil,
's bidh sinne 'nad dhéidh
'gad mholadh 's tu fhéin san ùir.

'S ged thug thusa spàirn
an aghaidh a' bhaìs gu dian,
gun thréig do chom
fo thinneas bha trom gun rian,
ach fhuair thu do shlàint
an àite nach fhairichear pian,
's bidh t' anam gu bràth
am Pàrras bheannaicht' aig Dia.

'S e eiseimpleir àrd
a thug thu do d' chàirdean riamh,
do gach piuthar is bràthair
nochd thu do gràdh gu fial,
bha fianuis do chàch
an àm bhith 'gad adhlacadh sios
air a' ghaol 's air a' bhàidh
thug Uibhist do ghràidh do d' chliabh.

'S an té shaothraich thu òg
chan iongnadh a bròn bhith mòr,
a bhith smaointean gach là
gun deach thu cho tràth fo'n fhòd,
am fear taice 'ga dith
's nach till e a ris ri beò,
's e bhristeas a crìdh,
's bidh ar faireachdainn fhìn 'na còir.

Ged leanainn gu bràth
bidh rud ùr ri àireamh 's ri luaidh,
's cha chuir briathran air dòigh
gach maise bh' air seòd nam buadh,
bidh ionndrain gach là
air sàr a bhuineadh do Thuath —
O sìth dhut, a Chaluim,
ann an glòir nam Flathanas shuas!

41

MOOR LOCHAN, WESTER ROSS

TOP OF BEALACH NA BA, CROWLIN ISLANDS AND THE ISLE OF SKYE BEYOND

"THE LORD'S DAY", INVERASDALE, WESTER ROSS

ANCHORS AT ACHILTIBUIE

INTRODUCTION

THE Highland area, if we may rightly use such a term, is divided from the Lowlands by a line which is clearly observable on orographical maps and extends from Stonehaven through Comrie and Aberfoyle to Helensburgh on the west. To the south of the line the terrain is one of plains and rolling uplands — a wealthy land, fertile above and rich below. To the north is a land of rugged mountains and deep valleys, the result of folding, fracturing, horizontal and vertical displacements and volcanic extrusions, where in places are exposed the very bones of old Mother Earth. These consist of gneisses, schists, indurated sandstones and quarzites that give character to a landscape, often barren of vegetation or covered by a layer of thin, sour soil that affords scanty sustenance to man or beast. Hence, while this portion comprises more than half the area of Scotland, its population is but one-eleventh of the country as a whole.

Weathering agents, such as waters, frosts, winds and glaciers have been potent factors in the sculpturing of the land. The action of the last, particularly, is reflected in the many flat-bottomed, smooth-flanked valleys, as against those produced by rivers which are V-shaped in cross-section and have accentuated offsets. That the carving was effected on what was originally a far-spread plateau is shown when, on the approach of winter, the summits with their fresh snow seem to rise to a uniform height, or, better still, when the valleys and the slopes are clothed in mist, the clear summits above are like islands in a sea of red cloud.

A major fracture, running from Tarbat Ness in Easter Ross, through the Great Glen, Loch Linnhe and the Firth of Lorn, separates the Grampian area from the North-west Highlands; minor fractures, represented by the line of Loch Maree, the valley of Strath Conan and the striking abyss of Loch Morar, indicate the extent of crustal adjustments that happened here. It also accounts for the impressive features to be seen on our western seaboard and adjacent islands, where masses of land subsided or were disrupted from the mainland. Such movements occasioned volcanic activity on a vast scale. Extruded lavas covered much of Skye, Rum, Eigg, Mull, etc., giving rise to their diverse geological formations and their grand mountain-systems. Similarly the Outer Isles represent a ridge of Archean rocks, isolated by fracturing and foundering along the line of the Minch. To the same origin are traceable the sinuous fjords, penetrating inland for many miles — a boon to transport, especially in the past, a generous source of wealth in the varieties of fish that frequented them and a source of pleasure to the wayfarer.

As the watershed of the Highlands is so close to the west and the decline so steep, waters draining to the Atlantic are short, swift and of great scooping power because of heavier rainfall, as compared with those tending eastwards over gentler slopes. The latter form broad and fertile valleys as those of the Spey, Findhorn, Don, Dee, and the Tay with its subsidiaries, particularly the Lyon. Because of the difference in the conditions mentioned, the watershed is tending towards the east, a phenomenon clearly exemplified, among others, in the encroachment of the catchment area of the Spean on that of the Spey.

As far as prehistory is concerned the Highlands cannot be regarded as distinct from the rest of Scotland. The earliest inhabitants came probably from Europe and North Africa by way of Ireland and England and eked out a precarious livelihood on the shores of our country. Relics wrought of flint and stone tell of their existence. Later came the long-headed Megalithic peoples, who built the massive stone chambers and circles, such as we see at Callernish in the Isle of Lewis. They fed on shell-fish and limpets, but there is evidence too that they had

47

domesticated animals and ate mutton and veal. About the year 1700 B.C. the round-headed folk called the Beaker people, from the type of vessel they buried along with them, made their appearance among the Megalithic communities. The Beaker people appeared to have become a dominant element. They made use of copper and bronze and were mainly pastoral. With the coming of the Iron Age, the communities able to use that metal acquired dominance over the less skilled users of bronze. At this time a form of Celtic culture, which was dominant in France, Spain and Central Europe as far down as the Danube, was adopted. The use of iron led to the clearing of forests and the cultivation of land for crops.

To the Romans the inhabitants of the region north of the Forth and Clyde valleys were known as *Picti*, "the tattooed folk". The Roman Empire had its most northerly limit in the chain of forts between the Forth and Clyde. While expeditions were made and battles fought north of this line, the *Picti*, nevertheless, remained unconquered and were left as an intact fighting-force to harass the defenceless Britons to the south on the withdrawal of the Imperial legions. The *Picti* were of the Celtic-speaking group and spoke a language related to that from which modern Welsh derives descent. Certain scholars maintain that there are still survivals of a pre-Celtic speech, as far as can be judged from the study of place-names. To the south-west of the demarcation line between Romanised Britain and the unconquered territory of the *Picti*, in the area between Loch Lomond and the Solway, the Christian kingdom of Strathclyde with its capital at Dumbarton was founded, the Christian faith having first been brought to *Candida Casa* near Whithorn on Solway. Towards the end of the fifth century the Scots arrived from Ireland and established themselves in what is now Argyll. In the year A.D. 563 Columba followed them from Ireland, and from Iona, his centre, began the evangelisation of the Scots and later the *Picti*. Columba was aided in his work by Pictish converts, who solved the difficulty of spreading his teaching among a people not familiar with the saint's own language. The Scots belonged to another family of the Celtic-speaking peoples and spoke the language from which come the modern dialects of Scots and Irish Gaelic. It was probably due to the spread of Gaelic influence and culture, coupled with the propagation of the Christian faith brought by the Scots, that the Pictish kingdom became merged with that of the Gaels under Kenneth MacAlpin in A.D. 843. With Kenneth MacAlpin the Gaelic dynasty of Alba begins. In the year 908 the grandson of Kenneth became king of Strathclyde. To the east the Anglo-Saxons had penetrated as far as the Forth, but in the early years of the eleventh century Malcolm II crushed the Anglo-Saxon forces at Carham-on-Tweed and thereby fixed the southern limit of the Scottish kingdom and nation.

Towards the end of the eighth century, however, a new force had appeared on the scene: the Vikings from Denmark and from Norway, the former designated as *Fionnghaill*, the fair strangers, and the latter as *Dubhghaill*, black strangers. They conquered Shetland, Orkney and the Hebrides and colonised them from Norway. They settled on the mainland of Argyll, and a Norse earl ruled over the province of Cait, the modern Caithness and Sutherland, and held his possessions nominally from the Scottish king. For the purposes of coastal defence *mormaers*, sea stewards, were appointed by the Scottish Crown. On the east coast there were the stewardships of Moray, Buchan, Mar, Mearns and Angus, while, on the west, the *mormaer* of Lennox defended the Firth of Clyde and the steward of Morvern, the approach to the Great Glen. There are evidences that many coastal areas at least paid some form of tribute to the Vikings, and the names of many places around the western and northern coasts, as well as the islands, bear witness to Norse infiltration.

Prior to the death of Malcolm II in 1034 the crown had passed from the monarch to collateral branches of the royal house, but, by a new law, direct descendants took precedence

THE BEAULY RIVER AT AIGAS

over the king's brothers, nephews and cousins. The promulgation of this law led to dissension over disputed successions in which the Highlands were embroiled for almost two centuries. Duncan, as successor to Malcolm II, was opposed by two powerful claimants, Macbeth and Gruoch, who further strengthened their claim by marriage. In 1040 Macbeth defeated and slew Duncan in battle and reigned until his defeat seventeen years later by Malcolm Canmore, Duncan's son. Canmore's second marriage to Margaret, sister of Edgar the Atheling of England, resulted in the Anglicisation of the Scottish Court, and the three sons of Malcolm and Margaret, who in turn ascended the throne, were reared under Norman influence. They furthered the introduction of feudalism, a new departure resented by the Gaelic elements within the kingdom, and a series of rebellions, the first of which, led by Donald Bàn, Malcolm Canmore's brother, marked the reigns of the Scottish kings down to the time of Alexander II. After Donald Bàn, resistance to central authority was led by the MacHeths, descendants of Gruoch, and later by the MacWilliams, descendants of a son of Duncan II. Feudal baronies were granted to Norman families and the influence of the Church helped the incomers to consolidate their position. The feudal barons were pledged to provide the king with an army and thus they helped him to deal with recalcitrant elements within his realm. To this period belong the beginnings of families that were later to play an important role in Scottish and Highland history, families such as the Comyns, Frasers, and Chisholms.

On the west, all the Hebridean islands, as well as the Isle of Man, were part of the Norse Kingdom of the Isles, established by Godred Crobhan in 1079. The Scottish Crown was later forced to recognise the Norse as sovereigns of all the islands on the west coast of Scotland except those in the Firth of Clyde. To this day Norse influence in the Hebrides can be traced in house-types, local narrative tradition, in place and personal names and in the very great number of loan-words that have come from Norse into Gaelic. Some of the almost pure Norse became gaelicised and Highland clans such as the Nicolsons, Macaulays, and Macleods prided themselves on their Norse descent. There were undoubtedly Norse settlements on the western mainland, but, in the earlier half of the twelfth century, a powerful figure appeared in the person of Somerled Mór, the son of Gille Bride. He drove the Norse from the mainland and founded a Gaelic principality in South Argyll. Somerled was of mixed Norse and Gaelic stock and his importance in Highland history cannot be over-estimated. He was the progenitor of the Macdougalls of Lorn and also of Clan Donald. Somerled was later to rule over part of the Norse Kingdom of the Isles, and his successors were subjects both of the Norse and Scottish kings. That dual role continued until 1266, when the Norse Kingdom of the Isles was ceded to Scotland.

The deaths of Alexander III and his grand-daughter, the Maid of Norway, left the realm under the covetous eyes of Edward I of England and the throne contested by rival claimants, Baliol and Bruce. The Highlanders who threw in their lot with Bruce benefited considerably when the independence of Scotland was finally recognised and the cause of Bruce supreme. The Macdougalls of Lorn, the MacSweyns of Knapdale, the Comyns of Lochaber and Badenoch and Alexander of Islay, the head of Clan Donald, were in the Baliol faction, while Angus Og, Alexander of Islay's younger brother, the MacRuairis of the *Garbhchriochan* — "the Rough Bounds" between Loch Duich and Ardnamurchan, favoured Robert Bruce. Angus Og led the Clan Donald at Bannockburn, and, although he subsequently surrendered to the Crown his lands in Kintyre, in compensation he was given Mull, Coll, Tiree, Ardnamurchan, Appin, Glencoe, and a large part of Lochaber, to augment his existing territories in Jura, Islay and Colonsay. Part of Lochaber, lost by the Comyns, was given to the MacRuairis to be added to their existing lands, comprising the *Garbhchriochan*, the Uists and Benbecula, Barra, Rum and

ABANDONED SALMON FISHING STATION, INVERASDALE, WESTER ROSS

KYLE OF TONGUE AND BEN LOYAL BEYOND, SUTHERLAND

Eigg. Further north the Earl of Ross changed sides in time to save his lands. In the east the Earldom of Mar had aligned itself with Bruce. The earls of Angus and Atholl sided with the Comyns and were both forfeited. The earldom of Mar was loyal to Bruce and later it passed temporarily to a scion of the royal house, when the Countess of Mar was forcibly married by Alexander Stewart, a grandson of Robert II.

Angus Og of Islay laid the foundations of what was later to become the Lordship of the Isles, a veritable kingdom within a kingdom and a continual threat to central authority for over a century-and-a-half. Lewis was granted by David II to John of Islay, the son of Angus Og, and John later acquired the MacRuairi lands when his wife, a sister of Ranald MacRuairi, fell heir to them. By his second marriage to Margaret, daughter of Robert the High Steward of Scotland, John of Islay acquired Kintyre and half of Knapdale to the north. The possessions of John of Islay, the first Lord, were even more widespread than those of the earlier Norse Kingdom of the Isles, and the earldom of Ross was added to the principality on the death of the last Earl, whose sister was married to Donald the second Lord of the Isles. Despite the fact that the Duke of Albany, Regent of Scotland, had succeeded in obtaining the earldom for his own son, Donald's claim to it through his wife was conceded by James I in 1424. Donald had previously fought the indecisive battle of Harlaw in vindication of her right. Alexander the third Lord of the Isles succeeded his mother to the earldom.

John the first Lord of the Isles, having appointed Donald, the eldest son of his second marriage, as his heir, gave the MacRuairi lands to Ranald, the youngest surviving son of his first marriage. Ranald thus founded the Clanranald branch of the Macdonalds. To Iain Fraoch, John's own brother, was given Glencoe and in this way another branch was founded. Donald the second Lord of the Isles gave estates in Islay and Kintyre to his brother, John Mor, who had married the heiress to the Glens of Antrim in Ireland, and from John Mor come the Macdonalds of Dunyveg, later designated as the Islay branch. To another brother, Alasdair Carrach, he gave Brae Lochaber and from him came the Macdonells of Keppoch. John the fourth Lord granted the lands of Loch Alsh, Loch Carron, and Loch Broom to his brother Celestine, and part of that territory passed later to Alexander Macdonell of Glengarry, while another brother, Hugh, was given Sleat in Skye and his direct descendants are still there.

The fundamental difference between the principality of the Isles and the Scottish Court was that the Lords of the Isles were Gaelic and the Court to a large extent Anglo-Norman in tradition and no longer Gaelic, although even as late as the beginning of the sixteenth century James IV had an excellent command of Gaelic. The Lords of the Isles had their own legal system and administration, and in reality they were in closer cultural contact with their kindred in Ireland than with the Lowlanders of Scotland. During the Lordship of the Isles the Gaels were often in league with the kings of England against the Scottish Crown, and during the struggle for supremacy in Ireland the claymores of the West Highlanders were often drawn on behalf of their Irish kindred with the connivance of the Scottish Court, and were unsheathed too in the pay of the English monarchs intent on crushing Irish resistance. The West Highlanders, of course, were not the only villains of the piece. To them the Scottish and English Courts were alien alike. The large numbers of clans that were vassals of the Lords of the Isles were at times sufferers from conflicting loyalties. It became Crown policy to strengthen the lesser clans to offset the power of Clan Donald, and when the Lordship of the Isles was finally forfeited in 1493, the lesser clans rose to prominence. From 1493 onwards there were, for at least half a century, intermittent armed attempts to restore the Lordship of the Isles. The accession of James VI to the united thrones more or less put an end to the activities of the West Highland mercenaries in Ireland. At that very time and even later the MacKays and Sinclairs,

NORTH SUTHERLAND LANDSCAPE: "SUTHERLAND IS A WIDE, DESOLATE AND BEAUTIFUL COUNTY, CERTAINLY THE MOST DESOLATE IF NOT THE MOST BEAUTIFUL OF ALL SCOTTISH COUNTIES."

north-eastern clans, distinguished themselves as mercenaries in the armies of the Scandinavian and continental kings. All over the Highlands there was no lack of fighting man-power. The social structure of clanship made that possible at all times.

What is termed a "clan" was a community of people claiming descent from a common ancestor, whether real or fictitious, living in a particular area, and bound together by common environment and interest. The member of the clan owed allegiance to the head of the family or chieftain and he could rely on them for military service. In return the chief took his clansmen under his protection; not only was he their superior but they were generally regarded as his kindred by blood. The lower grades of clansmen were the mere tillers of the soil, but, as most clans remained pastoral till a late date, there were always large bodies of fighting men available whenever need arose. In battle they were led by the chief or captains of the clan. The retainers as a rule adopted the name of the head or founder of the clan. The clan lands were absolute property, and a family holding land for a considerable length of time came to be regarded as its possessors. Under feudalism all land was the absolute property of the king and all landowners were subject to services due to the sovereign. The imposition of feudalism on the clans was by no means an insurmountable hurdle, for the two systems had elements in common, but the clansmen were now torn between loyalty to the chief on the one hand and to the king on the other. Most clans in the western and eastern Highlands were Gaelic communities upon whom feudalism had been imposed. Other clans were originally feudal units that had evolved as clans and were influenced by the culture and civilisation of their neighbours, as, for instance, the Frasers, Chisholms, and Grants. The feudal units became Gaelic clans like the rest.

The fifteenth and sixteenth centuries saw the rise of three very powerful clans, the Campbells, the MacKenzies, and Gordons. Although most of their land lay outwith the geographical Highland area, the Gordons were for long superiors of a great part of Lochaber and Badenoch. The Campbells were descended from Duncan MacDhuibhne of Lochow and were granted full possession of their lands as a result of having supported Bruce in the War of Independence. The barony of Lochow comprised much of central Argyllshire. By further grants from the Crown, such as the Knapdale lands which had formerly belonged to the Lord of the Isles, the Campbell territories grew enormously until, by the end of the fifteenth century, they owned extensive tracts in Glenorchy and Breadalbane. In 1457 Colin the fifth Lord of Lochow was made Earl of Argyll. To begin with the Campbells had enriched themselves at the expense of the Macdougalls, the MacSweyns, the Lamonts, and Macnaughtons, who had paid the penalty because of their alignment with the Comyn-Baliol party. They were later to encroach on the lands of the MacGregors. They acquired Glen Lyon through marriage with a Stewart heiress and the lands of Calder near Nairn in the Eastern Highlands by reason of another useful marriage. They also gained control over the MacNab lands in Lawers, Perthshire. In 1602 the Macdonalds of Ardnamurchan were forced to resign their lands to the Earls of Argyll. Four years later Argyll was granted a *feu* charter of the lands in Kintyre and Jura that had belonged to Clan Donald. The Islay Macdonalds and the Macleans had weakened themselves considerably as the result of a disastrous feud over possession of lands in the Rhinns of Islay. The Macleans are reputed to have been encouraged to attack the Macdonalds by the Scottish central authorities, while Argyll was a very interested spectator on the side-lines. His eyes were on the Maclean lands too and he was to acquire them eventually. Soon the whole of Islay was to go to Sir John Campbell of Calder and the Macdonalds of Islay were completely ruined. The failure of the Jacobite Risings were later to bring more grist to the mill of the astute Campbells.

The MacKenzies came originally from Kintail, where three glens, Glenshiel, Glen Lichd and Glen Elchaig, were noted for the rearing of cattle. During the period that the Lord of the Isles

"THE SEVEN MEN OF MOIDART – SEVEN HUGE OAK TREES – MARK THE SPOT WHERE PRINCE CHARLES LANDED..."

was Earl of Ross, the MacKenzies were his vassals, but on the forfeiture of the Lordship, MacKenzie was granted a royal charter of the lands of Strathconan, Strathbran, and Strathgarve in Easter Ross. Sometime about then the MacKenzie chiefs had moved their residence from Kintail to Easter Ross. Much land accrued to the MacKenzies later as the result of lease or charter, especially land in Easter Ross that had been Church property before the Reformation. Their new possessions in the Black Isle and in the area around the Cromarty Firth were very fertile and valuable. In the west the MacKenzies came to possess the lands of Loch Alsh, Loch Carron, and Loch Broom by purchase and marriage and also by driving out the Macdonells of Glengarry. They also got possession of the Church lands of Applecross, and by 1610 they had driven the Macleods from Gairloch and were next to gain possession of the Isle of Lewis after the failure of the Fife Adventurers to colonise the island with the support and backing of the central authorities. Later the MacKenzies wrested the lands of Coigeach and Assynt on the north-western mainland from the Macleods of Lewis. So powerful was MacKenzie of Kintail that he was able to defy the King's Lieutenant in the north, Huntly. In 1609 the chief of Kintail was created Lord MacKenzie and in 1623 he took the title of Earl of Seaforth. The triumphant progress of the MacKenzies was watched with anxiety by their neighbours, the Frasers, the Munroes, the Sutherlands, and others.

The main territories of the Gordons were in Aberdeen and Banff. The family was Norman, and the foundations of its power were laid when Robert Bruce granted Strathbogie in Aberdeenshire to Sir Adam Gordon of Gordon in Berwickshire. By marriage with a Fraser heiress further land was acquired in Deeside. The male line then died out, but the son of an heiress assumed the name and arms of Gordon and was created Earl of Huntly and Lord of Badenoch. Despite the fact that the principal men of the clan remained Catholic, the power of the Gordons did not wane. Huntly was several times appointed the King's Lieutenant in the north, but, in their relations with their neighbours, the Gordons were not quite as ruthless as the Campbells, for they entered into Bonds of Friendship and Manrent with them. Huntly was, however, the feudal superior of the Clan Chattan and the Camerons and was thus nominal overlord of lands stretching from Braemar through Badenoch to Lochaber on the west. The Clan Chattan was a group of clans, the Mackintoshes, Macphersons, Macbeans, Davidsons, all of whom claimed a traditional ancestor, Gille Chatain, the servant of St Catan. The original patrimony of the Children of St Catan was the area west of the loch and River Lochy to Knoydart and Morar, what latterly became known as the lands of Glen Loy and Loch Arkaig. South of that area was the land of Cameron of Locheil, lying between Locheil and Loch Leven. Towards the end of the fourteenth century the Camerons came to possess the lands of Glen Loy and Loch Arkaig and pushed the Clan Chattan eastwards into Badenoch. There the territories of the group extended northwards into Strathdearn and Upper Strathnairn and across the Grampians to Braemar, where the Farquharsons established themselves as the principal branch of the clan. At one juncture Huntly succeeded in inducing the Macphersons to break away from the Mackintoshes and constitute themselves as an independent clan. When Huntly became the feudal superior of the Camerons he attempted to make the MacSorlies of Glen Nevis break away from Locheil but without success. The Clan Chattan had Crown charters to the lands of Glen Loy and Loch Arkaig, but the Camerons and the Macdonells of Keppoch kept what they had in spite of everything.

In Perthshire the Earls of Atholl were in the unusual position of enjoying the allegiance of the Stewarts, Robertsons, Spaldings, Fergusons, and others, merely because they were their feudal superiors. To the very north there were four clans, the MacKays, Sinclairs, Gunns, and Sutherlands. The earldom of Sutherland, which was created for a branch of the Norman family

ARDCHATTAN PRIORY, LOCH ETIVE-SIDE, ARGYLL

of Feskin, passed through an heiress to a branch of the Gordons. The Norse earldom of Caithness reverted to the Crown and was granted to the Sinclairs, a family of French origin. The Gunns, themselves a Norse family, were closely identified with the Sutherlands. The MacKays originally held Durness in Sutherlandshire and were later to acquire most of the land from the border of Caithness westwards to Cape Wrath. For a long time there was bitter strife between the Sutherlands and the MacKays, because the former claimed to be feudal superiors of the MacKay lands. The MacKay estates finally became the property of the Sutherland family. Unlike Huntly, the Earl of Sutherland threw in his lot with the Protestant cause. The Grants, who held lands in Strathspey and Urquhart, were another important clan.

The main events of the seventeenth and eighteenth centuries are too well known to require recapitulation. The brilliant campaign of Montrose, during which the Campbells were rendered useless as a fighting unit, was soon to be followed by the Cromwellian occupation of Scotland when retribution overtook the Covenanters for having thrown the king to the wolves. The Macleans suffered grievous losses in the attempt to halt the Cromwellian forces at Inverkeithing on the Forth and all Scotland was completely and deservedly vanquished except Lochaber, where the valiant Ewen Dubh of Locheil held out to the last. The Restoration of Charles II was welcomed by the Highlanders mainly because they were not preoccupied with the religious controversies that engaged the attention of their contemporaries in the Lowlands, and it also meant that the English yoke was thrown off, at least temporarily. That century saw the flowering of native Gaelic literature, even though the close cultural link with Ireland had been broken: John Macdonald of Keppoch was appointed Gaelic Poet Laureate to Charles II, and in Skye and other parts of the Highlands the art of pibroch, Scotland's finest contribution to the culture of Europe, was reaching its highest level. At the battle of Worcester the reigning MacCrimmon was presented to Charles II and it was there he composed the famed pibroch, "I got a kiss of the King's hand". Before 1688 a Highland force was raised to keep law and order in the Lowlands — something that would have been utterly unthinkable in the early years of the century. The Revolution found the Macdonalds, Camerons, and Stewarts in arms again on behalf of the old Scottish dynasty, but the death of "Bonnie" Dundee in the hour of victory left them leaderless. At one juncture it was feared that the Earl (and subsequently first Duke) of Argyll would join Dundee. The Massacre of Glencoe in 1692 horrified all Scottish patriots. In fairness to the Campbells it must be stated that criminal responsibility for the outrage must be shared by Sir John Dalrymple and King William himself. Tradition, even in the Macdonald areas, does not damn the Campbells: they were mere pawns in the game and reluctant ones at that.

The three Jacobite Risings followed the Union of 1707. The first in 1715 could have been the most serious if there had been competent leadership. Argyll was made a duke for his support of the incorporating Union and he commanded the Hanoverian forces. The Duke of Atholl too called out his tenants in support of the Hanoverians, but under his son, the Marquis of Tullibardine, they marched away to join the Jacobites, declaring that their aim was "to restore the king and the kingdom to its ancient independence". The cause of the Stewarts and that of Scottish Independence were one and the same to them. Even the Campbell Earl of Breadalbane was out with the Jacobites. The fifth Earl of Seaforth brought out all the MacKenzies and lost heavily at Sheriffmuir. As a comrade-in-arms he had the Presbyterian Sir Donald Macdonald of Sleat. Because of the Treaty of Utrecht, help from France was out of question in 1715. The rising, however, gave us one invaluable possession, a very beautiful pibroch, "The Lament on the Departure of King James". Earlier it had given us "The Prince's Salute", also very beautiful.

The next rising of 1719 again found Seaforth as the chief protagonist of the Stewarts. If the

RIVER SHIEL, MOIDART

unfortunate death of the Protestant Charles XII of Sweden had not completely upset the plans of the Catholic Cardinal Alberoni, there would have been no need for a "Forty-five". Charles XII was to lead the expedition to Scotland.

Recent enlightened historians have suggested that the Highlanders joined Prince Charles Edward because they were either Episcopalian or Catholic and that those who were not motivated by religious convictions were influenced by fear or hatred of the Campbells and that was why nominal Presbyterians were found in the Jacobite ranks. The important point, however, is that the common people of Gaeldom, whether Catholic, Episcopalian or Presbyterian, were almost completely in sympathy with the Stewart cause. Whatever may have been the fault of the Stuarts, and the Highlanders were not quite sure that they possessed all the faults ascribed to them, they were, nevertheless, the direct link with Robert Bruce and the spirit of national patriotism that animated the Highlanders who fought at Bannockburn. What the Gaels did think can best be gauged from the spirit of eighteenth-century Gaelic poetry, which by the second half of the century had come to its finest flowering. Duncan Ban MacIntyre, a Presbyterian and tenant on the Campbell Breadalbane estates, fought in the Hanoverian ranks at the battle of Falkirk. He ran away as fast as he could, chuckling inwardly over the discomfiture of the Hanoverians or, as he called them, "the English-speaking folk", *luchd Beurla*. In his second poem on the battle he says that "the sons of Scotland are without esteem now that Charles has gone from us into exile". To Duncan Ban the terrible humiliation was in "submitting to England and enlisting in the forces of King George". Rob Donn MacKay of Durness, Sutherland, a Presbyterian and member of a Covenanting clan, composed songs both before and after Culloden, songs which to the Hanoverian régime were nothing but the rankest Jacobite sedition. No one in Durness seems to have remonstrated with him except the Reverend Murdoch Macdonald, the local Presbyterian minister, who seems to have been the only Hanoverian in the area. Today there are two books in every house in Durness, and sometimes there are only two, but they are treasured equally; one is the Holy (Protestant) Bible in Gaelic and the other, also in Gaelic, is an edition of the poems of Rob Donn, full of utter abhorrence of the Protestant Hanoverians and calling down the blessings of the Almighty on the Roman Catholic head of Charles Edward Stuart. William Ross of Gairloch, also a Presbyterian, composed a touching and very beautiful song on hearing that "ancient Scotland's royal heir was consigned to the earth in Rome in a narrow, polished coffin of boards". He goes on to say that "good as the clergy [Presbyterian] may be and despite all the joys that their lips promise us, I fear that we shall still be seen shedding tears for the White Cockade that is no more". Even to this very year and day oral tradition in completely Presbyterian Highland communities is full of stories about Gaelic-speaking officers and men in the Hanoverian forces who looked the other way when they saw, and could have captured, the Prince. It may be argued that oral tradition is not documentary evidence, but, more often than not, it is the completely faithful and irrefutable reiteration of the evidence of living witnesses.

After the "Forty-five" came the confiscation of the estates, the abolition of heritable jurisdictions and the sadistic and humiliating Disarming Act, which affected all Highlanders, whether they had been Jacobites or not. The Hanoverian régime recognised the fact — which most Highland historians choose to overlook — that every Gaelic-speaking Highlander, irrespective of creed or denomination, was a potential nationalist, a Jacobite and rebel. Towards the end of the century there was formulated the brilliant policy of enlisting the "secret enemy" to destroy him as cannon-fodder. Highlanders were again dressed up in kilts and, by the ingenious use of names such as Cameron, Seaforth, and Gordon, old loyalties were diverted into new channels. The end of the Napoleonic Wars almost necessitated another fresh policy to deal

THE OLD IRON-WORKS AT BONAWE, LOCH ETIVE-SIDE

with the same "secret enemy". Another way was soon to present itself, for the horror of the "Clearances" was now to be let loose on the luckless Gaels.

In the chapters that follow, and which deal with the mainland of the Highlands only, much of the history of the last century-and-a-half will be discussed. At the outset readers will be introduced to two valiant and loyal clans, whose patrimony was secured not by any written charter but by the sword, and there were and still are, at least remnants of them, in Lochaber.

DERELICT SHED, SEIL ISLAND, ARGYLL

SCOTS PINE, LOCH EILT

SOLITARY TREE GROWING IN CLEFT OF A BOULDER, RANNOCH MOOR

EVENING LIGHT NEAR STRONENABA, LOCH LOCHY

CASTLE STALKER, APPIN, ARGYLLSHIRE

EVENING LIGHT, LOCH LOYNE, WITH THE HILLS OF KNOYDART BEYOND

DUNADD, ARGYLLSHIRE – THE ANCIENT CAPITAL OF THE SCOTS

TREES BY THE SHORE, APPIN, ARGYLLSHIRE

BEINN GHOBHLACH AND LOCH BROOM AT DAWN

LATE ON A SUMMER'S EVENING AT LOCH BROOM IN WESTER ROSS

EVENING SUN ON THE MINCH FROM SOUTH ERRADALE, WESTER ROSS

SUN AND FALLING WATER

A STIFF BREEZE SWEEPS INTO THE BAY AT GAIRLOCH IN WESTER ROSS

KYLE OF DURNESS AND CRANSTACKIE, NORTH-WEST SUTHERLAND

A SUMMER'S EVENING, LOCH CARRON

GLEN SHIEL: "ON BOTH SIDES OF THE GLEN THERE IS A SERIES OF PEAKS RISING TO OVER THREE THOUSAND FEET. ONE DOES NOT EASILY FORGET GLEN SHIEL."

COTTAGE AT TORRISDALE, NORTH SUTHERLAND

INVERARAY ON LOCH FYNE, ARGYLLSHIRE

SHORE NEAR SALLACHAN, ARDGOUR WITH LOCH LINNHE BEYOND

CREAG RORY, BLACK ISLE, ROSS-SHIRE

A FROSTY WINTER'S MORNING IN GLEN SHIEL, WESTER ROSS

GLAS LEAC MOR AND THE OUTER HEBRIDES FROM POLBAIN, ACHILTIBUIE, WESTER ROSS

EDDRACHILLIS BAY, NORTH-WEST SUTHERLAND

ARISAIG BAY AND THE ISLE OF EIGG

PATTERNS IN THE SAND, KYLE OF DURNESS, SUTHERLAND

LOCH NA H-ACHLAIS AND THE BLACKMOUNT, SOUTH OF RANNOCH MOOR

ARDVRECK CASTLE ON LOCH ASSYNT, NORTH-WEST SUTHERLAND

MORNING MIST ROLLS AWAY FROM THE HILLS OF COIGACH

MIST ON LOCH LAGGAN-SIDE, SOUTH-EAST INVERNESS-SHIRE

JURA AND THE SOUND OF JURA FROM KNAPDALE

SANNA, ARDNAMURCHAN

CLOUD PATTERNS, STOB NAN CABAR, GLENCOE

DUCKS AT PORTUAIRK, ARDNAMURCHAN, INVERNESS-SHIRE

STAC POLLAIDH AND LOCH LURGAINN IN COIGACH, ROSS-SHIRE

UPPER LOCH TORRIDON AND BEINN DAMH, FROM ALLIGIN SHUAS

LOCH ETIVE

BEN NEVIS, LOCHABER: RISING TO 4,406 FEET, BEN NEVIS IS THE HIGHEST MOUNTAIN IN THE BRITISH ISLES. THIS VIEW IS FROM AN GARBHANACH IN THE MAMORE FOREST

ULLAPOOL AND LOCH BROOM

EVENING LIGHT, LOOKING DOWN LOCH LEVEN TOWARDS BALLACHULISH

BEN NEVIS, LOCHABER

Chapter One

LOCHABER

THERE would be no Highlands without Lochaber, the grand and wild Lochaber of the woods and majestic mountains, tarns and sweeping valleys, Lochaber with its wild and stormy past. Its grandeur impresses one not so much in the height of summer as in winter, when it lies deep in snow and the winds of winter; then I first came to know and love Lochaber. To the Gaelic mind it recalls the names of Montrose and Alasdair, the son of Colla Ciotach, Donald Dubh Ballach and the gentle Locheil. Here was the home of the loyal clans and the lost causes. Twice on the field of Inverlochy the Clan Donald won spectacular victories in campaigns that were doomed to end in failure and did end far away from Lochaber. The first time the victor was Donald Dubh Ballach, who defeated the forces of the Scottish Crown under the Earls of Mar and Caithness. That was in the year 1431.

> The pibroch of Donald Dubh, the pibroch of Donald;
> The pibroch of Donald Dubh, the pibroch of Donald;
> The pibroch of Donald Dubh, the pibroch of Donald;
> Pipe and pennon on the plain of Inverlochy.
>
> The Clan MacIntosh fled and fled,
> The Clan MacIntosh fled and fled,
> The Clan MacIntosh fled and fled,
> Away went the Clan Macpherson and Clan Donald stayed.

The second time was in the year 1645, when the Great Montrose and Alasdair, the son of Colla Ciotach, swept the Campbell clan into the ice-cold waters of Loch Linnhe. The Highland host had come with miraculous rapidity through deep January snows over the mountains from Fort Augustus and caught the Covenanting army unawares. John Macdonald, the Bard of Keppoch, brought word to Alasdair, the son of Colla Ciotach, that the galleys of Argyll had come to Inverlochy. "If that is not true," said Alasdair, the son of Colla Ciotach, "you will hang from the first tree I see in Lochaber."

Away went the Highland host to Lochaber and swept round the far side of Ben Nevis. As dawn was breaking on a cold Sunday morning, the Covenanting army was sighted at Inverlochy. The Bard of Keppoch escaped hanging and lived to sing the praises of the victors and of his beloved Alasdair, the son of Colla Ciotach.

"I ascended early on Sunday morning to the top of the Castle of Inverlochy. I saw the army being drawn up in battle order, and the victory of the day lay with Clan Donald.

Alasdair, son of the splendid Colla, right hand to cleave the castles, you have routed the wizened Lowland *carles* and, if they drank *kail*, you have made them spew it."

But not all the loyal clans shared the honours of the second battle. The story goes that the Clan Cameron did not take part in the rout of the Campbells. The Locheil of the time was an old man, too old to go to the battle although he would have dearly loved to cross swords with the Covenanting forces. He was married to a daughter of Maclean of Duart and from her had a son. This son was hardly a chip off the old block, but it fell to him to lead the Camerons to Inverlochy. Some distance from the field and away up on the hillside between the villages of Corpach and Banavie there is a copse called Bad Abraich. The young Locheil waited there all day with his men and watched the battle. Not one Cameron sword was unsheathed. Towards evening the old Locheil waited anxiously at Achnacarry to get news of his son and clansmen. A party of Camerons was seen approaching. The old man hurried towards them and accosted the first he met.

"How went it with my son and the men today?" asked Locheil.

"Your son," said the clansman, "did not go to the battle. He remained in Bad Abraich all day long and watched the fight."

"My son!" said the indignant Locheil. "He is not my son but the son of the bitch, the Maclean woman."

Later Locheils were to redeem the good name of the clan; no clan played a nobler part in the "Forty-five" than the Camerons.

Lochaber was always the bastion that never fell until the final defeat at Culloden. Here there was always resistance to central authority. There was something indomitable about the Camerons of Locheil and the Macdonells of Keppoch. At Mulroy, near where the present Catholic church at Roy Bridge stands, was fought the last clan battle in the year 1688. There the Macdonell chief, Colla of the Cows, inflicted a crushing defeat on the MacIntoshes, who apparently were trapped in a deep gully and almost entirely wiped out. The MacIntoshes based their claim to the Keppoch lands on a Crown charter, but the Macdonells held on to their inheritance by the strength of the sword-arm. Eight hundred Macdonells followed their chief to Killiecrankie and fought along with "Bonnie" Dundee. They came mostly from districts where there is not one living soul today.

There has been a heavy drain of population from Lochaber as elsewhere in the Highlands. Many of the remote glens are completely desolate. The folk are leaving the valleys of the Spean and Roy and moving either into Fort William or going to the south. The native Gaelic stock is decaying. I remember a retired shepherd telling that in his young days there was a thriving community at Achnasaul on the shores of Loch Arkaig. There they used to gather on winter nights to listen to storytelling. Only a few shepherds live along the sides of Loch Arkaig now. The people are gone; the storytelling a thing of the past. Nothing seems able to arrest the process of depopulation once it sets in. The young people no longer desire to remain country folk; their faith in the land is shattered. Crofting is no longer regarded as a means of livelihood. Sons and daughters of crofters now learn next to nothing about work on the land. What is worse: they no longer want to learn. In the old days crofting townships were practically self-sufficient. They clothed, housed and fed themselves, brewed their own ale and distilled their own whisky. They had their own social life and provided their own entertainment. Any money needed was used for buying luxuries that were not entirely indispensable. Every township or community had its own carpenters, wheelwrights, blacksmiths, shoemakers, dressmakers, and tailors. Very often the countryman could turn his hand to many crafts. Life was at times a hard struggle, but the straths and glens did breed a sturdy stock, a race more generously endowed both mentally and physically than the football fans and cinema devotees of the industrial centres of Scotland of our day. Highland depopulation began with the "Clearances" in the early part of last century. The initial causes were violent and completely criminal. The continuance of that depopulation ought to be a very heavy weight on the conscience of any civilised government.

I remember walking up Glen Roy to visit an old man who told me stories one evening in springtime four years ago. Glen Roy must be one of the most beautiful glens in the Highlands. In a few years it will be derelict and dead. The ageing population there at present will have gone because, among other things, they have no water supply and no electric light in their houses in Glen Roy. All these blessings of modern "civilisation" are available even as near as the village of

Roy Bridge at the entrance of the glen. There was a school at Bohuntine in Glen Roy once: today there is none. Yet Glen Roy is not so very far away from the railway line. Exactly a year from that evening I walked up Glen Roy, I was staying with Johan Persson in Långåskans in the province of Härjedalen, Sweden. Långåskans is about forty miles from the nearest railway terminus. Johan is a small farmer and owns some few acres of forest. Johan Persson has had electric light in his stables and byre, not to speak of his house, for many years now, and there I saw every conceivable labour-saving device operated by electricity. Young people will stay in Långåskans even though it is completely snow-bound almost from November till March. In both places there is to be found the same affection for the homeland. Långåskans will live. Glen Roy will be desolate. Why must that be so? I just wonder if the real reason is the difference between government from Stockholm and government from Westminster. One very important point must be stressed. It was in Glen Roy I found the only Gaelic-speakers in Lochaber under forty years of age. There also I found one of the best traditional fiddlers in Lochaber. With Glen Roy, a language, a culture, a civilisation passes into oblivion.

The object of my visit to Lochaber was to garner some of the traditions that had survived the ravages of time and were in danger of passing into the realms of the unknown. A new culture had penetrated the Rough Bounds (Garbhchriochan) of the Gael and was sweeping before it all traces, all memories of the past. Before it became too late, I had to recover something that would give our contemporaries and the generations of the future some picture of that past. My sources of information were not to be guide-books, travellers' accounts or the prejudiced writings of formal historians. They had to be living sources breathing the air and treading the soil of Lochaber. They are, of course, the people who know most about Lochaber. In the past, generation after generation of them returned slowly to the dust and left not one single record of what they ever knew or learned about their *patria*. Without doubt, the transmission of knowledge had proceeded orally for centuries. The time had come when the process had ceased or was about to cease. The process was about to cease because the younger generation was no longer interested in its continuance. The culture of Hollywood has certainly influenced youth in Lochaber today. Formal education during the past seventy years did not help much to instil into Highland youth a pride or interest in their native districts. There is hardly one child in any school in Lochaber today who will be able to read, write or even speak Gaelic on reaching school-leaving age. Yet English was a completely foreign language in Lochaber until the advent of the West Highland Railway in the final decade of last century. At the time of the "Forty-five", and prior to that, Highland chieftains in Lochaber and elsewhere sent their children to be educated in France. The Cameron of Locheil and Macdonell of Keppoch at the time of the "Forty-five" were Gaelic-speakers despite the fact that they were cultured gentlemen. Today the country families and the bourgeoisie of Lochaber send their children to be educated in England, if at all possible. The Mammon they worship speaks good Southern English. The people of quality in Lochaber today have two distinctive markings: they wear kilts and have the "received pronunciation". The less intelligent lower strata of society talk English with an accent more akin to that of Glasgow and the industrial belt than the soft Gaelic accent of the western seaboard. Now that Gaelic is no longer spoken, the use of Gaelic sounds in English speech must be avoided at all costs. There is nothing worse than having the epithet "Heilant" hurled at one. That is one of the results of the Scottish education system. There has always been some subtle insinuation that Highland and barbaric are synonymous. Formal Scottish historians did not quite say so. Nevertheless, they implied as much. At present the only remedy seems to be to close every school in the Highlands for ten years and send Highland children to be educated in the Scandinavian countries, in Germany, France and Italy. If something of that nature were

CHURCH AT GLENFINNAN

practicable, one thing is certain: there would be hell to pay if these children returned to Scotland after an absence of ten years on the Continent. They would certainly not return as monoglot English speakers. As well as that they would have learned to value language and nationality. They would return as very good Highlanders with a European outlook. To the peace of Her Britannic Majesty's realm they would be a source of very grave danger. The "Clearances" would be all in vain. If I were not a Highlander, I should say that it would be a good thing if the Gaelic language and all Gaelic traditions went into outer darkness. For what would it be a good thing? Any Highlander worth anything ought to say that his language and nationality must be saved at all costs. To hell with transient powers, principalities, and empires! The things of the spirit are what really matter.

To get the traditions of Lochaber I did not have to go to the homes of the county people. I did not have to go to the people with social prestige or status. I had to look for what the Irish poet, the late F. R. Higgins, described as "the lowly, the humble, the passionate and the knowledgeable stock of the Gael". Even in the Lochaber of today the Gael is not far to seek. I did not expect to see kilted stalwarts coming down the Lairig Leacach brandishing Lochaber axes. I knew it was useless to try to conjure up the spirit of the reiver-songster, Donald Donn of Bohuntine, or the Hag of Beinne Bhric or the malevolent Glaistig of Lianachan, who pronounced a curse on the Kennedy clan and promised them that they would "wax like the rushes, decay like the bracken, grow grey in childhood and die in the prime of strength". I had to find living people whose memories were not dead.

It was on a cold Sunday morning in January 1951 that I first met little John Macdonald of Highbridge or John the Bard, as he is called. He had just come from Mass in the church at Roy Bridge. That morning he had cycled over eight miles to church through showers of sleet and hail. That was not bad for a man of seventy-five years of age. He wore no overcoat. John Macdonald is a sturdy man, somewhat under medium height, but very alert and active. His little grey eyes seemed to pierce right through me as I approached him. I greeted him in Gaelic. On hearing his own language, he immediately shed his reserve and smiled. He was John the Bard. He could not remember how many songs he had composed, perhaps a hundred or two. He had just composed a song in praise of the young Scots who removed the Stone of Destiny from Westminster Abbey. The Stone was then at large. We crouched down behind a wall and he sang the song. It was full of vigour and fire. The historic Scottish nation still lived. The Stone of Destiny really belonged to Scotland. John the Bard did not give a damn if the police never set eyes on it again. Of course, he would tell me stories. His father knew everything that ever happened in Lochaber. He would meet me that afternoon. He sprang up, mounted his cycle with the agility of a youth of seventeen and was gone. I knew I had met a real character.

That afternoon John Macdonald did come to see me. It was the first of many afternoons and evenings together. We continued to meet once weekly for a whole five months. Day after day he came and poured out the unwritten history of Lochaber. Everything that ever took place there seems to have left some imprint on his memory. Figures like St Columba, Robert Bruce, the Red Comyn, Donald Balloch son of the Lord of the Isles, the Earl of Mar vanquished at the first battle of Inverlochy, Montrose and Alasdair, the son of Colla Ciotach, Charles Edward Stuart — no pretender but the rightful heir to the throne — and the patriot Dr Archibald Cameron, brother of Locheil, flitted across the stage with which John the Bard was so familiar. We were one lovely summer day walking along from Roy Bridge to Spean. Away to the west Beinn Bhàn at the lower end of Loch Lochy was silhouetted against an unusually clear Lochaber sky.

"The Prince," said John the Bard, "was coming over the top of the mountain from the Achnacarry side. As soon as he came over the ridge yonder, he saw a party of redcoats down below him in Mucomer. They were looking for him but did not see him, for he threw himself down among the heather and waited there until night came. He was quite safe here in Lochaber. They had all been out with him. I heard my father telling that there was a very strong woman living over at Stronenaba then. She was then an old woman and her son was at Culloden along with the Prince's army. Her brother's son was there as well. News came that the battle had gone against the Gaels, but there was no sight of the sons. The old man walked all the way to Culloden and found his son lying sorely wounded among the dead. There was still life in him, and the father carried him on his back all the way down Loch Ness-side and down the Great Glen. Over there at Letterfinlay, just as they were coming in sight of home, the son gave up the ghost. His father carried the corpse home to Stronenaba. When he was passing his sister's house, she came out and said:

'Were you at the field of battle?'

'Yes,' said the brother.

'Did you see my son there?'

'I did,' said he, 'but I had to leave him behind.'

'Was he dead?' she asked.

'He was not dead, but there was not much life in him. He was sorely, sorely wounded and the redcoat devils must have thought he was dead.'

'Ah!' she said, 'if I had been there, I would have taken the two of them with me.' "

I do not know what the woman's name was but she may have been a Cameron. In that district of Lochaber there are still some very fine physical specimens. The late A. A. Cameron, the most noted of all Highland athletes, belonged to Mucomer. In the years immediately before the Second World War, ten Camerons from Stronenaba played for the Spean Bridge shinty club. Physically they were much the best shinty team in the Highlands. Shinty is still the most popular game in Lochaber. Three senior shinty teams, Fort William, Kilmallie and Brae Lochaber, represent the district in competitions open to the Highlands. The once-noted Spean Bridge team plays now in junior competitions, although some young men from Spean Bridge play for the Roy Bridge team, Brae Lochaber. There is still much keen interest taken in the game despite the fact that the running of clubs is a costly business owing to the exorbitant price of shinty sticks. In pre-war years hickory shinty clubs cost seven shillings and sixpence. Hickory clubs are no longer obtainable, but the ash sticks now used cost as much as thirty-five shillings although they are not nearly as good as hickory sticks. In the course of one game several sticks may be broken. For teams run on a purely amateur basis the cost of clubs can be a heavy item during a season usually starting in November and lasting as long as the following July. In districts where there is a long tradition of shinty-playing every effort is made to carry on out of a sense of loyalty to a game regarded as distinctly Highland and national. Shinty was the game played by Cuchulainn, the hero of the early Gaelic sagas. In the Highland glens where teams can be mustered it is played still. Two thousand years have almost gone since Cuchulainn played. The shinty-players of today are heirs to a long tradition. A handful of Highland exiles still have their clubs in Glasgow and Edinburgh. The game is mainly played in the Upper Spey Valley, Lochaber, Lochfyneside, Oban and Lorn, the Caledonian Canal Basin, the area from Inverness to Strathpeffer and westwards to Kintail and Lochalsh. The Isle of Skye alone of all Scottish islands entered into senior competitions. Shinty is very like the Irish game "hurling", but does not have nearly the following that game has not only in Ireland but also among exiles in Britain and America. Irish hurling teams occasionally play against Scottish shinty teams. Some years ago some pompous member of the Scottish Camanachd Association disapproved of such fraternisation on the grounds that the Irish were not loyal subjects of His Britannic

Majesty. It appeared that the Highlanders who went across to play in Dublin were tremendously impressed by everything they saw and heard in what is now the Republic. After all Cuchulainn was an Irish Gael despite all Scottish attempts to establish sole claim to him.

The greatest game of all took place in Invergarry two centuries or so ago between the men of Keppoch and Glengarry. The Keppoch men were victors thanks to the swiftness and prowess of a man named Iain Dubh Seang (Slim Black Iain), a man who as a motherless child was suckled by a greyhound bitch. The night after the game the Keppoch men kept watch from their native hilltops in case the smarting Glengarry men brought fire and sword to their very homesteads. After the game Slim Black Iain had to flee for his life across the hills from Invergarry to Glen Roy. That night, however, the men of Invergarry did not raid the Keppoch country. Before the days of the Camanachd Association and standardised shinty rules, parish played parish in games in which everyone participated, even women and children. A team was deemed victorious if it brought the ball well within its own parish boundary. The contests usually took place on New Year's Day.

Fort William is the biggest centre of population in the area. Its history dates back to the times when English government set up garrisons within the Highlands to quell the turbulent natives. Within recent years the town has grown considerably and is now one of the most prosperous in the Highlands. Fort William nestles right at the foot of Ben Nevis and is consequently a favoured tourist centre. The loveliest parts of the Highlands are within striking distance of the town, with its numerous hotels and boarding-houses. Here there are two distilleries and a museum. The West Highland Museum possesses a very fine collection of Jacobite relics and tartans. It also displays the interior of an old-time Highland cottage, replete with furnishings and utensils. The museum is certainly worth a visit. A couple of miles east of the town-centre and on the very spot where the first battle of Inverlochy was fought, stands the factory of the British Aluminium Company. The advent of industry has also brought in its train an influx of English-speaking workers from the south. Only a small percentage of the natives of Fort William are of old Lochaber stock. On Saturday afternoons, when the farmers and shepherds from the countryside come in to do their shopping, one still may hear Gaelic spoken in the main street. Once a year a race is run from the town square to the top of Ben Nevis. Noted cross-country runners from all parts of Scotland compete. In recent years the race has been won mostly be local runners. The finest view of Ben Nevis it to be had from the shore of Loch Eil beyond the village of Corpach.

In any account of the Lochaber of today mention must be made of the Great Glen Cattle Ranch owned by Mr Hobbs. An almost complete transformation has taken place here within recent years. Here a really serious and furthermore a successful attempt is being made to turn a waste into smiling arable and pasture land. Land that was not much more than bog a few years ago now supports a large and thriving herd. Acres of land that had not been tilled for probably a century or so now yield crops. Mr Hobbs has certainly shown what can be done when determination and the necessary capital are both available to back an undertaking. Mr Hobbs' estate stretches from Inverlochy along the valley of Allt Achadh na Dalach almost to Spean Bridge. His property can be recognised easily, as the stonework of all buildings on his estate has been painted a sickly yellow. No doubt, he is a first-class rancher, but aestheticism is not his forte.

If one approaches Lochaber by the railway line, the summit at Corrour may be taken as the march of Lochaber. One then goes along the steep northern shore of Loch Treig on to Tulloch. To the left the mountains rise steeply and here begins the ridge that stretches westward to Ben Nevis. The two highest peaks next to the Ben are both over 4,000 feet. To the right one can almost see Badenoch and in the valley to the north-east, the British Aluminium Company has

FISHING BOATS IN LOCH MORAR

built a huge dam to trap the waters flowing out of Loch Laggan and convey them by tunnel through the mountains to Loch Treig. We then come into the narrow valley of the Spean. To the left is the farm of Inverlair. It was here that Alasdair Buidhe, the instigator of the murder of the two young Keppoch chiefs, lived. The murder is to this day commemorated by the gruesome monument at the Well of the Seven Heads at Invergarry. It was Iain Lom, the Bard of Keppoch and Poet Laureate to King Charles II, who had the murderers brought to justice. Farther on to the right is the church of St Cyril (Cille Choiril). It stands high on the slope of a hill over-looking the railway line. Here it is that Iain Lom, the Bard of Keppoch, has found his last resting-place. The tradition is that he expressed a wish to be buried with his face towards his beloved Corrour. A stone taller than all others in the graveyard has been raised in his honour. All other headstones face due east; Iain Lom's headstone looks southwards to Corrour. The actual spot where his remains lie is not known now. It will never be known, for the last tradition-bearer who knew for certain is long dead. My kind friend, Mr Archibald MacInnes, caretaker of the graveyard and the most accurate authority on the history of Lochaber, does not know where Iain Lom lies although he knows every other grave marked and unmarked in St Cyril's.

A hundred yards or so further west, just where the pathway to the graveyard branches from the main road, there are a number of cairns. Here funeral parties had their last rest before bearing the corpses up the slope to the graveyard. Wherever the funeral party rested a cairn was raised in honour of the person about to be interred. As a mark of respect every member of the party had to place a stone on the cairn. At this spot are several cairns. Near Auchandaull there are three very fine cairns side by side on the verge of the main roadway. They are in honour of the three Kennedy brothers of Lianachan whose funeral parties passed that way. All of them had risen to the positions of eminence and all had died almost in the prime of life. The size of the cairn was the measure of the esteem in which a person was held. It was utter sacrilege to remove stone from a memorial-cairn. Many years ago that was done by someone engaged in building a house near Roy Bridge. The consequence of that act was an early death.

Funerals in Lochaber today are hardly like what they were two generations ago. Cairns are not raised now, as the motor-hearse has displaced human bearers and funeral parties no longer walk long distances. It was a common belief in Lochaber as elsewhere in the Highlands that the person last buried in a graveyard had to keep watch over the dead until the next interment took place. In Gaelic the term *faire chlaidh* was applied to this. Highland superstition, one will say. Nonsense! The belief is widespread and common to many European countries. In Sweden, for instance, the being that watches over the graveyard is called the *kyrkogrim*. This, of course, is not the same thing as the protection of burial-grounds by living persons against body-snatchers. The belief is much older than the birth of anatomical science. The spirit of the last person buried in a graveyard had to continue watching until relieved when the next corpse arrived, and, of course, it was never desired that a long period of watching should fall to the lot of any spirit. Rival parties approaching the same burial-ground strove to reach it first and bury the dead to ensure that the spirit's watch would not last long. Very often fights occurred between rival parties. John Macdonald tells that a Lochaber clergyman of long ago was one day walking on the banks of the Spean. As he came to a ford on the river, he noticed two little dogs converging on it from different directions on the faraway bank. They met and fought long and viciously until one of them was no longer able to move and the other crossed the river. In an instant both dogs vanished. The dogs, however, were but a shadow of what was to come. A week later two funeral parties were making for Cille Choiril. They met at that very ford and disputed the right to cross. An amicable settlement was impossible and a bloody fight ensued. The victorious party crossed the river and reached Cille Choiril. They buried the remains and that spirit's watch lasted only until the other party arrived.

In this part of Lochaber the Catholics are buried at Cille Choiril and the Protestants at Kilmonivaig near Spean Bridge. In one of the headstones at Kilmonivaig there is a hole made by a bullet. Away back in the days of the "body-snatchers", John Macdonald's father was one night watching the Kilmonivaig graves. He was armed with a muzzle-loader. Towards morning he was tired and drowsed off to sleep. Suddenly he awoke and saw what he thought was the figure of a body-snatcher. He shot. The figure did not move. The bullet, however, went clean through his victim — the headstone. Real body-snatchers did visit Lochaber. One of the Kennedy brothers of Lianachan was a student of medicine at Edinburgh. One day a corpse was brought to the dissecting laboratory. It was that of an old woman, and young Kennedy marvelled at the fine set of teeth. They reminded him of the teeth of the wife of Donald, the son of Iain, at home. That night he wrote to ask if anyone had died recently at Lianachan. In due course word came that the wife of Donald, the son of Iain, was dead. In haste young Kennedy wrote again to say that the graveyards of Lochaber were not being properly watched.

Only a few forestry workers live at Lianachan now. The Kennedy clan has decayed "like the bracken" as the malevolent Glaistig of Lianachan promised their progenitor. The Glaistig was a supernatural being in the form of an old, shrivelled woman of small stature. One day Big Donald Kennedy was riding home to Lianachan. On the way the Glaistig accosted him and asked to be allowed a pillion-ride on his steed. Her request was granted. Kennedy caught her and would not let her go until she promised to build a mansion for him that very night and have it finished by next morning. The Glaistig, true to her promise, summoned the craftsmen of the "little people" to her aid. Their number was legion, and they arrayed themselves in a long line and passed stone and timber from one to another all night long. Morning came and the mansion was finished. The Glaistig came to Big Donald Kennedy and said: "I have done what you asked. May I now shake you by the hand?" At that very moment Big Donald Kennedy was heating a plough-iron for the anvil. He took it from the fire and held the red-hot end towards her. She grasped it as if to crush his hand but caught the red-hot iron. Screaming she fled to the hills. "May your progeny wax like the rushes, decay like the bracken, grow grey in childhood and die in the prime of strength." The three cairns at Auchandaull are to this very day silent reminders of the power of the Glaistig's malevolence.

East of Lianachan a stream called The Cour flows down from the mountains to join the Spean at Inverroy. On the stream there is a waterfall called Finisgeig. Below the waterfall is a deep pool and slightly farther down there is a ford that was much used in days of old by travellers from Keppoch and the Upper Spean Valley going and coming from Fort William. One of the most fascinating of John the Bard's stories is told about Finisgeig. One day, and it was a dark winter's day, a young man on his way to Fort William came to the swollen waters of The Cour and was just about to cross the ford. From the dark depth of the pool came a hollow voice:

> Young man, listen to the word of counsel. When Finisgeig has one calf a boy may cross The Cour. When Finisgeig has two calves a horse and boy may cross The Cour, but when Finisgeig has three calves, neither a host nor clan can cross The Cour. I did not heed my mother's warning and here I was drowned. Go home and tell this to your kith and kin.

Needless to say the young wayfarer did not cross the ford, for on that day Finisgeig had three calves — there were three rivulets tumbling over the edge of the waterfall as well as the main stream. The Cour was in spate and the ford impassable. Ever after that, wayfarers first looked at Finisgeig before attempting to cross the ford. In the tradition of Lochaber, as well as other parts of the Highlands, the dead return to warn the living.

The ruins of Inverlochy Castle may still be seen at Lochyside north-west of Fort William. The second battle was fought within a stone's throw of its walls. Past the town to the south-west the main roadway to Glencoe and the south skirts the steep eastern shore of Loch Linnhe and turns eastwards along the northern shore of Loch Leven. This part is called Nether Lochaber: Upper or more usually, Brae Lochaber is the name of the district from Fort William to Tulloch. There is a glorious view of Loch Linnhe and the hills of Ardgour all the way from the Fort to Onich and from then on to Kinlochleven an equally fine view of the hills of Glencoe and Appin. Nether Lochaber is Cameron country.

No railway line in Britain passes through more beautiful country than the line from Fort William to Mallaig. It runs along the northern shore of Loch Eil past the villages of Banavie and Corpach. The names of both are interesting. Banavie was so named by early Gaelic settlers from Ireland whose homeland was of old called Banbha. Corpach is the place of corpses. Here the corpses of chiefs and others of high birth were embarked on the way to interment at Iona. At Corpach there is a very fine obelisk in memory of Col John Cameron of Fassifern who commanded the Gordons on the eve of Waterloo. He was killed at Quatre Bras on the eve of the battle. His body was brought home to Lochaber and his was the most magnificent funeral that Lochaber has ever seen. One hundred and thirty-nine years have passed since the eve of Waterloo. The monument raised in memory of Col John Cameron stands to this day, but in Lochaber another tradition has long outlived the oldest veteran of the Napoleonic Wars. I doubt if any formal historian knows what Col Cameron's last words were, but most formal historians would not understand them in any case, for they were spoken in Gaelic. In Sweden a fierce controversy has raged for many years between formal historians and the brilliant director of the Marburg Museum on the west of Sweden. The point at issue is the nature of the death of Sweden's heroic king, Charles XII. There has been a persistent tradition that Charles XII was shot by one of his own men. Dr Sandklef's researches have gone a way towards proving that the tradition was based on actual fact. The formal historians have written lengthy volumes to disprove that thesis. Recently Dr Sandklef seems to have had the best of the argument. I do not wish to precipitate another controversy regarding a Scottish hero. In Lochaber it is still said that Col John Cameron was not killed by a French bullet. He met his death at the hands of one of his own men. As he lay dying, he said to his Gaelic-speaking adjutant: "*Chan e mo nàmhaid a rinn siod.*" (It was not my foe that did that.)

The adjutant replied: "*Biodh fhios agat nach e do charaid a rinn e.*" (Be assured that it was not your friend that did it.)

The bald account of Col Cameron's death lacks most of the trappings of stories told about commanders shot by their own men. We are not told that anyone had an "animus" against him, nor that he had an Achilles heel. The event was probably too recent for any account of it to have acquired the normal, traditional pattern. It was foretold of Charles XII that he could be killed only by a button from his own clothing and his vulnerable spot was his forehead. According to tradition in the Clanranald country, the most noted of all their chiefs died at the hands of one of his own followers, an unwilling follower, as the story goes. Allan Mor of Clanranald was mortally wounded on the field of Sheriffmuir. Before leaving South Uist, a charm (*seun*) was put upon him to protect against leaden shot. When his doublet was examined it was riddled with holes, but not one single mark was there on his body except the one wound that proved fatal. Allan's weak spot was his right armpit. From Uist he had brought in his train a widow's only son, much against the mother's wishes. The widow was determined that Allan Mor would pay dearly for his action. She gave her son a sixpence of silver that had been cursed seven times and told him to aim at his right armpit, when the first chance came. In the heat of battle, Allan Mor raised his right arm to urge on his men and then the widow's son saw his chance. The silver sixpence did the rest.

Had Charles XII of Sweden not met his death at Fredricksten in 1718, the whole course of Scottish and British history might have been changed and changed utterly. At the time of his death, a continental expedition to Scotland to effect the restoration of the Stuarts was being planned and Charles was to lead it. No Hanoverian force could ever have stood up to Charles XII leading the Highland clans alongside his own trained, seasoned veterans. But for one single button there might have been no King's English, no British Empire, no Disarming Act, no shipping of Highlanders to the Barbados and to slavery, no more of the blood and race of the "Butcher Cumberland", none of the barbarity of the Highland "Clearances", no thrashing of children for talking Gaelic in Highland schools and the Clan Donald would have had the power to make another retaliatory Glencoe of the whole Campbell country. The death of the heroic Charles XII of Sweden was about the greatest tragedy that ever befell the Gaels of Alba. But for that fatal button the Orkney and Shetland Islands would be governed not from Westminster but from Oslo, as they ought to be. But for that very button, An Gearsadan Dubh (the Black Garrison), as Fort William is called in Gaelic, would have been rechristened Baile Mhuire (Maryburgh). Had the heroic Charles lived to lead his expedition and make contact with the loyal clans, thousands of Highland hearts might have been spared the terrible anguish of "Lochaber no more".

On calm days the waters of Loch Eil are the most placid in all Scotland. The loch is long and narrow like a leather thong: its Gaelic name is most appropriate, for it is Loch Iall (Thong Loch). During the years of the Second World War Loch Eil was full of tankers and other ugly naval vessels. On its shores at Annat and Corpach squalid clusters of prefabricated houses sprang up and to them came the scum of the industrial midlands of England and Scotland. Most of that has now been cleared up again, and Locheil-side now looks more like what it must have been in the days of Eoghan Dubh Cameron of Locheil away back in the Cromwellian times. During the occupation of Scotland the English soldiery were stationed in Lochaber. One day a party of Camerons under Eoghan Dubh encountered a band of English soldiers out gathering firewood by Locheil-side. Eoghan Dubh and his men were not the kind to shun a scrap. In the ensuing fight Eoghan Dubh grappled with an enormous English officer. They wrestled and the Englishman threw Eoghan on the flat of his back and held him to the ground. Eoghan's hands were pinioned but like a flash he caught the Englishman's throat in his teeth and did not let go until he had torn out his windpipe. Some years after the Restoration, Eoghan visited England and happened to go into a barber's shop to be shaved. The barber, noticing his strange dress and appearance, asked him if he hailed from Scotland. Eoghan replied in the affirmative. As he held the razor to Eoghan's throat the barber said: "There are some terrible savages in Scotland. Do you know that a Highlander tore the windpipe out of my father with his teeth. If I had the throat of the villain who did it, I'd waste little time slitting it with this razor." Eoghan never again entered a barber's shop.

I shall always associate Kinlocheil with someone whom I have never seen, someone I shall never see. During my months in Lochaber I paid many visits to the late John Macleod, a Fort William newsagent. John was a fine storyteller as well as being one of the very finest of Highland gentlemen. He was passionately devoted to the Gaelic language and Gaelic traditions. We spent many pleasant hours together. John always told me that his brother, Joseph, who was station-master at Kinlocheil, had scores and scores of old songs and other lore as well. The Macleod brothers were natives of Glen Finnan and knew the whole history of that lovely, fateful glen. Joseph had songs that no living person knows now, songs that had been sung in Glen Finnan long before it ever saw Charles Edward Stuart, the last rightful prince of the Gael. Joseph was a comparatively young man. I left Lochaber in June 1951 and did not succeed in visiting him. I was away for over a year. When I returned Joseph Macleod was dead. The recording of folk-songs has become quite fashionable in Scotland during the last few years. Certain singers have had their songs recorded by as many as a dozen collectors. All Joseph Macleod's songs went with him to the grave. His brother, John, died shortly afterwards. Two authentic Highland voices are now silenced for ever.

Across the mountains due north from the head of Loch Eil is Glen Dessary at the western end of Loch Arkaig. Here Lochaber marches with the lands of Glengarry. From the shores of Loch Arkaig "the Gentle Donald" brought a great many of the fighting men who followed him to Culloden. In the following century a less noble and less Gaelic Locheil cleared the Camerons from the shores of Loch Arkaig and scattered them to the four winds of heaven: their land he gave to alien tacksmen and sheep-farmers. The martial Cameron clan was dealt a blow more cruel than it received at Culloden: after Culloden there was hope that the French would still come and that Charles would again be at the head of the Highland host. After the "Clearances" there was no hope — only bitter and terrible despair. Today the shores of Loch Arkaig are deserted — silent as the grave. During the first week-end of February 1951 a terrific snowstorm swept Lochaber. On a dark afternoon the factor of the Locheil estates went to inspect fences on high ground near Loch Arkaig. The storm struck in its fury, and when the unfortunate factor did not return home, sufficient men could not be found in the neighbourhood to organise a search-party. The factor's body was not found until months afterwards. The hills and mountains of Lochaber have often claimed victims during snowstorms.

I first heard Loch Arkaig mentioned in a lovely song I heard in the Island of Raasay. It was a love song sung to an enchanting melody. Like so many of the traditional Gaelic folk-songs it was simple yet something of absolute sincerity and intensity.

> Hi eile ho gu
> Dh' fhalbh mo rún air an aiseag.
>
> Hi eile ho gu
> My love has gone across the sea.
>
> My love has gone on the boat;
> Safely may he come home.
>
> My love left a year ago
> And my reason left me this week past.
>
> The red doe and her fawn
> Will my beloved bring home.
>
> And the green-headed wild duck
> That comes from the banks of Loch Arkaig.
>
> Yours is the hand to steer a boat
> And no surly sea wearies you.

110

BRIDGE OVER THE RUSSEL BURN AND SGURR A GHAORACHAIN, ON THE WAY TO APPLECROSS

You are the swimmer of the strait
Who does not call for the ferry.

Since you went by way of the ford
You did not choose to visit me.

Since you have tied a knot firmly
Often tears fall from my lashes.

My love left a year ago
And my reason left me this week past.

The song has been recorded in Cape Breton also, for many of those evicted from Lochaber went thither. In Lochaber I sought in vain for the song: it is certainly not known to anyone within miles of Loch Arkaig. I doubt very much if it will ever be taught in any school in Lochaber, certainly not as long as the Inverness-shire County Education Committee continues to litter the schools of the country with monoglot English-speaking headmasters. A knowledge of Icelandic is an indispensable qualification in the case of every public appointment in Iceland. The same is true of Finnish in Finland, Norwegian in Norway, Swedish in Sweden, Danish in Denmark, Faroese in the Faroes and English in England. There is no reason whatsoever why a knowledge of Gaelic should not be quite as indispensable in the case of all appointments within the Gaelic-speaking areas. Norwegian educationists approve of the teaching of the three world-languages, French, German, and English, as well as Norwegian in Norway. I agree with them. They will certainly agree with me regarding the teaching of the three world-languages as well as Gaelic in Scotland.

Locheil's residence, Achnacarry, is at the eastern end of Loch Arkaig. Part of the old house burnt down after the "Forty-five" may still be seen. The Royal Mile of trees planted hurriedly by Locheil when news of the Prince's arrival reached him, may be seen also, although a great many trees have been cut down. The last time I saw the place, it had a very untidy appearance. Forestry workers and timber merchants had been at work. I have never seen any part of the Highlands where young trees shoot up so rapidly and in such profusion as here. Achnacarry was used as a commando training-centre during the Second World War. A memorial to the commandos stands on an eminence by the roadside near Spean Bridge.

It was John Macdonald of Highbridge who told me of the sequence of events that led to the capture of Dr Archibald Cameron, brother of Locheil. Seven years after Culloden, Dr Archibald returned to Scotland. He stayed for some time at Achnacarry, where a nephew of his, a young boy, was ill. The local physician at Fort William had been attending the boy, but under his treatment the patient showed no signs of recovery. The physician continued the same treatment, when, quite unaccountably, the boy made a rapid and complete recovery. Some skilled hands had been at work and the physician immediately thought of Dr Cameron. Out of professional jealousy rather than out of a sense of loyalty to the Hanoverian régime, the medical gentleman decided to contact the military authorities. The noble and humanitarian Archibald Cameron was captured and went to his death as befitted one of his name. The execution of Dr Archibald Cameron was an act of unpardonable sadism on the part of the British Government. All through the campaign the doctor's duties were non-combatant and he had given his services readily to the wounded on both sides. As long as true Highlanders like John Macdonald of Highbridge remain, even the commandos will have come, gone and been forgotten while the name of Dr Archibald Cameron of Locheil will still be revered and honoured. The memorial to

Dr Archibald Cameron is more lasting than any edifice of stone or bronze, for it is deep in the hearts of the Gael.

During the fishing season Loch Arkaig is very popular with anglers. In this area I once had the good fortune of meeting anglers who were a decided exception to the rule; so far from being boring they were charming and fascinatingly amusing. It had been a beautiful day in 1951, and I had walked a distance of over ten miles back to Spean Bridge from Bohene in Glen Roy, where James Macdonald of Bohene had shown me a stone used as a mortar for grinding herbs by Donald MacEoghain, a noted medical man of old-time Lochaber. I was very thirsty after the long walk, and my friends John and Milly Macdonell joined me in the bar of Spean Bridge Hotel. There we fell in with the anglers. They had spent the whole day on Loch Arkaig but with little success, for the day had been much too bright. They were three young Glasgow businessmen. We discovered that we had a friend in common. They had fished in the Outer Hebrides and especially at Creagorry, Benbecula. At Creagorry their ghillie was none other than my friend, Donald MacKinnon or, as he is popularly known, Domhnall Curstaidh. Donald must be about the most unorthodox ghillie alive as well as one of the most popular. He is the complete antithesis of the subservient, cap-touching, monosyllabic Highland ghillie. Even in his lifetime he has become a legend. He has led more than one unsuspecting angler a pretty merry dance. He has a special penchant for dropping stones into lochs and streams behind the backs of unwary fishermen. He is so adroit at his job and his victims testify to the exact weight and size of the non-existent fish they see leaping but completely fail to catch. "I bought a light salmon-rod," said one of the anglers. "It was rather expensive and I was quite proud of it. It was my first day in Creagorry and I hired Donald to fish Loch Bee for the day. I showed him my rod.

'It is a very fine rod,' said Donald, 'but it won't catch any fish.'

I was frankly amazed, for I was not quite used to this. We started fishing and Donald rowed for some time. All of a sudden I hooked a huge fish, but before I could say Jack Robinson away it went with the line, leaving the bare rod in my hands. There was dead silence for about one full minute. At last I looked round. Donald was resting on his oars. With the quietest and gentlest of voices he said, 'You stupid bu——r,' and dipped his oars into the water again. I did no more fishing that day."

About the most noted of Lochaber's local heroes was Donald Cameron who was factor to the Huntly and Gordon estates in Lochaber during the early part of last century. In tradition he is known as Domhnall Mor Og (Big Young Donald). He was a powerful figure and an unsurpassed marksman. Many stories are told about him, some of them quite remarkable. A very fine elegy was composed on his death. It ran into sixteen stanzas, and was very popular with old Lochaber singers. One man came into possession of a copy of several stanzas of the song, which were written down in Cape Breton from a descendant of Lochaber stock and mailed across the Atlantic. He was extremely proud of his acquisition and showed the copy of the song to everyone he met. Then one day he met John Macdonald of Highbridge. They met halfway across the bridge at Spean. The copy of the song was produced and the old man read through the five or six stanzas. The other listened with interest and patience. When he finished, John was asked if he knew the song. He did.

"Sing it then," said the other.

John put his back to the parapet and went through sixteen verses. The other crumpled the paper he held into a ball and threw it into the Spean.

"To the house of the bitch with it!" said he. "That is only half the song."

The old man was illiterate according to modern standards, yet one song meant as much to him as a herd of prize cattle. So much for the barbarism of the Highlanders!

A story goes that a spirit used to meet Domhnall Mor Og and it told him when he would die.

"The wife will tell you," said the spirit. "She will let you know when you are going to die, for you will ask for something and will not get it."

"In that case, I shall take good note of it," said Donald. "The wife never refused me anything, but was always good and kind to me."

"Oh!" said the spirit, "put not your trust in a broken sword. Do you not know that it was the woman who was fanning the fire with her apron when Christ was being crucified so that the smith should make the nails to go in His hands and feet? The smith said:

'I am afraid that we have not enough fire for four nails.'

'Oh!' said she, 'what need have we of four nails?'

'Yes,' said he, 'we need four.'

'Put one foot on top of the other and drive the nail through the two and that will secure them', said she. 'You need no more than three nails.'

'Oh! woman,' said he, 'in every difficulty in which you ever were there was always a tongue in your mouth to get you out of it. It will be so. There will be only three nails.'"

And to this day women are forbidden to fan the fire with their aprons, and they will on no account do it. They all know about this.

The legend about the nails in the Cross is known in many European countries, but the number of nails varies. In Gaelic tradition the woman is invariably master of every situation. "Why is a woman like an echo?" asks the Gaelic riddle. "She will have the last word in spite of you."

It appears that Domhnall Mor Og was very fond of the fair sex and his reputation lived long after him. Fifty years after his death and burial in the churchyard of Mucomer, a crofter in the neighbourhood had a very troublesome ram which always chased women, never men. The ram's behaviour seemed inexplicable until one of the local characters ventured a serious and plausible suggestion.

"Perhaps," said he, "the ram is really Domhnall Mor Og."

The belief that spirits of the dead return in animal form is widespread; it is by no means Highland or Lochaber superstition. Actually there is surprisingly little of what may be termed as superstition in Lochaber. There is very much more among the fishing communities on the east coast of Scotland.

I regret that lamentably little of the fine traditions of Lochaber are being passed on to the younger generations. Men like John Macdonald of Highbridge, Archie MacInnes of Achaluachrach and the late Allan Macdonell of Inverlochy could stand anywhere on the highway between Fort William and Roy Bridge and name every valley, every stream, every copse and every peak in an absolute sea of mountains as far as the human eye could reach. Their knowledge did not, however, stop at mere names. They knew the why and wherefore of them all.

Early in the seventeenth century, and probably before that time, a hag known as the Hag of Ben Breck frequented Lochaber. She was always accompanied by a herd of deer over which she exercised some occult power. She used to milk the hinds, and also had the power of giving luck in the chase to hunters and withholding it when she chose. One of her favourite haunts was a corrie on Ben Nevis where the sun never shone. The Hag of Ben Breck was sometimes said to assume the form of a white hind. The song she sang when milking the hinds is still known to some of the older singers:

Old hag of Ben Breck, horo,
Breck horo, Breck horo,
Old hag of Ben Breck horo,
Great hag of the high mountain-spring.

I'd never let my band of deer,
My band of deer, my band of deer;
I'd never let my band of deer
To lick the dun shells of the shore.

Much they'd rather water-cress green,
Water-cress green, water-cress green;
Much they'd rather water-cress green,
On the banks of the high mountain-spring.

Pipers too still play a very beautiful pibroch called "The Old Wife's Croon" or, to give a closer rendering of the Gaelic title, "The Croon of the Hag in Ben Breck". The melodies of both the song and the pibroch are enchanting. They are not quite the same.

Contemporary with the Hag of Ben Breck was the famous hunter-poet Domhnall Mac Fhionnlaigh nan Dan (Donald, the son of Finlay, of the Songs). Donald Finlayson was the surest and most unerring archer ever to hunt Lochaber hills, but at one time he was down on his luck utterly. Then one day he met the Hag of Ben Breck. She asked him if he had killed many deer of late. Donald, the son of Finlay, had to confess that he had killed none at all.

"Which would you rather have," asked the Hag, "that the eye or the nose be taken from them?"

"You take the nose from them," said Donald, "and I myself shall take the eye from them."

After that all went well with Donald's hunting; he killed as many deer as he could approach without being seen, for the Hag had taken their sense of smell away from them.

The Hag had one favourite hind, a large hind that Donald, the son of Finlay, had long sought but failed to shoot. One day the Hag was milking this hind and it became restive and kicked away the milking-vessel out of her hands.

"Would that an arrow from Donald, the son of Finlay, were in you!" said the Hag angrily. That very day an arrow from Donald's bow did kill the hind.

In his old age Donald, the son of Finlay, composed one of the very finest poems in the language. He was married to a young wife who one day brought home an old and feeble owl to keep company with the aged hunter and his hound. The poem is in the form of a dialogue between Donald and the Owl of Strone. The poet dwells on the glories of the chase and is full of descriptions of the scenes of his past prowess. He also mentions the great heroes and hunters of his youth. The poem breathes the spirit of an age far removed from ours.

Many were the wars and forays
In Lochaber at that time.
Where did you then go into hiding,
Little bird of the sad brow?

The Owl then answers:

Whenever I saw passing by
The forays and the terror,
I'd turn a little from the way
And for a space I'd be at Creag Uanach.

The rock of my heart is Creag Uanach,
The rock where I got part of my rearing;
The rock of the hinds and fleet stags,
The wholesome, joyous, bird-haunted rock.

The rock of my heart is the great crag,
Dearer to me is the stream underneath its face
And the dell at its back
Than the plains and ramparts of the Saxon.

Chapter Two

MORAR, ARISAIG AND MOIDART

THE railway line from Fort William to Mallaig passes through what I consider to be the most beautiful country in all Scotland. Four or five miles westwards from the head of Loch Eil one comes all of a sudden into Glen Finnan. It is a deep, wooded glen shut in by very high hills. Away to the south-west stretch the waters of Loch Shiel. The Prince's Monument stands as a silent, gaunt reminder of the day, 19 August 1745, when the standard was raised to strike a last blow for the Stuarts. The monument was erected by Macdonald of Glenaladale. It was the same Macdonald who built the beautiful Catholic church overlooking the loch. We are now in Moidart and Moidart has always been predominantly Catholic. I was delighted to learn that the Glen Finnan estate has now reverted to the Gaels. Two Gaelic-speaking natives are joint-proprietors of Glen Finnan; they are Mr Mackellaig and Mr Gillies. Mr Mackellaig lives in Glen Finnan, and Mr Gillies in Glenaladale. For many years Mr Mackellaig owned the local Stage House Inn. He is an expert angler and an authority on local tradition. I did not wait long in Glen Finnan the first day, as the place and its association depressed me. I was glad to learn that the sacred but ill-fated soil on which the Royal Standard was raised did belong to a Gaelic-speaking Highlander.

The heart of Moidart beckoned me westwards again. A launch named *Loch Ailort* plies daily on the loch, up from Acharacle and down again in the evening. The launch belongs to David MacBrayne & Co and quite recently replaced the old *Clanranald*, owned by a local concern. Here too the cancer of mammoth companies is eating into the very heart of local endeavour. MacBrayne's new boat rejoiced in the very English name, *Rosalind*, until some brave spirit, Wendy Wood, if I remember rightly, obliterated the offending name and painted *Clanranald* on it instead. Messrs MacBrayne & Co very wisely had the boat rechristened *Loch Ailort*. Local opinion accepted the compromise.

At the risk of being accused of an undue Highland bias, it must be said that, in comparison with Loch Shiel, Loch Lomond leaves me entirely cold. At the moment I cannot say that I have yet seen Loch Maree in Ross-shire. If Loch Maree is lovelier than Loch Shiel, it must be a sheer joy. A distinguished Swedish scholar, Dr Björn Collinder, Professor of Finno-Agrian Languages at the University of Uppsala, accompanied me on the trip down the loch. "I have visited eleven European countries," said he, "but this exceeds all I have yet seen. There are places in Lappland and Northern Italy that almost approach it in beauty, but they do not quite equal it." Dr Collinder is a magnificent linguist. That morning he was able to translate the Gaelic inscription on Prince Charlie's monument as I had read it slowly twice. He had neither heard nor seen hardly any Gaelic before.

Unfortunately, Dr Collinder's stay in the area was all too short. He saw Moidart for three days only. Had he stayed a bare week longer, he would, undoubtedly, have added one more to the number of eminent Gaelic-speaking Scandinavian scholars. Going down Loch Shiel he recited passages from his Swedish rendering of the *Kalevala*. To have translated the Finnish *Kalevala* into Swedish and to have retained not only the spirit but also the rhythmical construction of the original was certainly no mean feat. As the Gaelic saying has it: "No sea without steering came upon him." (*Cha d' thàinig muir gun stiùireadh air*.) Dr Collinder had certainly steered the

Kalevala into Swedish waters. His immediate and enthusiastic interest in the Gaelic language was something that would make every professor in the Arts Faculties of the Scottish Universities blush with shame. Another Swedish professor, Dr Nils Holmer of Lund, electrified a crowded gathering at the official opening of the Jubilee National Mod a couple of years ago in Oban by delivering the best speech of the evening in the purest Argyllshire Gaelic. To every Gaelic-speaking member of that huge audience every word was clear as crystal, and every single word of that magnificent speech would have been lost on the ears of Scottish university professors, had they been there to listen.

The shores of Loch Shiel are steep and wooded, especially the shore with a southern exposure. The southern shore does lose a great deal of sun, and sunshine is a rare commodity here at times. The average rainfall of this district must be about the highest in Scotland. Three times I travelled the waters of Loch Shiel and on each occasion the sun blazed from a cloudless sky. I have never seen anything so beautiful as Loch Shiel in the sunshine of an early June morning. But the beauty of Loch Shiel makes one sad, for on the wooded slopes can still be seen clear traces of tillage, and the furrows of plots or "lazy beds" were never filled in, but were left to be overgrown with grass when the tillers left over a hundred years ago to face an uncertain future and to start life anew beyond the seas. Could the forests of Canada or the Australian bush have assuaged their grief in parting with Loch Shiel? Material prosperity at best could not have been more than a poor recompense for what they had lost.

I had no idea where Glenaladale was until that afternoon I first went down the loch. It is about half a dozen miles from Glen Finnan on the northern shore. In that beautiful glen there is only one homestead visible today; the home of the present proprietor. The gallant Macdonalds of Glenaladale have gone for ever. Professor Charles W. Dunn of the University of Toronto informs me that in 1772, Capt. John Macdonald of Glenaladale sent three hundred Catholics to Prince Edward Island as tenants on land he purchased there. In 1947 I recorded from the lips of my dear friend, the late Angus Maclellan of Benbecula, an account of this movement of people from Glenaladale. Lest there be any smirch on the good name of a loyal Highland chief, I should hasten to add that this was no "Clearance" in any shape or form. Macdonald of Glenaladale was prompted by only the very finest motives. The clan had taken a prominent part in the "Forty-five" and it was a predominantly Catholic clan. At the time Catholics in Scotland suffered from many disabilities; among other things a Protestant education was foisted upon them and their freedom to practise their own religion was far from complete. By sending his people out to Prince Edward Island, Macdonald of Glenaladale removed them from the clutches of the proselytising Society for Propagating Christian Knowledge. The religion of the "Yellow Stick" was still fresh in the memory of Catholic Highlanders. About the year 1725 the "Yellow Stick" was very much in evidence in the island of Rum to beat recalcitrant Catholics into attendance at Protestant schools and churches. The proselytisers were still at work for a good century after 1772. During the years of the potato famine in the middle of last century they resorted to the subtle means of doling out meal to half-starved Catholics who were prepared to renounce the Pope of Rome. Some did accept the meal and satisfy the inner man and then told their benefactors to go to the devil.

I looked in vain for smoke rising from the chimneys of the few houses by the lochside. They were roofed, but otherwise seemed deserted. They were probably shepherds' houses, and today it is not easy to get shepherds to live in solitary places, especially married men with families. At Polloch on the left there is a new Forestry Commission settlement. A week earlier I had met Mr Richardson, the postmaster of Loch Ailort, and was told that he had been appointed to a similar post at Polloch. Mr Richardson plays the drums and is a member of the most remarkable dance-band in Britain, a band that has to walk sometimes distances of over ten miles on rough paths over high mountains, play until five or six in the morning and then retrace their steps carrying fiddles, drums and accordions until dawn sees them go home. I had heard of such in the Highlands fifty or sixty years ago. I had not dreamt that something like that was still done. It was my pleasure to have made some very fine recordings of that band. The other players live at Loch Ailort except Dugald MacRae, who lives farther down the loch at Achnanellan, where his elder brother has a sheep-farm. At Inverailort is another brother, Farquhar, also a splendid musician who plays both the fiddle and piano-accordion. The other two members of the band are Mr John Begg, the local station-master and Angus MacNaughton of Inverailort. Mr Begg is a native of Speyside and a member of a family of noted fiddlers; he is the only one of the band able to read music. The others play by ear, but they too play exquisitely. They think nothing of trudging over the hills on winter nights to play at Kinlochmoidart or Glenuig over ten miles away, and the young ladies and men of the district invariably accompany them. They seem to enjoy these long treks immensely. They dance the most strenuous reels and schottishces all night and then walk miles in the cold dawn. It is not difficult to understand why the people of Moidart were so heroic. Life must have been like this before the "Forty-five".

Glen Finnan gets its name from Saint Finnan, a saint of Ireland who came to spread the light of Christianity in this area long, long centuries before any pseudo-Christian political group. As he came northwards he climbed over Ben Resipol and looked down on the green waters of Loch Shiel. Nestling in a little bay he saw a greener isle and here he chose to build his monastery. The ruins of an old foundation can still be seen on St Finnan's Isle, which has been the burial-ground of the district for long ages. It is not unusual to find burial-grounds on islands in lakes and rivers. In olden times such places afforded newly buried corpses some protection against wolves. The present-day Lapps bury their dead in temporary graves on islands in lakes and river-beds. Probably the chief reason for the choice of St Finnan's Isle was that here there was soil consecrated by a saint. On the island many roughly hewn pillars and some recent headstones mark the graves. There is one huge pillar which was taken from high up the hill on the northern shore of Loch Shiel on the back of one strong man and thence by boat across to the isle to serve as a headstone. Funeral parties still come to the isle by boat down from Glen Finnan, and from Moidart and Acharacle by the rough pathway along the Moidart shore until they reach the little headland opposite the island. There is a stone jetty where the remains are embarked and brought sun-wise to the jetty on the isle. Funerals from Glen Finnan must approach the isle sun-wise also. Above the jetty on the Moidart shore there is a green, mossy hillock with a couple of very large spreading trees. In the old days funeral parties rested there on their return from the isle and had whisky, biscuits and cheese. The older generation remembers great gatherings resting on that hillock. Funerals to St Finnan's Isle must have been very impressive. Unfortunately, there are fewer people to attend them now. A famous chief of Clanranald was buried at St Finnan's; he was John of Moidart, who annihilated the Frasers at the "Battle of the Shirts" fought at the head of Loch Lochy in 1544. At one time his bones could have been seen in one of the ruins on the isle, and they were, of course, quite enormous. Tradition has it that by some powers of sorcery John's birth was delayed so that another embryonic claimant to the chieftain-ship would have precedence over him. John of Moidart was kept in his mother's womb for nine months longer than he ought to have been and was born with a full set of teeth. The clan, however, considered him as chieftain and supported his claim against that of Ronald Gallda, whose mother was a Fraser. Ronald was killed at the "Battle of the Shirts".

The farm of Dalilea is to the right on the way down the loch. The farmhouse hidden among trees was the birthplace of Alexander Macdonald, the greatest of all Gaelic poets. Alexander

Macdonald was born about 1700 and died at the age of seventy. He was the poet of the Jacobite army and Gaelic tutor to the Prince at the "Forty-five". His father was an Episcopalian clergyman and a man of enormous strength and physical resource. He often travelled distances of forty miles in one day to hold services at Ardnamurchan, and his physique stood him in good stead when quelling fights after funerals to St Finnan's Isle. Alexander was for a period a teacher under the aegis of the Society for Propagating Christian Knowledge and under the patronage of the society, he published his *Gaelic and English Vocabulary*, the first published Gaelic dictionary, in 1741. He entered heart and soul into the "Forty-five" and his rousing songs must have rallied hundreds of Highlanders to the Royal Standard. He became a commissioned officer in the Jacobite army.

I was quite astounded by the beauty of Moidart, especially the country round the lower end of Loch Shiel. Little has ever been said or written about it: it has yet to be discovered. A stone bridge spans the Shiel River which flows out of the loch to the west. To the south of the bridge is Ardnamurchan and the Protestant country, to the north is Inverness-shire and Catholic Moidart. The line of demarcation is very clear but there is a complete lack of sectarian animosity. Here, as in practically the whole Highlands, Protestants and Catholics live side by side and are a shining example of tolerance and good neighbourliness. That was very forcibly brought home to me shortly after my arrival. I was the guest of the genial and popular parish priest of Mingarry, Moidart, and on the following evening I had to recross the bridge to record songs from old Sorley Cameron in Realann on the Ardnamurchan side. Fr. Campbell accompanied me and I was very struck by the cordial welcome extended to him in this Protestant household. I doubt very much if any English-speaking clergyman of the Reformed Church would have received such a welcome as this Gaelic-speaking Catholic priest. Gaelic is still very strong in Moidart and Ardnamurchan and devotion to the language is still strong enough to overcome religious differences. The Catholic population of Moidart is diminishing rapidly, but so also is the Protestant community across the river.

The ruins of Caisteal Tioram, the mainland stronghold of the Clanranald, will long remain my most vivid memory of Moidart. It came upon us with such suddenness as we turned a corner of the road down from Shiel Bridge. The first sight of it takes one's breath away, for there it stands silent and majestic on a high rocky island set against the lovely background of Shona Isle. A narrow spit of sand joins in to the mainland at ebb-tide only. Fortunately, we were able to walk across and climb the hill into the courtyard. The stonework is practically as it was the day the castle was burnt in 1715. There is a hole in the wall on the seaward side and this is said to be the result of a cannon-ball fired from the galleys of Argyll on one occasion when the castle was under siege. The building is an imposing three-storeyed structure, but it was the old room that obviously served as a kitchen that I found most interesting. In the wall and down for a couple of feet below the level of the floor there is a well of clear water. There was a built-up fireplace in one corner and it appears to have been canopied with mortared stone, but the canopy is now broken. At one time Caisteal Tioram must have been a formidable stronghold. There is a high wooded hill on the mainland across from the castle and it was from this eminence that Allan Mor of Clanranald watched his castle going up in flames as he was on the point of leaving for Sherrifmuir to join the Old Pretender. He ordered that the castle be burnt lest it should fall into the hands of the English. His other castle out at Ormicleit in South Uist went up in flames on the night of Sherrifmuir; the fire started in the kitchen where venison was being roasted. The wraith of Allan Mor, who fell mortally wounded in the battle, appeared before the watchman, Donald Ruadh MacIntyre, Donald Ruadh immediately blessed himself.

"Well has the consecration served thee, Donald Ruadh?" said Allan Mor. "Ormicleit is on fire."

STRATHMORE, LOOKING DOWN TOWARDS LOCH BROOM

The end of Clanranald's glory was drawing near. However, it cannot be denied that the most notable of the loyal clans owned about the most beautiful and enchanting part of Scotland, for all Moidart is lovely. The road to Kinlochmoidart skirts the northern shore of Loch Shiel, passes by the townships of Mingarry, Dalnabreck and Langal and climbs over a wooded ridge to give one an unforgettable first glimpse of Glen Moidart. There is no other road leading to the glen and in the glen it ends and gives way to a rough track over the hills to Glenuig on Loch Ailort. Fr. Joseph Campbell has often to walk miles and miles over this rough track to minister to the needs of his flock in Glenuig. With him it is always a pleasure and a labour of love. The four fiddlers from Inverailort walk over an equally long and arduous track to play at dances in Kinlochmoidart. In their case too it is not only a duty but a pleasure.

Glen Moidart must have supported a huge population at one time, for there are good stretches of land on the floor of the glen as well as on the slopes and everywhere there is good shelter for cattle and sheep. There are but few inhabited houses now. I hardly remember seeing more than one living soul in the glen. Natives of the area are quite positive that the *La Doutelle* sailed up the narrow North Channel between Shona and the mainland and that the Prince landed on the flat stretch on the northern shore of the loch. Today the "Seven Men of Moidart" — seven huge oak trees — mark the spot where he landed. One of the trees is smaller than the others, for it was planted to replace one blown down by a storm. The landing of the Prince has left its imprint on tradition. It is related that two men of Moidart were digging for sand-eels on the strand when they first heard that Charles Edward had arrived. They immediately crossed the little shovels they were using and commenced to dance and that was how the "Sword Dance" originated. In Shona Isle I was told that four men of Moidart were cutting turf when the glad tidings reached them. They stuck their irons in the ground and using them as dance-partners danced the "Eight Men of Moidart". I must confess I have never seen the "Eight Men of Moidart" danced. I must return to Shona to learn more about it. A MacIntyre piper of Rannoch composed a lovely pibroch called "My King has landed in Moidart". The pipers of today play it often. To this very day old women in Barra sing a beautiful song called "*An Fhideag Airgid*", "The Silver Whistle".

> Who will play the silver whistle?
> Ho ro hu a hu il o
> Hi ri hil u hil oro
> Hi ri hil u hil oro
> The son of my king has come to Alba.

The Catholic church hall at Mingarry houses one of the very few relics of the "Forty-five": a glass case which holds the banner of Glenaladale's men. The banner escaped capture at Culloden and came into the possession of the late Dr MacVicar, a relative of the Glenaladale family, who bequeathed it to the church of Mingarry. It is a beautiful banner of green silk and bears the coat of arms of the Macdonalds of Clanranald. It is singularly fitting that it should find a haven so near Caisteal Tioram. There was no one to tell who brought the banner home to Moidart and how. The people who did know are today mingled with the dust of Prince Edward Island, far away from Moidart.

I left Mingarry on a beautiful June morning to sail up Loch Shiel. The trip up to Glenfinnan took about three hours, but these were hours that I shall never forget. All the way the mountains and slopes on either side were mirrored in the placid waters of the loch and light silvery clouds were wafted leisurely from the Argyllshire hills northwards to the ridges high on our left. Only the bleating of sheep or the song of birds broke the stillness of the morning. The launch put in at the jetty at Dalilea and crossed the loch to Achnanellan, where we picked up Dugald MacRae, one of the fiddlers from Inverailort. He was on his way home and I was on my way to an International Folklore Conference in Paris, but that night I had to spend in Inverailort to record the playing of the MacRae brothers and their colleagues. Mr Begg, Angus MacNaughton and the two MacRae brothers fiddled all night long until four in the morning. I took the train south at eight.

I returned to Moidart two months later and sailed down Loch Shiel again. The second visit was longer and gave me more time to get to know the district and its people. It was on my second visit that I met Alex Dan Henderson of Newton, a direct descendant of the piper to Macdonald of Glencoe, who fled on the night of the massacre and made his way to Ardnamurchan. There have been pipers in the Henderson family ever since 1692, and Mr Henderson's son figures in the prize list at the local games. Alex Dan Henderson is a piper as well as being a very fine singer. He sang one beautiful elegy composed about a daughter of Campbell of Lochnell who was drowned crossing Loch Etive to see her sweetheart, young Macdonald of Glencoe. I had never heard the song before, but it may very well have been brought to Newton by the piper who fled the massacre. According to Alex Henderson, Campbell of Lochnell was bitterly opposed to his daughter's friendship with Macdonald of Glencoe and she was drowned crossing the dangerous waters at Connel in a small boat which she launched under cover of darkness and unknown to her irate parents. It appears that the young lady communicated with her lover by putting letters in bottles of skin which the tide carried to the northern shore of Loch Etive. The song obviously belonged to the seventeenth century.

The day following my visit to Alex Dan Henderson I crossed over to Eilean Shona. From the Moidart shore the island is most attractive. We passed by Caisteal Tioram, which looks equally imposing from the sea as from land. I attempted to photograph the castle from different angles, but I am afraid that the result left much to be desired; the photographs completely failed to reproduce the grandeur of the place. Shona is privately owned and is one of the few model estates on the western seaboard. The population was large at one time, but now there are only estate-workers and their families left. The small population is Catholic, and here again I was fortunate in having Fr. Campbell along with me. The boatman was young John Maclellan, and it was to his mother's house we went. Mrs Maclellan's brother, Donald Kennedy, had come across the island to meet me. He was full of the traditions of the island and the surrounding district and was an excellent storyteller. Mrs Maclellan herself sang and her son, a very fine piper, is, incidentally, a direct descendant of Ronald Macdonald (Raghnall Mac Ailein Oig), a noted hero and piper of Arisaig who lived away back in the seventeenth century. In that Shona family a piping tradition has lasted two centuries and probably more.

Donald Kennedy started telling a most interesting story about the MacCrimmon pipers of Skye. One of the very noted MacCrimmon pipers was named Padruig Caogach (Squint-eyed Patrick), and a pibroch called "Lasan Phadruig Chaogaich" (Squint-eyed Patrick's Flame of Wrath) commemorates his name to this day. Patrick was a hasty hot-tempered fellow, as the name of the pibroch suggests. At one time Patrick was up in Glen Shiel, where he had a foster-brother. Patrick and the foster-brother quarrelled, and one day, when Patrick was washing his face in a stream, the foster-brother, taking advantage of the situation, drew his sword and killed him. The news of Patrick's death reached Dunvegan in Skye, and Donald More MacCrimmon, Patrick's blood-brother, took up his bagpipes, went straight to Dunvegan Castle and threw them on the table before Macleod. Macleod asked what all that meant. Donald More told him that Patrick had been killed and that he was going to Glen Shiel to avenge his death. Macleod asked him to wait for a year and that he would see to it that justice was done. A whole year elapsed and Patrick Caogach's death went unavenged. Away went Donald More without telling anyone and made for Glen Shiel to avenge his brother's death. When he arrived in Glen Shiel, he heard the murderer was in Kintail. Donald More proceeded to Kintail, but no one in Clachan Duich of Kintail would tell him where the murderer lived. Donald More promptly set fire to some of the houses in the clachan with the result that several people were burnt to death. The great MacKenzie of Kintail, on hearing this, set a price on the head of Donald More. Donald took fright and made for Glen Shiel, where the laird MacRae of Glen Shiel told him that one of his shepherds lived in a very remote place and would keep him hidden in his house. Thither went Donald More. At night he stayed in the shepherd's house, but made for the hills as soon as dawn broke and returned again at nightfall. MacRae's wife was none other than the daughter of MacKenzie of Kintail, and it was not long until the chief of Kintail heard that Donald More was hiding in the house of one of MacRae's shepherds. Donald More always left the house at daybreak, but on this particular morning there was a fearful deluge and Donald More stayed at home . . .

At that very point in the telling of the story our recording machine broke down and Kennedy came to a sudden stop. I still have not got the end of the tale, but I have never heard the story from anyone else and, as far as I am aware, it has never been in print. The story has evidently been in Kennedy's family right down from the time of Ronald Macdonald of Arisaig, who flourished somewhat later than Domhnall Mór MacCrimmon. Thus does one piping family preserve the traditions of another. However, I must return to Shona to get the rest of the story. Donald Kennedy will, of course, continue from where he left off.

Across the hills from Kinlochmoidart is Glenuig and there is an almost forgotten but happy little community. Sad to say it is a dwindling community and it really is a great loss to Scotland that such communities should vanish. There was a quiet and strangely remarkable dignity about the people here. I spent only two days amongst them, but these are days I shall long remember. A rough track leads over the hill from Kinlochmoidart and another, longer and more arduous, skirts the southern shore of Loch Ailort for a distance of over eight miles. The easiest way to Glenuig is by sea from Inverailort and that was the way I chose to go. Twice or thrice weekly Ronnie the Whaler's motor-launch plies between Glenuig and Inverailort. Ronnie spent some time with the whaling ships in the Antarctic; hence his name, but, of course, he is one of the real Macdonalds of Clanranald. He is a fine singer as well as a bard and an expert seaman. He composed a very lively song about one of his poaching expeditions to Inverailort and later sang the song to Mr Francis Cameron-Head of Inverailort, the very proprietor on whose preserves the doughty Whaler had been poaching. Mr Cameron-Head was delighted with the song.

It was a very wet afternoon as we left the jetty at Inverailort. The local doctor, Dr Rodger of Arisaig, a post office accountant and I were the only passengers. The inner end of Loch Ailort is full of little islands and reefs, but Ronnie the Whaler could make his way among them blindfold. To our left the hills rose sheer out of the water to a height of almost three thousand feet, while to the right lay the lower, rocky headland of Ardnish. Ardnish was our first port of call, but there is no port there, not even a trace of a slipway or jetty. The boat was brought in to the rocks and Ronnie the Whaler slung a sack of flour on his back and clambered with it ashore and left it high and dry against a stone dyke. There is only one dwelling in Ardnish now and it is occupied by a native of Harris, who spent most of his life sheep-farming out in South America. He now farms the whole of Ardnish, and there are good patches of land there. We could see several empty houses, some still roofed but others roofless. The older people in the district remember the time when there were fifty families in Ardnish.

DETAIL, LAIDE CHURCHYARD

It was still raining when we got to Glenuig and it rained continually all that evening and night. Ronnie the Whaler had to return to Inverailort with the doctor and it was late when he came home. Tired and wet as he was, he was still game enough to sing. He has a lovely natural tenor voice and knows many old songs, learned mainly from his parents. His father is now dead but his mother still lives not very far away from him. Ronnie is married to a very charming young lady from South Uist and they have two little children, a girl and boy. They spoke only Gaelic to the children. It is only in cases where two Gaelic-speakers marry that the language stands any chance at all of passing on to the next generation.

For years I had thought about Glenuig and hoped to have the opportunity of visiting it. One September evening away back in 1946 I crossed the Minch for the first time on my way to Barra. I was then on the staff of the Irish Folklore Commission and had just started the systematic collection of folklore material in the Western Isles. At that time there was very little talk about Scottish folklore and folk music or even about Scottish culture or our Scottish heritage. In fact, there was none at all. I was a salaried official of a cultural institution established by the Government of Eire. I met very few people who shared, or even understood, my interest in old tales and songs. But on that night I first crossed the Minch I met one who both understood and shared that interest; I met what I first took to be a Highland drover on his way to the September sales in the Long Island. The Highland drover was none other than the late Mr Graham Croall of Glenuig. We spoke of old tales and songs, and he told me that a neighbour of his in Glenuig had a tale about the son of the King of Tethertown (*Mac Rìgh na Cathair Shìomain*). The tale took twenty minutes to narrate, and Mr Croall had thought of writing it down from the old man's dictation and entering it for the folktale competition at the National Mod. I do not know if that was ever done, but Mr Croall kindly invited me to stay with him at Glenuig and there I would have ample opportunity to record the tale. Over eighty years before Hector Maclean of Islay had recorded it from a man at Inveraray, Argyllshire, and in the noted collection of John Francis Campbell of Islay the story goes under the name of "The Battle of the Birds" (*Cath nan Eun*). It is a complex wonder-tale about a young prince who was helped by a grateful raven whom he succoured in the battle between the birds and quadrupeds and whose son later eloped with the fair daughter of a giant even though he almost lost her through being given a kiss that induced forgetfulness by his favourite hound. The story is a well-known international tale, but I was quite thrilled when Mr Croall told me it was still narrated in Moidart. It was only later I learned that Mr Croall was not exactly a Highland drover but the owner of the Glenuig estate. I was still more amazed to discover that his knowledge of Gaelic had been acquired in his early manhood. Mr Croall learned Gaelic better than anyone I have ever known, better than anyone I shall ever know. Mr Graham Croall will long be remembered in this part of the country and remembered with affection by many humble singers whose songs he was given so readily, even in places as far distant as Druimnin in Ardnamurchan. During the years I had feared that the old storyteller would not be there when I got to Glenuig. By the strange irony of fate it was Graham Croall who was not there to welcome me, for he died in the prime of life away out in South Africa. To all lovers of Gaelic he was an inspiration and a shining example, and by his untimely death all were affected with a sense of deep, personal tragedy.

Ronnie the Whaler brought me down to Samalaman to visit Mrs Croall, Graham's mother, and I was invited to lunch there later in the day. Mrs Croall is a very charming and extremely intelligent lady, keenly conscious of all the problems that confront small, isolated rural communities. She regards all the tenantry on her estate as one large, happy family, and her main mission in life is to bring as much joy as possible into the lives of those people whose land, language and traditions her son loved so dearly. I still remember the wave of emotion that swept over the huge audience at the official opening of the National Mod at Oban in 1953 when Mr J. M. Bannerman announced Mrs Croall had donated £1,000 to the funds of *An Comunn Gaidhealach* in memory of her son.

Over a century ago there was a seminary for the training of priests at Samalaman. Mrs Croall now lives in the house which was the college. Mrs Macdonald, Ronnie's mother lives about two hundred yards west of the estate house. It was here I found the storyteller I had long wanted to visit. I found Angus MacPherson, still hale and hearty although so crippled with rheumatism that he walked with the aid of two sticks. Until a couple of years ago Angus and his sister lived in the now deserted township of Smearisary a mile or so to the west and facing the full fury of the Atlantic. From Smearisary they removed to Samalaman to live with their sister, Mrs Macdonald. They were too old to continue alone on their croft, and there were no younger people to take their place.

I spent over four hours with Angus and Mrs Macdonald, four hours that passed all too quickly. Of course, Angus told the story about "The Battle of the Birds", and a very fine story it was and excellently told. Since Graham Croall had died, no one listened much to his story-telling and the old man was quite delighted to meet someone interested in what he had to tell. He also told me an equally long and fine story about Young Iain, the Son of the Scottish Soldier, and the many hardships he had to undergo in quest of his lost wife, the Daughter of the King of the Green Mountains. Angus learned his stories from Charles MacPherson of Smearisary who died over thirty years ago. The two stories, however, are well over a thousand years old, and they belong to many lands.

Before I left Mrs Macdonald sang two waulking songs. As a young girl she had taken part in the waulking or fulling of cloth and that was over fifty years ago. In those days all cloth was homespun, and there was a loom in almost every house. When the roll of cloth came off the loom, it had to be washed and shrunk to the required width and thickness. When the housewife decided to have a waulking (*luadhadh*), she invited all the women and young girls of the neighbourhood to her house. The waulking usually took place in wintertime. The web was first soaked in ammonia or soap and water and sometimes in stale urine, the last mentioned being often considered the best detergent. When the women were assembled, the door was taken off the hinges and placed on stones or some other support in the middle of the floor. Several women sat on either side and one at either end. At one end sat a woman who knew many waulking songs and who could sing them well; the woman at the other end handed out the web to the fulling-women, who rubbed the cloth vigorously while passing it around the board from one to another. To lighten their work they sang the waulking songs and pounded the cloth in keeping with the rhythm of the song. The woman at the head of the table sang the verses while the others joined in the refrain. Usually each verse was sung twice. There are still hundreds of waulking songs to be heard, although they are more commonly met with in the Outer Hebrides, where waulking belongs to the less distant past and is even carried on still in certain places. I have never seen a waulking on the mainland, but was present at several in the Outer Hebrides. In certain districts the cloth was rubbed with the feet instead of the hands. In Moidart the hands were used. From time to time the width of the web was measured with the thumbs to see if it had shrunk sufficiently. By the time it did shrink to the proper width and had been given a fine, even nap the young men of the township began to arrive and stand around with their backs to the wall of the room or crowd about the door. The waulking was finished and now the web was coiled and in the process the women clapped the coil to remove creases. At this point they sang the clapping songs, light songs with a set refrain but lending themselves to extemporisation in such a way that the name of some girl was coupled with that of her sweetheart or some young man in the audience, and the bantering and fun continued until the work was at an end. After some refreshments the company would dance till morning. The waulking was an important social event in the life of the community, for it served more purposes than one. For any young woman it was a serious slight not to be invited to a waulking, for it was there many young girls met their husbands. There was also a great deal of friendly rivalry between the women who led the singing. A woman who was much in demand at waulkings had a high social status. In Benbecula I noticed that the two outstanding singers were never invited together to any waulking. I suppose it must have been much the same in other parts of the Highlands. The problem of precedence would have been too much for the diplomacy of any Highlander.

One of the songs Mrs Macdonald sang for me was actually a clapping song I had not heard before. There were other women singers in the district, including the late Miss Peggy MacDougall who lived in a little cottage right behind Samalaman House. When I left Mrs Macdonald's house, Angus MacPherson, despite his disability, insisted on accompanying me all the way to the garden gate of the cottage where old Peggy MacDougall lived with her nephew and his wife. Peggy MacDougall was then ninety-eight years of age but, despite that, sang from morning till night. She was rather deaf but otherwise very alert and her voice was still good. I recorded seven songs from her. They were mostly local songs and I had not heard any of them before. That wonderful, happy old lady has since gone to her eternal rest.

All that night it rained incessantly and the rain continued all the following morning. I returned to Inverailort with Ronnie the Whaler. The next few days were spent in Inverailort at Glenshian Lodge, an old shooting-lodge now converted into a guest-house. All the time the weather was dreadful and it rained incessantly. Most of the other guests were anglers and did not seem to mind the rain. There must be heavy rainfall at Inverailort, for that was the last week of June when better weather might be expected. The place is so shut in by high hills that no rain clouds can ever pass overhead, but in bright weather it is very lovely. The rain never seems to damp the spirits of the people there, for even the visiting anglers were a jolly crowd and had more or less become part and parcel of the community. They had evidently been visitors to the district for a number of years and knew everyone there. Strangely enough they were not English anglers and some of them, including Mr Stephens Orr, the noted photographer, spoke with pronounced Glasgow accents. Of course, most Scotsmen and Highlanders nowadays who achieve distinction and the social status that it entails tend to shed their native accents and try to ape southern English. I do not think Mr Stephens Orr has even tried to shed his native accent. All the members of his party definitely belonged to Glasgow. Commander Hamilton and his Greek friend, Mr Johanides, were the other party. Commander Hamilton was one of the officers in charge of the Naval Commando Training Centre at Inverailort during the Second World War. He was a very pleasant and generous old gentleman, even though he was glad that the "Forty-five" did not succeed in dethroning the "wee, wee German lairdie". Of course, he maintained that we had the British Navy to thank for that.

I had met Mr Francis Cameron-Head of Inverailort some years before as he was on his way to South Uist. He is one of the promoters of the seaweed industry which has brought so much prosperity to that island. Mr Cameron-Head has learned Gaelic well and is passionately devoted to everything that appertains to Gaelic culture. Mrs Cameron-Head is Irish and she too is deeply interested in all Highland problems, social and economic. Both are very concerned about the drift away from the Highlands, and will do anything in their power to keep as many people as possible on their estate. If all proprietors were like them, there would be a lot more hope.

The most pleasant memory of Inverailort will, of course, be the nights spent with the

PLOCKTON, WESTER ROSS: "PLOCKTON IS A VERY PRETTY LITTLE VILLAGE AND THERE IS HERE A VERY LIVELY COMMUNITY."

MacRae fiddlers and their three colleagues, Mr Begg, Angus MacNaughton, and Mr Richardson. Mr Richardson was postmaster at Inverailort, but has now gone to a similar post on the Forestry Commission estate at Polloch on the shores of Loch Shiel. It is to be hoped that he has not left the band entirely, for he played the drums. Farquhar MacRae played the accordion as well as the fiddle, but Mr Begg, Angus MacNaughton, and Dugald MacRae were the regular fiddlers. Mr Begg belongs to a family of noted Speyside fiddlers. A story is told about Dugald MacRae. The band had trudged the ten miles over the hills to play at a dance in Kinlochmoidart one night. While the dance was at its height and the fiddlers played fast and furiously, Dugald suddenly lost his temper with a huge bluebottle that kept buzzing around his head. With lightning speed the bow was raised on high and the bluebottle smitten to earth and Dugald went into the next bar as if nothing had happened.

Our sessions usually began at ten in the evening and continued until four in the morning. The company was always large, for we were joined by Matthew and Miss Morton and her two sisters from the next house and Mrs Thomas, a young lady from the south who spends all her time at Inverailort, having become so enamoured of the place and its way of life that she now finds it impossible to live anywhere else. Old Mr MacRae must be well over eighty, but he always stayed up with us all night, his foot beating time with the music without a stop. Twice during the night Mrs MacRae, with the help of the ladies, made tea for the whole company. Mrs MacRae is an extremely handsome old lady and both the sons have inherited her good looks. There was such an atmosphere of gaiety and friendliness about the household and the whole company that I was not the least surprised that Mrs Thomas never wants to leave the place. The number of tunes the fiddlers could play was amazing. On my final evening, or to be exact about two o'clock in the morning. I decided to record a selection of five tunes from each in turn. No two played the same tune, and no tune played earlier in the evening either individually or by the band as a whole was repeated. Each of the four fiddlers must know a couple of hundred tunes. It is quite remarkable in the case of players who play solely by ear and have to rely on memory alone. There is an old Gaelic proverb that says that the world will come to an end but music and love will go on. Long may the fiddlers of Inverailort cross the mountains to Glenuig and Kinlochmoidart and long may the sons and daughters of Moidart dance lightly to their playing!

Although their number is small, this community has a life that is rich and full, for each single entity matters and contributes to the joy and well-being of the whole. It was for this way of life that the men of Moidart went out to die at Culloden Moor.

A mile or so across from the head of Loch Ailort is Loch nan Uamh (Loch of the Caves). There is one cave there which I have seen, but I suppose there must be many more I have not seen. Loch nan Uamh, of course, has become part of history, for it was here that the Prince said farewell to Scotland. The actual spot where he embarked is not known to many, but away back in 1860 or so an old man living in Moidart saw to it that the spot would be known and remembered. At the place where the road from Fort William comes down to the side of the loch and turns sharply to the west there is today a dwelling-house occupied by a retired postman. About a hundred yards west of the house along the shore there is a little headland. From a little rock on that headland Charles Edward stepped into the little boat that brought him out to the ship that sailed with him to France. The spot is in direct line with two little islands named Eilean na Gobhlaig on Ordnance Survey maps. The spot was pointed out to me by my friend, Donald Macdonald of Bunacaimb, Arisaig. There can be little question as to the accuracy of Donald Macdonald's information. However, the way the information came to him was most interesting. Some years ago there died at Bunacaimb, Arisaig, a noted storyteller and tradition-bearer named Angus Campbell. He was aged at death, for he was born in the year 1849. About the year 1860, Angus Campbell was down at Loch Eilt and was wending his way home to Arisaig. He was still a very young boy, and at Loch nan Uamh he met a stranger, a very old man. The stranger asked him whence he had come and where he was going. Young Angus told him. The old man asked him who his people were. Again young Angus told him.

"I am a very old man now," said the stranger, "for I am over ninety years of age and you are young. I am going to tell you something today so that you will be able to tell it to those who come after you and that it will not be forgotten by the children of the Gaels. Down below us there on the shore is the stone from which Prince Charles stepped into the little boat that brought him out to the French ship the day he went away to France. Macdonald of Glenaladale, who was out with the Prince and said goodbye to him here, showed me this very place, and that is where the Prince stepped into the boat. Mark the place well, young lad, and make sure that it will not be forgotten. May the blessing of God be with you now."

Angus Campbell never discovered the identity of the stranger, but he never forgot the information that he gave him. It was he who passed it on to Donald Macdonald.

I was lucky enough to be able to spend a whole month in Arisaig and the surrounding district. The month of the year was May and the weather was glorious — for a number of years now May has been the best month in the West Highlands as far as weather goes. For the greater part of the time I was the guest of that fine Highlander, Lachlan Stewart, factor to the Arisaig estate. Lachlan lives in that lovely eighteenth-century house at Borrodale. Borrodale is a lovely wooded valley gradually opening out to the sea. At that time of the year it was like paradise. Every morning I went down to the shore of Borrodale, sunbathed and wrote my notes and diary. At nights Lachlan Stewart and I went out to visit storytellers and singers.

In his wanderings after Culloden Prince Charles is reputed to have hidden in numberless caves up and down the western coast. There are hundreds of Prince Charlie's caves that the royal fugitive never saw. Borrodale, however, can boast of a cave in which he did hide. When he was brought from Skye by John MacKinnon, he was committed to the care of Angus Macdonald of Borrodale. "I shall lodge him so secure," said Angus, "that all the forces in Britain shall not find him out." The Prince was then brought to the cave in the wooded rock-face above the strand at Borrodale. He hid there for sixteen days until the area was cordoned off by militia and Charles had to break through the cordon with the help of a few loyal friends. The cave at Borrodale was an excellent hiding place. I was given fairly detailed directions as to where it was, but succeeded in finding it the third day I went to search and not until then. The entrance to the cave is so narrow that it cannot be seen until one is within a couple of yards of it.

One would expect that in this area there would still be stories and traditions about the "Forty-five" and Prince Charlie. Strange to say, there is not so very much. One tradition, however, does persist and it persists in all Clanranald lands, although I have not come across it anywhere else in the Highlands. For some reason or other in all parts of the old Clanranald estate tradition-bearers are united in maintaining that Lord George Murray betrayed the Jacobite cause and was responsible for the defeat at Culloden. One of the very best and most reliable sources in this area stated that he had often heard the old people say that on the morning of Culloden, Cameron of Locheil sought the Prince's permission to shoot Lord George Murray but the Prince refused. The late Duncan Macdonald of South Uist, the greatest Gaelic storyteller of his generation, was quite positive that Lord George Murray was secretly in communication with Cumberland. Col John Roy Stewart, one of those who sailed with the Prince from Loch nan Uamh on 20 September 1746, refers to Lord George Murray in one of his Gaelic poems on the Battle of Culloden and makes it clear that there were doubts about Lord

George Murray's loyalty, but he is not quite certain that the charges against him could be substantiated: "If the story be true, there was an Aachan in the camp, the utter rogue of deceit and falsehood. He sold his honour and mantle for a larger purse and that spelled ruin to the heroes of King James." Col John Roy Stewart had distinguished himself in the French service before the "Forty-five" and was one of the ablest officers in the Jacobite army. Of course, towards the end of the campaign Prince Charles had come to regard Lord George Murray with suspicion and distrust, and that is probably why such a tradition persists until this very day in the country of Clanranald.

Donald Macdonald of Bunacaimb did, however, have one very fine story about four young men who had taken part in the "Forty-five". They were summoned to appear before the authorities in Edinburgh. The four leave and one of their number is Farquhar Og. Farquhar is accompanied by his faithful dog, Bran. Some time during the first day of their journey, Farquhar and his three comrades decide to part company and go different ways. His comrades leave him and young Farquhar goes his way accompanied by his dog. Night overtakes them, but Farquhar finally sees a lonely bothy and decides to shelter in it for the night. He makes himself as comfortable as possible and in a short time he is sound asleep. In his sleep he dreams, and a voice comes to him saying: "There is hope for the man of the host, but there is no hope for the man of the tomb." (*Bidh dùil ri fear feachd, ach cha bhidh dùil ri fear lice.*) He awakens and is perplexed, for before setting out he and his comrades had grave doubts about the wisdom of answering the summons of the authorities. A black cat enters the bothy and Bran snarls. The cat begins to increase in size and grows and grows until it assumes the form of a woman. Farquhar tries to restrain Bran, but the dog attacks the uncanny creature and drives her out of the bothy. A terrific fight ensues outside and Farquhar listens to the shrieking of the woman and the howling of the dog until they fade away into the black night. Much later the faithful Bran returns torn and bloody, falls at his master's feet and dies. The long night passes and day dawns. Farquhar continues his journey but with greater misgivings than ever. Finally he reaches Edinburgh, and there he is given the choice of transportation or decapitation for his part in the "Forty-five". Nobly he chooses to be beheaded. There can be hope for the return of the man who leaves to join a host but none for the return of one who is claimed by a tomb. The story is most fascinating as it reveals how factual historical tradition and folklore motifs become interwoven.

Donald Macdonald of Bunacaimb is a surface-man employed by the British Railways. He must be close on sixty years of age, but it is very difficult to tell his age, as he still is fresh-complexioned and is really a magnificent physical specimen. I was told later that he comes of a stalwart, athletic stock. There must have been many such as Donald Macdonald on the Clanranald lands in days gone by. Donald belongs to the Children of the Son of Dugald (Clann Mhic Dhughaill), the Macdonalds of Morar. He inherited his great fund of tradition mainly from an uncle and aunt who died abut thirty years ago. Donald is a magnificent storyteller and declaims his stories like one reciting verse from memory. Stories about Fionn and Ossian and their band of warrior-hunters were told in the Highlands a thousand years before James MacPherson of Ossianic fame saw the light of day. These stories are told still and Donald Macdonald tells them, although I doubt very much if he ever heard of MacPherson.

From Bunacaimb there is a glorious view over the sea to the hills of Skye and out to Eigg and Rum beyond. This district must be the artists's paradise. The first evening I walked over to Back of Keppoch and on to Bunacaimb I had to hurry to escape an approaching rainstorm. The morning had been exceptionally fine, but long before noon I was told there would be rain ere long, for there was mist on the Sgurr of Eigg, and mist on the Sgurr of Eigg is always a sign of approaching rain. Before dusk the rain came and with a vengeance.

MOOR LOCH, NORTH SUTHERLAND

Above Bunacaimb there is a wide and dreary expanse of bog stretching almost to Morar. Much of this could be properly drained and converted into good arable land. In some areas the Department of Agriculture for Scotland has made attempts at land reclamation, but only on a small scale and, no doubt, a great deal more could be done. Recent experiments carried out by Major-General Costello in the west of Ireland have gone a long way to prove that reclaimed peatland makes the best arable land. Experts from the Scottish Department of Agriculture have recently studied Major-General Costello's experiments and it is to be hoped that what they may have learned will influence agricultural policy in the future. At present there is so much arable land going out of cultivation and slowly reverting to bog all over the Highlands that it would seem over-optimistic to hope for any large-scale schemes of reclamation.

The districts of Morar, Arisaig and Moidart had their share of evictions and emigration, forced and otherwise, in the past and the drift away from the land has by no means ceased, especially in Moidart. Donald Macdonald told a very moving story about an old man who was to be evicted from Camusdarrach near Morar. At one time about the beginning of last century, the estate, on which Camusdarrach is, belonged to Col Simon Macdonald, a distinguished soldier of the Napoleonic Wars. A native of Camusdarrach served under Col Simon Macdonald in Egypt and Ireland and returned to his ancestral home at the end of hostilities. Unfortunately the gallant colonel contracted fever and died. He was buried in the churchyard of Arisaig, where his grave can still be seen. On the death of Col Simon the estate passed to one named Aeneas Macdonell. The accession of a new landlord brought in its train many changes, and now evictions became the order of the day. The veteran soldier at Camusdarrach was told that he would have to leave his house and patch of land on a certain day or he would be forcibly evicted. The hapless old man could not leave his house for he had nowhere to go. Early in the morning of the day he was to be evicted, he wended his way to the churchyard of Arisaig, to the grave of Col Simon Macdonald. The burial-ground of Arisaig is right beside the highway and later on that day the estate-bailiff was passing in his coach on his way to Camusdarrach to evict the old soldier. In passing, the bailiff's attention was suddenly arrested by piteous cries within the graveyard. He came out of his coach and looked over the wall. There at the grave of Col Simon was the old soldier kneeling down, beating the grave with his two hands and calling upon the dead in the hopelessness of his grief.

"Arise, arise out of there, Colonel Simon! Arise and help me! Many a day I followed you in Egypt and in Ireland, and today I am in dire need! Arise out of your grave and help me!"

Needless to say, the bailiff turned about and went home. The old soldier was left in peace. Not even the direst necessity would force the Highlanders of old to call upon the dead to help them. The bailiff was so terror-stricken by what he heard that he could proceed no further.

The bay of Arisaig is very pretty and sheltered. At the mouth of the bay are a number of islands and reefs, each with its own name. A story is told that a party of Swedish sailors landed at Arisaig once and saw a very pretty girl on the shore. They promptly abducted her and she was brought to Sweden, and probably married one of her captors. Long years afterwards a party of Highland sailors in a port on the west of Sweden were heard talking Gaelic by this same girl. She approached them and recited a rhyme in Gaelic, and the rhyme she did recite was about the islands and reefs at the mouth of Loch nan Cilltean, Arisaig Bay. The sailors brought back to Arisaig the news that the abducted girl was alive and well. Old Donald MacEachan who told the story was inclined to think that the incident took place in the Viking age, but the islands got their names first from the Vikings and were gaelicised later.

Keppoch House on the northern side of Loch nan Cilltean is on the site of the residence of Aonghus nan Corc (Angus of the Knives), a ruthless character, who finally met his end at the hands of his own son-in-law. There was an old burial-ground at Keppoch, and tradition has it that it was closed on the orders of Aonghus nan Corc. The belief that the last person buried in a graveyard had to keep watch over the dead until the next corpse took over, has already been mentioned; and it was because of this belief (*faire chlaidh*) that the old burial-ground was closed. One of Angus' sons died and was to be buried in the old ground. At the same time the son of a poor widow over at Back of Keppoch died also, and he too was to be buried at Keppoch. During the night before the burial of Angus' son was to take place, the widow's friends brought the corpse of her son over the hill and buried it under cover of darkness to ensure that the period of watching would not be too long. When Angus of the Knives arose the following morning, the grave of the widow's son had been filled in and the corpse buried. In his anger Aonghus nan Corc gave orders that there were to be no more burials in the graveyard of Keppoch.

"I shall see to it that the widow's son will have to watch over the graveyard for a long time."

Angus' own son was buried in the crypt of the church at Arisaig, and a new burial-ground was opened south of the church. The watch of the poor widow's son has never ceased.

The main entrance to the Catholic church at Arisaig faces west and the burial-ground is on the south side of the church, while the main road is right at the eastern gable of the church. There is a fairly high wall of stone all around the burial-ground, and it has two entrances, one on the eastern side leading from the main road and another on the northern side leading to the grounds of the church. I attended a funeral in Arisaig, and was interested to observe that the old practice of approaching the graveyard "sun-wise" (*deiseal*) with the remains of the dead has not yet been abandoned. The practice was general all over Scotland and in many European countries, both Catholic and Protestant. Here too I noticed that all graves were on the south side of the church, for according to old belief the south side of a church was hallowed and only murderers, suicides and so forth would be consigned to the unhallowed ground on the north side of the church. That belief was common both to Catholic and Protestant communities, and we find it even reflected in the sermon of a noted Presbyterian divine of Skye, who, while castigating some of his flock, addressed them from the pulpit.

"Ye people of Glenmore and Mugarry, go ye to the north side of the church for your sins are as black as the droppings of vultures."

It was a Catholic funeral I attended at Arisaig. After the service the remains were taken out of the church and the cortège proceeded to the north-eastern entrance to the church grounds, then along the road southwards and then it turned westwards to enter the burial-ground. It had proceeded clockwise right round the church, although the obvious route would have been straight from the church door to the entrance by the northern wall of the burial-ground, for the grave was just beside that entrance.

Over a generation ago there were two famous pipers in Arisaig, the brothers Angus and George Macdonald. Angus died shortly after the First World War and George many years earlier. Angus was never married, but three of George's sons live in Arisaig still. Unfortunately, they are not pipers although all are very interested in piping. I had the pleasure of visiting one of the sons, Charles, and by him I was shown the gold medal for pibroch won by Angus at the Northern Meetings at Inverness in the year 1886. Angus was the exponent of pibroch, while George excelled as a player of marches, strathspeys, reels and jigs — the lighter music. Pibroch is the classical music of the bagpipe. Every piece is involved and intricate, and some take as long as twenty minutes to play. All through each piece there is a basic melody or groundwork that undergoes from three to four variations and ends with a return to the groundwork. Angus Macdonald's favourite pibroch was "The Desperate Battle of the Birds", a magnificent piece beginning with the challenge and followed by the fighting and beating of wings until it finally ends with the moaning of the wounded and maimed.

Charles recalled visits paid to his uncle Angus by notabilities in the piping-world, such as the late Pipe-Major John Macdonald of Inverness, Lt-Col J. P. Grant of Rothiemurchus and Pipe-Major William Maclean of Kilcreggan. There was one particular time that Pipe-Major Maclean came to see him. Angus was then an old man over seventy and had long ceased to play the pipes, although he still played the practice-chanter. Pipe-Major William Maclean is still an outstanding player and an unrivalled authority on pibroch. He was a much younger man at the time of his visit to Angus Macdonald and consequently a better player than he is today. For a long time he played for the old man, but could not induce him to play himself. Finally he succeeded, and old Angus took up his pipes and played "The Desperate Battle". When he finished, Pipe-Major William Maclean laid his own set aside with the remark: "After that I can now stop." The veteran had not lost the touch.

There is one very lovely pibroch called "MacCrimmon's Sweetheart". One tradition has it that this pibroch was composed by one of the MacCrimmons to a favourite brown polled cow that fell into a bog. The English name is quite fictitious, for there is nothing in the tradition to suggest a sweetheart, especially a fairy sweetheart: the Gaelic name is *"Maol Donn"*, meaning "the bare or hornless brown one". Tradition in the Arisaig district has it that the pibroch was composed not by a MacCrimmon but by Raghnall Mac Ailein Oig to a sea-shell that he picked up one day as he strode along the shore.

Despite the lapse of over three hundred years Raghnall Mac Ailein Oig (Ronald the son of Young Allan) remains the outstanding local hero. Ronald had at one time driven cattle to the southern markets and on his way home was overtaken by nightfall. He wandered on in the darkness until finally he saw a distant light. He made for the light and it came from a small bothy. The night was cold and stormy and he knocked at the door and asked for shelter. An old woman answered his knock and told him that she could not admit him. Ronald begged her to let him in to the shelter and warmth of the fire. Still she refused, but Ronald put his foot to the door and forced his way in. "There will soon come one," said the old woman, "and she will not take long in putting you out." They both sat down by the fire. It was not long until the daughter, a huge red-haired woman, arrived. Immediately she seized Ronald and began to put him outside. She was so strong that she put him down on his knees. The shame of being beaten by a mere woman incensed him and he sprang up and wrestled with her until she was finally thrown. The struggle then ceased and Ronald was made heartily welcome. He spent the night in the bothy and the result was that he fathered a natural son. Long years afterwards the son came to Morar to see his father. He was not recognised until he came into the kitchen of his father's house and took up a set of pipes that lay on a table and began to play. Ronald heard the playing and came in to see who the piper was. It was then he realised that the piper was none other than his son. Some time later Ronald put his son to a further test. A filly had died in his stable and he and the son went to remove the carcase. Inside the stable it was quite dark, but the son caught hold of the hind legs and proceeded to drag the dead animal out through the door. The father took the fore legs and pulled against the son. Not knowing what his father was doing, the son pulled and pulled until the carcase was torn in two and the son fell outwards with the hindquarters in his grasp. After that Ronald had no doubts but that he really was his son.

It was during Ronald's time that the district of Morar and Arisaig was haunted by a dread spectre called the Colann gun Cheann (Headless Body). The Headless Body was the spirit of a decapitated woman who returned from the dead to wreak vengeance on the living. John Francis Campbell, the noted folktale collector, noted down the story in 1860, but it was not until William Macdonald of Cul na Ceapaich told me in the summer of 1954 that I learned how the whole thing originated. The irascible chief of Siol Dughaill (the seed of Dugald) as the Macdonalds of Morar were called, caught a woman with a suckling baby stealing ears of corn in his field and promptly cut off her head with a sickle. The spirit of the beheaded woman appeared in the district and waylaid and killed as many of the seed of Dugald as it met. The whole district was terrorised and no one could be found brave enough to challenge the Headless Body. At last Ronald the son of Young Allan decided to rid the land of the scourge and he met the Headless Body on the strand between Morar and Arisaig. A desperate struggle took place until Ronald overcame the monster and had it firmly pinioned and helpless in his strong arms. The Headless Body begged him to let it go. Ronald refused to loosen his grip until he received a solemn promise that the Headless Body would never again interfere with anyone who had one single drop of the blood of the Seed of Dugald in his or her veins. Ronald then let go, and away went the Headless Body singing:

> Far from me is the foot of Beinn Eadara,
> Far from me is Bealach a' Mhorghain.

The tune sung by the Headless Body was noted by Ronald the son of Young Allan and it is still played by pipers in many parts of the Highlands.

Ronald the son of Young Allan was called upon to deal with an even more formidable adversary than the Headless Body. The most notorious chieftain of Clanranald was Evil Donald (Domhnall Dona Mac 'ic Ailein) who lived in the seventeenth century. Donald sold himself to the Devil in return for power and glory all through his life. Donald continued merrily on his evil course, but the Devil saw to it that he was never allowed to forget the contract between them for very long. Donald was continually followed by a frog-like creature as large as a bullock. All attempts to dispose of it were unavailing, and wherever Evil Donald went the gigantic frog was bound to make its appearance. Often he left Moidart and sailed across to South Uist fondly imagining that the frog was secure in the dungeon of Caisteal Tioram only to discover that it would appear out of nowhere and clamour to be taken aboard. On his return to the mainland the frog would be locked in the dungeon of the castle of Ormicleit and again it would appear swimming in the wake of his boat. The years rolled by and Evil Donald drew close to the end of his alloted span. He had been out in South Uist and was overtaken by the frog on the journey homewards. Evil Donald landed at Canna, and the frog gave him a lingering look as it got out of the boat and disappeared not to be seen again. Evil Donald observed this and knew that the end was not far off. Word was sent to Ronald the son of Young Allan asking him to go to Canna to be beside Evil Donald as the end approached. Ronald arrived in Canna and spent the night at the bedside of the dying chief. On this particular night Evil Donald was very low, and in hushed tones he told Ronald of his contract with the Devil.

"I sold myself to the Destructive One for success and vainglory in this life and tonight he comes to claim me. All through life I delighted in doing evil. At the battle of Inverlochy I could not get my fill of Campbell blood. There is no evil thing that I have not done, and tonight I must meet the master I served so faithfully."

Midnight approached and a shrill whistling was heard outside. Someone looked out, and there on a high rock by the shore stood a dark figure. As soon as the whistling was heard, the dying man made to get up. but Ronald the the son of Young Allan held him down. A second time the whistle was heard and again the old man struggled to get up but Ronald held him down. The third time the summons came the old man almost reached the door and only the great strength of Ronald succeeded in bringing him back to bed. As the hour of midnight struck a fearful noise was heard outside. Again they looked out and the dark figure had gone and the rock on which he stood was cleft in twain. As the noise died away Evil Donald of Clanranald sank back on the bed and gave up the ghost.

Ronald did compose one very noted pibroch called "*An Tarbh Breac, Dearg*" (The Dappled Red Bull). He was invited down to the Cameron country where an inveterate enemy let loose a wild bull in a field which Ronald had to cross. The bull attacked Ronald and almost succeeded in goring him to death. The bull, however, was killed by Ronald, but he never recovered from his injuries and his exertions in the struggle with it. It was on that occasion that he composed the pibroch.

The district of Morar is extremely pretty with its white sands and hills clad with birch. Loch Morar is reputed to be the deepest fresh-water loch in the British Isles. The loch is now a North of Scotland Hydro-Electric Board reservoir, and although there is a dam and power-station at its western end, the beauty of it remains unaffected. Simon Fraser, Lord Lovat of the "Forty-five", was captured on one of the wooded islands on the loch and from there made his way to his execution in London. There is a roadway up for a couple of miles on the northern shore of the loch, while there are only one or two scattered houses on the southern shore. I met a young shepherd who lived alone at Meoble miles away from anyone. He never felt lonely and seemed to enjoy life very much. He was accustomed to walking long distances to Morar and Arisaig. He laughed heartily on being asked if he were afraid that he might encounter the legendary Grey Dog of Meoble. The Grey Dog of Meoble makes its appearance when any one of the Macdonalds of Morar, the seed of Dugald, is about to die. There are several people still living who maintain that they have really seen the mysterious dog. It appears only before the death of that particular branch of the Macdonalds. Over two hundred years ago a Macdonald of Meoble had a greyhound. He had to leave home to take part in some campaign and at the time of his leaving, the hound was in pup. When he left, the bitch swam out to an island on Loch Morar and there gave birth to a litter. Months went by and Macdonald returned home again, but his greyhound was missing. He happened to go to the very island where the bitch had her litter. The pups had now grown up into huge dogs, and not recognising their master, attacked and killed him before the mother appeared on the scene. Ever since that time the Grey Dog has appeared as an omen of death.

The township of Bracara is on the southern side of Loch Morar, and it was there I found one of the finest traditional fiddlers in all Scotland, Donald Macdonell. Donald Macdonell is now over sixty years of age. On several occasions he has won awards for traditional fiddling at National Mods, but he has never received due recognition. He started to play in his early teens, and is completely self-taught. He first started to play the pipes but soon found that he preferred the fiddle. He has been a traditional fiddler for almost fifty years now, and he brings to his playing an artistry that is quite superb. By clever manipulation of the strings he can make his fiddle sound like a set of bagpipes played at a distance, and he always resorts to this when playing marches. He did play the groundwork and first variation of the famous pibroch "Mackintosh's Lament", composed by the bride of the Mackintosh chief, a bride widowed on her wedding day when her husband died as the result of a fall from a horse. I had never heard a fiddler attempting to play a pibroch until I heard Donald Macdonell play "Mackintosh's Lament". It was heartening to discover that there are so many fiddlers in this part of the country still. There were several fiddlers in Arisaig such as Lachlan Gillies who was also an expert Highland dancer in his younger days, the late Ewen Cameron, John MacQueen and young John MacMillan of Millburn. This is the only part of the Highlands that can compare with Shetland as far as traditional fiddling goes. Fortunately, this area, being to a large extent Catholic, was not influenced by the belated introduction of Calvinism into the Highlands and the hedonistic excesses of the evangelists of the early part of last century. It was in the Island of Eigg, not far distant from Morar, that old Donald MacKay was forbidden to play by a hide-bound lay preacher, and his fiddle, reputed to be a Stradivarius, was sold to a pedlar for ten shillings although he had given ten young bullocks to buy it. In the Isle of Skye an eminent divine, Rev. Roderick Macleod, set fire to a pile of bagpipes and fiddles as high as a house with the remark: "Better is the little fire that warms in the day of peace than the great fire that consumes in the day of wrath."

There is one memory of Morar that I shall always retain. I happened to go to Mass in the Catholic church one Sunday about Christmas-time seven years ago. Towards the end of the service a young girl with a most exquisite voice started to sing the beautiful Gaelic hymn "*Tàladh Chriosd*" (the Lullaby of Christ). The hymn was composed by a Fr. Rankin who emigrated with his flock from the Arisaig district last century. I had never heard the hymn until that day, but I shall never forget that young girl's singing. I think the girl's name was Maclellan, and she received whatever tuition she had from the late Mrs Macleod, who was school-mistress at Morar for many years. It was from Mrs Macleod that the late Mrs Kennedy-Fraser noted down the world-famous "Eriskay Love Lilt". I revisited Morar about eight months after Mrs Macleod's death. One of her pupils, Ronald Maclellan, has composed a very fine pipe-tune in her memory.

The village of Mallaig has sprung up within the last fifty years, when it became the terminus of the West Highland Railway. It is now an important herring port and boats fishing in the southern stretches of the Minch and out beyond Barra Head land their catches there for transit to southern markets. The village itself is perched on bare rocks, and there is an all-pervading stench of fish and crying of gulls to remind one that it is not just another fishing port, but a fishing port not quite dead like so many others up and down the western coast. The herring industry has resulted in a large influx of strangers from the east of Scotland and other places and the village differs considerably from the surrounding districts, although a number of natives have settled in Mallaig, and some Gaelic may still be heard there. At one time there was no habitation in Mallaig except a small shoe-maker's bothy, but old Marjorie Gillies and the late Archibald Maclellan remembered the time when there was nothing there except a small cluster of thatched houses, and it was in that little township that they were born and there they spent their youth. Marjorie Gillies is a remarkable old lady. She is well over eighty years of age, but still sings and she has scores and scores of songs. It was she who told me that it is unlucky to fish on mountain lochs. She told the story of a man who went to fish on a loch in the hills of North Morar and never returned. "Fresh water," said she, "is crossed, but the water of the sea is blessed."

LOCH NAN UAMH, MOIDART

Chapter Three

ARDGOUR, ARDNAMURCHAN AND MORVERN

IF ONE asks where this almost forgotten corner of Scotland is, I suppose the answer would be that it lies west of Lochaber and south of Moidart. It lies slightly out of the way of heavy tourist traffic, but no area is more deserving of attention than it and no area could recompense the visitor more fully. Ardgour and Morvern are bound on the east by the waters of Loch Linnhe, on the north by lovely Loch Shiel, on the south by the Sound of Mull, while Loch Sunart — a beautiful winding fjord, its name means Svend's fjord — enters from the ocean to separate Morvern from Ardnamurchan, winds its way eastwards and almost cuts Morvern from Ardgour. The former is popularly called Morven, possibly due to the influence of MacPherson's Ossian lays, but the real name ought to be Morvern which is the proper rendering of the Gaelic *Mora-bhearna*, meaning sea-gap. Loch Sunart, of course, is the gap. Ardnamurchan juts out into the Atlantic and Ardnamurchan Point was a noted landmark and danger-spot for shipping in the days of sail and seamanship. The area may be approached from Oban by sea or by road round the end of Loch Eil or across the car-ferry at the Corran of Ardgour south of Fort William.

I have always had, as it were, a clannish interest in Ardgour, "the high land of the goats", as it is called in Gaelic. For long now it has been the territory of my clan and still is. There are still Macleans of Ardgour although their number is now almost reduced to the only family, but the principal family nevertheless — the family of the proprietrix, Mrs Maclean of Ardgour. The story of how Ardgour came into the possession of the Macleans belongs to the past, but it is a story that does not do much credit to the good name I bear in common with the rest of my clansmen. Like all other Highland clans the Macleans monopolised neither vice nor virtue. The story, however, goes right back to the days of the Lordship of the Isles, to the time that we were mere vassals of the great head of Clan Donald. Today the ruins of Ardtornish Castle stand on a bare headland overlooking the Sound of Mull at Lochaline on the west of Morvern. Ardtornish was one of the principal seats of the Lord of the Isles. Across the Sound of Mull there was another seat belonging to the same potentate, the castle of Aros. From both seats there was a commanding view up and down the sound. The two first Macleans were gentlemen bearing the names of Wily Lachlan, Lachlainn Lùbanach, and Eachann Reangannach, Wrinkled Hector. Both, it appears, had qualities in addition to those suggested by the epithets applied to them, for neither of them were weaklings. They came to Aros of Mull and were given food by the ploughman of the Lord of the Isles. They were given no forks and knives by their host, who politely told them to put on hen's bills and eat away. The guests promptly took off the ploughman's head and went on their way to meet the great Macdonald himself. They took Macdonald prisoner and brought him to Dunolly, to MacDougall of Lorn. MacDougall, however, would have nothing to do with the very important captive, and on the advice of an old man they returned to Aros with their captive and induced him to give his daughter to one of them. Wily Lachlan married the daughter and became the possessor of Duart in Mull. Thus the family of Duart could claim descent from the Lord of the Isles. Some generations later a son was born to Maclean of Duart and, when he came of age, the father had to look for some lands for him. The person to whom he appealed was, of course, the then Lord of the Isles, and this lord was married to a close relative of Duart in any case. Some time before, the Lord of the Isles was lying ill at Ardtornish in Morvern. MacMaster of Ardgour came to visit the invalid, and on his arrival gave vent to some expression of disgust regarding the lack of proper ventilation in the sick-room. The Lord of the Isles heard the remark, and decided that it would not be forgotten. When Maclean of Duart came to him looking for lands for his son, his advice was: "Jump the wall where it is lowest." Duart was not slow to take the hint and he gave to his son a company of men and a boat. The young Maclean made for Ardgour, and defeated MacMaster in a battle. One of MacMaster's sons, who went by the name of the Fox, fled from the field and made his way across to the mainland at the Corran of Ardgour. His father's fisherman, who went by the name of the Son of Carrusglach, was fishing for coal-fish near the ferry. Young MacMaster called to him to row him across to the mainland. The fisherman turned a deaf ear to his request and went on fishing with the remark that the coal-fish were taking well. MacMaster had to go and hide in a wood near by. When the Macleans appeared on the scene, the son of Carrusglach told them that the Fox of the MacMasters was hiding in the wood. The young MacMaster was found and put to death. The fisherman then approached Maclean and asked him for a reward for having refused to help the fugitive. Maclean replied that if he had treated his master's son as he said he had, it might be his turn to be so treated at some other time. Three oars were set up to serve as gallows, and Maclean hanged the fisherman at a spot known to this day as the Hangman's Cove (Port a' Chrochaire). Ardgour has belonged to the Macleans ever since. The sudden death of Maclean of Ardgour in the late 20s robbed the Highlands of one of the very few Gaelic-speaking chieftains, but his widow has brought up the family in the true Gaelic faith and all her daughters are fluent Gaelic-speakers and have figured in the literary prize-lists at National Mods. Mrs Maclean herself has taken a prominent part in the affairs of the country of Argyll and interests herself in Gaelic and Highland problems.

It was autumn when I first crossed the ferry at the Corran and the wooded shore of Ardgour was a blaze of colour. All down from the head of Loch Eil there are good stretches of arable land and the farms and crofts are obviously well worked, but most of Ardgour is very high ground and quite sheltered in parts. The whole parish is within easy reach of Fort William, which is the shopping-centre for this area.

The road to Strontian and Ardnamurchan skirts the shore of Loch Linnhe and turns due west at Inversanda, while another road to the south-west brings one to Kingairloch and thence to the coast of Morvern. We were warned that the road to Kingairloch was in a poor state and we chose to go west to Strontian. The distance from Inversanda to the head of Loch Sunart is about eight miles. It is a fairly stiff climb and the mountains on either side, Garbh Bheinn on the right and Creach Bheinn on the left, rise to a height of almost three thousand feet. At the top of the incline we were rewarded with the first glimpse of Loch Sunart. Away behind us we could see where Loch Leven begins to wind its way in among the mainland hills. My companion on this journey was Francis Collinson, the well-known composer and broadcaster, and I had come with him to help in the recording of songs and stories in Ardgour and Morvern. He had been to the district before, but it was my first visit.

It was a dull day and windy, but when we got down to Strontian the waters of Loch Sunart were as calm as glass. The high hills on all sides broke the force of the wind completely. Strontian is a very pretty township, and I was surprised to see so many dwellings, especially in the valley of the Strontian River. The estate is now owned by the Department of Agriculture for Scotland, and there are a number of crofters here. An old shooting-lodge has been converted into an hotel. Shootings invariably go when the Department of Agriculture takes over. There was a rough pathway from the upper end of the river valley over the hills to Glen Gour on the Loch Linnhe side. This was the way used in the olden days by drovers and travellers to the south. It more than halved the distance to the Corran of Ardgour. The valley of the Strontian River and the northern shore of Loch Sunart is clad with birchwood. The sun broke through the clouds momentarily and we saw the countryside at its loveliest.

In other parts of the Highlands I had heard of a famous warrior, Ronald Glas (Grey Ronald) of Strontian; I failed to get any information about him here but heard plenty about him later when I visited Shona Isle in Moidart. However, I did hear about the floating church of Strontian, but that belonged to the less distant past. At the time of the Disruption in 1843, when the Free Church broke away from the parent Church of Scotland over the question of lay patronage, the proprietor of the district refused to give the adherents of the new denomination a site on which to build a church. Not to be outwitted, the Free Kirkers collected money and bought an old ship on the Clyde. It was fitted up with a church, roofed and all, and towed from the Clyde up Loch Sunart and anchored near Strontian. Every Sunday the preacher and worshippers rowed out in boats to the floating church and had their services. Seldom, if ever, were the waters of Loch Sunart rough, and the size of their congregation was always gauged by the depth of the ship in the water. The floating church was in use for a long time, but the Free Church finally acquired a site on which to build.

There are a number of Camerons in this area, although this is not quite their traditional territory. Many may have come westwards from the clan lands around Loch Eil and Loch Arkaig after the disaster at Culloden, for the defeat of the Jacobite forces resulted in greater displacement of persons than is generally realised. A great number of fugitives fled to places where they were unknown. Macleans from Mull, for instance, fled as far north as the borders of Sutherlandshire, and some of their descendants still live there. MacPhersons from Badenoch went as far as the Outer Hebrides, and the famous smith who distinguished himself at the Rout of Moy fled for refuge to the Isle of Lewis.

On the road to Salen we met Alexander Cameron who writes under the name of "North Argyll". He is an extremely able man and a first-rate scholar. Incidentally, he is employed as a road-mender and all the formal education he ever got was what the local primary school could give him. Nevertheless, Alexander Cameron is a Fellow of the Society of Antiquaries of Scotland and has written a great deal of valuable stuff including a booklet on the Floating Church of Strontian. All his articles on Highland history are most authoritative. How he can write them is quite beyond me, for, although he may have a small, private collection of books, he is miles and miles away from libraries and sources. Whenever he does have any time for study or writing it is always after a long day of heavy manual work.

Salen nestles in a pretty, wooded bay of Loch Sunart. Here the road to Acharacle and Loch Shiel turns due north and to the south-west is the road to Kilchoan in Ardnamurchan proper. This Salen is called in Gaelic "the Salen of Sunart" to distinguish it from Salen in the island of Mull to the south. I came across from Acharacle to the inn at Salen one Saturday evening in early September. It is only a couple of short miles from the western end of Loch Shiel across to Salen and the distance is not too long for the men of Acharacle and Moidart on a Saturday night. That day there had been sheep-dog trials at Acharacle, and I guessed that, if any of the local worthies were to have a day off, they would end the day in the inn at Salen. I went across in the hope of discovering singers. Highland public-houses can be fairly noisy on Saturday nights, and the ridiculous licensing laws of the country do not help matters much, for there is always a frantic rush against time. Highlanders are not beer-drinkers as a rule. If they do drink beer, it serves only to wash down their whisky. They never dream of drinking whisky leisurely: it goes down in one gulp. I am sure there is a lot less drinking in the Highlands than in countries like France and Ireland, but signs of drunkenness may be more evident in the Highlands for the very simple reason that there is less time to drink and the system cannot absorb all the alcohol it has to cope with in one short hour or so. When I arrived at the inn, the dogs lay quietly outside, for most of them had been run in the trials during the day and were tired. Their owners were crowded in the tiny bar and in a small smoke-room beside it. Only Gaelic was spoken, except when a couple of young shepherds, obviously Gaelic-speakers normally, started airing their English when they had had more drink than was good for them. One of them, however, started singing, but, of course, it was in Gaelic he sang. It was a recent composition in praise of the Isle of Mull, or rather the farewell taken by a native going into exile. The songs of the homeland have always a great appeal to Highlanders and do much to foster local sentiment and regional patriotism. At gatherings of Highlanders in the cities the songs expressive of longing for the glens and mountains of home are ever popular and their effect can be quite moving, for each district has its own anthem. I imagined the young shepherd belonged to Mull, for he was completely carried away by the song he sang. Two other singers followed in turn. Both were men from Glen Borrodale in Ardnamurchan; one of them sang a rollicking song in praise of whisky and the other, two songs which he himself had composed, one being about his experiences during a visit to Glasgow and the other telling of the hardships he endured working as a road-maker under an Irish foreman. Both his songs were humorous and brought an immediate response from the listeners. He was the local bard and his art was still a living one. The two young shepherds had quietened down considerably by the time the bard got under way. Closing-time came at 9.30 and the innkeeper had to clear the bar. It was then he had to face the most difficult task of the evening. He succeeded after a good deal of pleading on his part and bantering on the part of those reluctant to stop drinking. The dogs, however, had become restless by this time and itched to be on the way home. There had been much drinking during the evening, but no one showed signs of being ill-tempered or bellicose, and owners and dogs finally disappeared quietly into the darkness of the mild autumn night.

From Salen the road to Kilchoan in Ardnamurchan skirts the wooded shore of Loch Sunart, turns due west at the mouth of the loch and then climbs round the back of Ben Hiant. Kilchoan is a pretty little village lying in the shelter of the hills and looking south across the sea to the lovely Isle of Mull. This was, and is still, the home of seafaring folk and there are several master mariners living in retirement in and around Kilchoan. The bare walls of the castle of Mingarry stand by the shore some distance east of Kilchoan. It was in this castle that the valiant King James IV of Scotland received the submission of the powerful western chiefs in May 1495. The castle was later razed to the ground by Sir Donald Macdonald of Lochalsh who was proclaimed Lord of the Isles after the disastrous defeat and death of King James at Flodden. The castle must have been rebuilt, for it was captured by Alasdair Mac Colla, the lieutenant of Montrose, in 1644. The history of Mingarry has now entered its final chapter and only the bare walls retain the memories of a stormy and now hidden past.

As we left the shores of Loch Sunart to climb the steep hill on the way to Loch Aline, we passed what must be about one of the smallest schools in the Highlands; a neat structure of corrugated iron barely twelve feet in length and breadth. It stands by the roadside at Liddesdale, for there is a Liddesdale here too. Away back in the time of the evictions, a crofter was turned out of his home and left to die along with his wife and family of small children unless some shelter could be found somewhere. In desperation he went down to the shore and built a rude bothy for his family underneath high-water level. Underneath the tidal mark he was immune from any interference by landlord or factor, and there he remained and brought up his family.

His great-grandchildren were the pupils who attended the little school at Liddesdale. However, the desolation caused by the evictions is still painfully evident throughout great stretches of Morvern. Even the surface of the road testified to a lack of traffic due to an utter lack of people, and an unbroken hedge of green rushes had sprung up through the tarmacadam along the whole length of the road, but on both sides of the hedge the surface that remained was surprisingly good.

Our little car battled bravely up the incline and over the top. Down below us there was a great glen, absolutely desolate, without the slightest trace of habitation. Down in the depth of the valley, the road from Kingairloch joined the two parallel lines that had stretched before us all the way. Again we began to climb, but this time we had not so far to go. On the very brow of the hill we were met by another vehicle — much to our surprise — and we had to back for almost a hundred yards to allow it to pass. We met no other traffic on the road; it was late in the season and tourists had long gone. Once again we sped down into a lovely, wide, sweeping glen, and in the gathering darkness we caught a glimpse of a solitary house. We saw no more of Morvern that night, but there was a fresh wind blowing across the Sound of Mull when we got to Loch Aline. We were hospitably received at the Loch Aline Hotel, and that night we slept heavily.

Next morning the wind still blew across from the hills of Mull and the sky was dull and overcast. Across the narrow mouth of the loch the ruins of Ardtornish stood gaunt and silent, but still seemed to keep a watchful eye on Duart Castle away to the south across the Sound of Mull. Loch Aline means "beautiful loch", and when the sun appeared the next day it was quite beautiful. The loch is long and narrow and its shores are wooded. The silica sand mine, which is in operation at Loch Aline, has to some extent stemmed the flow of the district's life-blood, for several men are employed there. A little hamlet of prefabricated houses has sprung up on the face of the hill overlooking the pier. The most direct communication is with Oban by sea and the boat that plies between Tobermory and Oban calls twice daily, in the morning on its way to Oban. The locals can thus do their shopping in Oban and return by the evening boat. It is much cheaper to shop in person than pay carriage for goods ordered from Oban; freight costs exceed the price of the commodity often. Circumstances being as they are, one can see why it is so difficult to halt the tide of depopulation.

The Forestry Commission owns quite a stretch of land in this area and there are young plantations westwards along the coast from Loch Aline. Up from the head of Loch Aline and around Larachbeg the woods have grown well. It was to Larachbeg that the Government evacuated the people of St Kilda in 1930. There they were housed and given employment as forestry workers. It is difficult to see how governmental planners decided that forestry work was suitable for a community of people coming from an island where there are no trees and, indeed, it is questionable if even half of them had ever seen a tree prior to their arrival in Morvern. Still more difficult to understand is why they should have been sent to a place from which they could not even see the sea although Loch Aline is barely more than a mile away. Only persons born and reared on small seagirt islands can really understand how much the sight, the sounds and smell of the sea become almost an integral part of life itself. I should imagine that the mental suffering of the older members of the St Kildan community must have been intense. But the feelings uppermost in the minds of the evacuees on their arrival at what was to be their new home were, according to what I gathered over twenty years after, not so much longing for the sea but a feeling of overwhelming loneliness, for a couple of families were sent to live at Loch Aline on the Sound of Mull and this was the first time that the community had ever been broken up. Those unfamiliar with the geography of the west of Scotland must remember that St

145

Kilda lies almost a hundred miles out from the mainland and only on occasional days of exceptionally clear weather can it be seen from the western shores of the Outer Hebrides. To the St Kildans the difference between the old home and the new must have been enormous; true they had come to live among a community of the same race and speech as themselves, but before them was a way of life with which they were completely unfamiliar, a way entirely different from the old one which had been their way and that of their fathers for generations back. In 1930 even the St Kildan community lived as a family or a group of closely knit families and their system of social relationships was still much as it had been in Morvern prior to the decay of the clan system after the "Forty-five". That gentle and kindly community of St Kildans had to come a much longer way than the merely physical space of two hundred miles; they had to bridge an abyss of two centuries of time. Their bearing and their physical appearance made a very favourable impression on their newly acquired neighbours in Morvern, but strangely enough it was an almost insignificant detail that struck the people of Morvern most of all and that was that the St Kildans all spoke with much louder voices than they had been accustomed to hear. Of course, the reason was that the islanders had to make themselves heard above noises of wind and sea all their lives. If any change did come about, it came gradually, and the few remaining St Kildans I met had very musical voices, and spoke about the loveliest dialect of Gaelic I have yet heard. Unfortunately there is only one St Kildan family living at Larachbeg now and one other near Savary on the Sound of Mull. The community has scattered, some in Glasgow, some in Easter Ross-shire and elsewhere throughout the country. I doubt whether they will ever come together again.

Francis Collinson and I visited both St Kildan families. The old lady at Savary was rather shy and reticent; she did not remember any songs for, as she said herself, she had always been too busy to have time to sing songs. Somehow or other I think that we ourselves were to blame; we had come without any warning. Later in the evening we visited the family at Larachbeg. Here we were more successful and found this family more communicative. We assumed the man of the house was a widower, but his two daughters lived with him as well as a lovely old lady whom we took to be his mother. They sang for us and the good man himself told a couple of St Kildan legends; even the old lady joined in when she overcame her shyness. There was a little poem she remembered, a poem by a minister about a well on St Kilda. She lingered lovingly over the words, for they must have recalled memories of the times when she drank of the waters of the well as a little girl and later as a grown woman. We all listened while she repeated the verses she knew over and over again. Only in her mind's eye would she ever see the well again.

We left Larachbeg and motored through the night to Druimnin along the coast to the north-west. It was a narrow road full of twists and turns. At Druimnin the road came to an end. Across the sound we could see the bright lights of Tobermory in the island of Mull; on our side there were only dim lights from scattered homesteads. Druimnin is a dead end, but it is the most Gaelic part of Morvern. Here the school-children speak Gaelic as their habitual language, and that hardly can be said for any other area on the mainland of Argyllshire. We had come to Druimnin to see Sandy Cameron, the retired ferryman. All spoke of him as being the authority on the traditions and songs of Morvern. We expected to see an old, decrepit person, but found a man whose appearance completely belied his years even though he was recovering from a serious illness and had spent weeks and weeks in hospital. Sandy Cameron was full of information, of good spirits and gaiety. He must have been over sixty, but looked less than forty. He sang song after song, all the while bemoaning the fact that he had just come out of hospital and was still off colour. To us he seemed quite fantastic; we could have waited with him till dawn. We both knew that we would have been quite welcome to do so. The late Mr Graham

STAC POLLAIDH AND LOCH LURGAINN, COIGACH

Croall had often come all the way from Glen Uig in Moidart to visit him and they had spent long evenings together recalling and learning old songs. On our way back to Loch Aline, Francis Collinson and I could not help thinking what a rich and charming character we had met in Sandy Cameron.

The following afternoon we left Loch Aline and motored back to Strontian. We traversed the road we had come, but for the first part of the way it was a sunny autumn evening, an evening alive with colour. On the hillsides all the way along, the stags were belling. It was the rutting season.

Chapter Four

BADENOCH

BADENOCH may be regarded as the very heart of the Highlands, for it lies equidistant from the Atlantic and the North Sea and nestles between the great mountain barrier of the Cairngorms to the south-east and the Monadh Liath hills to the north-west. Its western limit is the end of Loch Laggan and it marches with Lochaber, while it stretches along the Upper Spey Valley in a north-easterly direction to Granton-on-Spey and the borders of Moray. Perhaps we ought to say that Badenoch and the upper valley of the River Spey mean much the same thing. Now we are in the country of the Clan Chattan, the Macphersons and MacIntoshes, loyal clans both.

The Spey rises high up in the Corrieyairack Forest and flows southwards for about a mile and enters Loch Spey. It then flows north-east and after four miles or so veers to the east. At Laggan it is joined by the Mashie which rises in Meall Cruaidh above Loch Ericht and flows almost due north to join the Spey. Two miles west of the Mashie and flowing parallel to it is the River Pattack which also rises above Loch Ericht. For five or six miles the rivers run in the same direction, but only one of them joins the Spey, for the Pattack, once it reaches low ground, turns due west and flows into Loch Laggan. Right in between the two streams must be the boundary between the eastern and western half of the Highlands. The strange course of the Pattack gave rise to the old Gaelic saying which in translation is: "The black, bubbly Pattack running against the water of Scotland." This part of Badenoch is a land of deep valleys and steep hills whose slopes are well wooded, often with birch.

If we approach Badenoch from Lochaber and the west, the only road is the one from Spean Bridge along Loch Laggan to Newtonmore, where it joins the main Perth-Inverness highway. The road from Spean to Newtonmore passes through enchanting country. The waters of Loch Laggan have been dammed by the British Aluminium Company and brought by tunnel to Loch Treig. The dam is an imposing structure, but even so it hardly spoils the grandeur and beauty of the valley. The loch proper begins at Moy Lodge and the road skirts the north-western shore all the way to Kinloch Laggan. Both sides are thickly wooded and the hills rise and tower on left and right. Across the loch on the right stands Ardverike House, one of the finest mansions in the Highlands. It is on the site of an earlier house owned by MacPherson of Cluny. The little hotel at Kinloch Laggan is in prettier surroundings than any hotel I have seen in the Highlands. It is a favourite resort of anglers who come to fish in Loch Laggan and other lochs in the area. It was there I met old Archie Cameron who lives in a little cottage beside the hotel. It was he who induced me to visit the old kirkyard of St Kenneth, a little to the east of the hotel. The ruins of the old parish church still stand there roofless. Inside the walls of the church there is a dark patch of earth in the south-eastern corner. Here the ground is bare although nettles and weeds grow in profusion elsewhere within the walls. The bare corner marks the grave of a factor who evicted a poor widow with her fatherless children during the evictions. Because of the widow's curse no grass will ever grow on the factor's grave. No grass has ever grown and none will. Old Archie Cameron, who has been a gardener all his life, strewed the grave with grass-seed one spring but no grass ever appeared. Apparently the widow has had her wish. There is still another legend connected with the church of St Kenneth, a legend with a theme common to the lore of many countries. Two young lovers were prevented from marrying on the grounds that they professed different religions: one was Catholic and the other Protestant. The young man took ill and died and some time later the young lady died of grief. They were buried on different sides of

149

the church, but from their graves grew two rowan saplings which finally met and intertwined above the church. Beyond the grave there are no differences of creed.

The road to Laggan Bridge winds onwards through lovely woodland, first along the banks of the Pattack, the black river of eddies that refuses to run east and join the Spey, and thence into Strath Mashie, a really beautiful strath that has not quite recovered from the spoliation of timber-merchants during the Second World War, although happily enough the Forestry Commission has come on the scene to make amends. A lot of wood was cut down all over this area, and there were bare, untidy stretches a couple of years ago. I should love to see Strath Mashie when its woods grow up again. In Strath Mashie lived Lachlan Macpherson, a friend and contemporary of James MacPherson the translator, or rather the creator, of the Ossian that ushered in the Romantic movement in European literature. Lachlan Macpherson knew a great deal more about the real Ossian than his more eminent and successful clansman. It is said that Lachlan helped him to translate his Ossianic poetry back into the Gaelic from which James MacPherson himself averred that his English rendering had come to begin with. The main difference between the two was that, while Lachlan Macpherson of Strath Mashie remained a Gaelic poet, James MacPherson never became one, for his genius expressed itself in the language of the people who honoured him with a last resting-place in Westminster Abbey. I doubt if more than two people in Badenoch today know where poor Lachlan Macpherson turned to dust. The authentic, traditional poetry ascribed to Ossian the son of Fionn must have survived in Badenoch as elsewhere in the Highlands long after James MacPherson was laid to rest in Westminster Abbey, but it survived on the lips of humble tradition-bearers whose names will never be known now. However, I do not think James MacPherson ought to have been maligned as he was, for in a sense he did no more and no less than the Finnish Elias Lönnrot who strung together in sequence the heroic ballads that went to the formation of Finland's natinal epic and proudest literary possession, the *Kalevala*. The important difference was that Lönnrot strung the ballads together in Finnish and not in Swedish or Russian, while the English language must have seemed strange in the mouth of Ossian the son of Fionn and very strange to the thousands of Highlanders who knew Ossian long before they ever heard of James MacPherson. Had James MacPherson written in Gaelic, and Gaelic only, he would have ended his days where they began, as an unknown schoolmaster in the now derelict township of Ruthven near Kingussie. All Badenoch people are immensely proud of James MacPherson, but to them his claim on their respect and affection rests not on his literary achievements but on his generosity to the poorer tenants of the Balavil estate which he acquired and his selfless efforts to have the Cluny lands restored to Ewen Macpherson, attainted for his part in the "Forty-five".

Along the road to Laggan Bridge, and to the left, there is a small enclosed copse. This marks the spot where Sir John Cope and his general staff decided to clear out of the way of the advancing Jacobites, then said to be more than halfway across the Corrieyairack. Tradition in Badenoch maintains that the Hanoverians caught sight of the advance guard of the Jacobites and beat a hasty retreat to Inverness, thus leaving the way to the Lowlands open to Charles and his men. It was about this time that the Jacobites captured young Ewen Macpherson of Cluny and the lot of the clan was cast with the Stuarts. From the fateful day of Culloden until he made his escape to France, where he died in 1764, young Ewen of Cluny spent years in hiding. His principal retreat was a cave high up in Ben Alder, and it was here he entertained the fugitive prince shortly before the latter left for France. His narrowest escape must have been when, disguised as a herder, he held the reins of the horse of the Hanoverian officer who was ransacking his house looking for him. The officer gave Cluny a shilling for holding his horse. After Culloden two rents were raised in the Macpherson lands, one to be paid to the

Hanoverian authorities and the other to the beloved and exiled chief. In the slums of Glasgow I recorded a merry little Gaelic song a couple of years ago, a song that ran:

> The lord of Cluny is coming over,
> The lord of Cluny is coming over.
> To me it is a joyous tale to tell
> That the lord of Cluny is coming home.

The Lord of Cluny never came home, and I never as much as heard a line of that little song in Badenoch. The estates were finally restored and many descendants of young Ewen of Cluny distinguished themselves in the service of the Hanoverian monarchs and their successors, but, of course, the star of the clan set in 1764 in France. On the death of Albert Cameron Macpherson of Cluny, the hereditary chief, the estate passed in 1932 into other hands and the last vestige of the link with young Ewen of Cluny vanished. Today the few clan relics that remain have been assembled in the Clan Macpherson House, a clan museum, at Newtonmore. There is to be seen the green banner of the clan, the green banner that always ensured victory when it accompanied the clan to battle. The Macphersons were not on the fatal field of Culloden, for they had gone out to forage and did not come up till the day was lost. They were present at Ruthven near Kingussie when the clans were disbanded after Culloden. There also is the black chanter of Cluny which fell from Heaven during the famous clan battle on the North Inch of Perth. It also brought victory to the side whose piper played it. Equally interesting, if not quite so venerable, is the broken fiddle of the noted James Macpherson, an honoured freebooter who robbed the rich to feed the poor and who was hanged on 16 November 1700, in Banff. Before going to his death, he asked to be allowed to play one last tune. He played "Macpherson's Lament" and, when the tune was finished, turned round and asked if there was anyone present willing to speak for him. No one would, so he broke the fiddle over his knee, sprang from the gallows and hanged himself. My friend, Mr Hamish Henderson, has recorded some very fine versions of the song, notably from Davie Stewart of Dundee and Jimmie Macbeath of Elgin, and the tune has long been a favourite with Highland pipers.

> Fare weel ye dark and lonely hills
>   Away beneath the sky,
> Macpherson's Rant will nae be long
>   Below the gallows tree.
>
> Sae rantinly, sae wantonly, sae dauntinly gaed he.
>   He played a tune and danced it roon'
>   Below the gallows tree.
>
> Fare weel my ain dear Heiland hame,
>   Fare ye well my wife and my bairns.
> There was nae repentance at my hert
>   While the fiddle was in my airms.
>
> There's some come here to see me hanged,
>   And some to buy my fiddle.
> But before that I do part wi' her
>   I'll brek her thro' the middle.

CAISTEAL TIORAM, MOIDART: "THE RUINS OF CAISTEAL TIORAM, THE MAINLAND STRONGHOLD OF THE CLANARANALD, WILL LONG REMAIN MY MOST VIVID MEMORY OF MOIDART."

The broken fiddle is still to be seen among the clan relics at Newtonmore. It is very fitting that it should have been given a place of honour, for "Macpherson's Rant" is much better known today than the black chanter or the green banner. Songs have always been, and still are, very potent things.

The old Wade road leading over the Corrieyairack can still be clearly seen along the banks of the Spey right up to Garvamore. In places the new road has been superimposed on it and some of the lovely old bridges still serve a purpose on the new road. The road had been newly tarmacadamed when I last walked up to Garvamore, but beyond that it was much as Wade must have left it before the snowstorms and floods of a couple of centuries began to play havoc with it. The old road over the Corrieyairack was the main drove route from the west and must have been used a great deal until within twenty or thirty years ago. The old house at Garvamore was built in 1739, but it stands still and is inhabited. It first served as a barracks, but later as an inn. In the old droving days it was the resting-place for cattle and drovers once they had got safely across the Corrieyairack. The very walls of that old, fascinating house must be replete with memories of long nights of drinking by sturdy men from Kintail, Knoydart and the Western Isles and still seem to re-echo the choruses of their Gaelic songs.

This part of the river valley is thinly populated, but I was quite surprised at the number of spacious mansions not far distant from each other. They all seemed empty, but undoubtedly they were let as shooting-lodges in the days when the "gentry" were more prosperous than they are now. These lodges must have displaced crofters and small farmers some generations ago, and the tragedy of it all is that they have outlived their dubious usefulness but the crofters they displaced will never return. Across the glen I could see the township of Crathie, now completely desolate. My friend, Mrs Milne of Laggan Bridge, who is still not so very old, remembers the time when large numbers of strapping, stalwart men came down to Laggan Bridge for divine service and funerals there. The people seem to have gone so quickly. I met the last resident of Crathie in Inverness and there he was spending the evening of his days in a rest-home.

From Laggan Bridge right on to the village of Newtonmore there are fine stretches of agricultural land reputed to be about the best in the north of Scotland. The farms are large and some are extremely well managed. Cluny Castle, the seat of the Macphersons, stands back from the main road and is hidden in trees. I do not think I have yet seen the castle properly. The road to Newtonmore can be beautiful on late summer evenings. The river winds its way through the low valley on the right and steep wooded hills rise on the left. As one nears the village of Newtonmore the valley widens and away to the north-east there is a splendid view of the Cairngorms. During my stay in Badenoch, Newtonmore was my centre. Every day I cycled to Laggan and back. That stretch of road I preferred to all others in the area and there are any amount of lovely byways in Badenoch.

Another road climbs over the hill southwards from Laggan to Dalwhinnie. From the summit there is a glorious view down the valley of the Spey as far as Aviemore. From this road may still be seen the ruins of a little cottage at Catlag, or Cat Lodge as it is in English, a cottage that in reality was a veritable college of piping. It was here that the late Malcolm Macpherson, piper to Cluny and deservedly styled "King of Pipers", lived and taught. Malcolm succeeded his father as piper to Cluny, and he was succeeded by four of his sons, each in turn. Malcolm Macpherson's father, Angus, was taught by the last of the MacCrimmon pipers of Skye and he also inherited the gift from another noted piping family, the Bruces of Glenelg. Angus taught his son, Malcolm, who also received tuition from Angus MacKay and Archibald Munro, both of whom were taught by pupils of the last of the MacCrimmons. Malcolm Macpherson taught five of his sons the art of pibroch and his pupils included some of the outstanding pipers of this century, such as the late Pipe-Major John Macdonald of Inverness, the late Angus MacRae, Callander, and Pipe-Major William Maclean of Kilcreggan. Old Malcolm Macpherson used no books, no musical scores; his method of teaching was entirely oral and he used a system of vocables called in Gaelic *canntraireachd*. That was the very system employed by the MacCrimmons and other piping schools. In that little cottage at Catlag old Malcolm enforced a rigorous discipline. Pupils sent to him started at ten in the morning and continued until ten in the evening with only short intervals for meals and a break of about an hour at four in the afternoon, when they were sent out for a walk. Sometimes young boys living in the Badenoch district walked distances of ten to fourteen miles in sleet and snow during the depth of winter for their nightly tuition and walked back home again.

Malcolm Macpherson, King of the Pipers, has long since become a legend in many parts of the Highlands. Often he walked over the Corrieyairack to visit piper friends in Skye and often also he walked with his pipes all the way to Fort William to compete at the Lochaber Gathering. Many stories are still told about him, but there is one which has wide currency. Malcolm was piper to Cluny Macpherson at the time of the story, and the patriarchal chief was always anxious that his piper should figure in the prize-lists at the various Highland Games. Cluny sent him off early one summer's morning to compete at the Kingussie Games. The piper had to walk the whole way, but Cluny himself was to follow later in his coach. The morning was hot and sultry and poor Malcolm was tired when he had covered the first number of miles to Newtonmore. At Newtonmore he repaired to the change-house and drank some ale and then continued on the way. Owing to the heat of the morning he rested by the roadside, and while resting he drowsed off to sleep. He was not long asleep when Cluny Macpherson came by in his coach. He saw his piper asleep by the roadside and decided to teach him a lesson. He alighted and as gently as possible removed the set of bagpipes from the sleeper's arms. Malcolm would have no pipes to play when his name was called, and that, thought Cluny, would serve him right. Cluny drove on. When Malcolm awoke his pipes were gone. Nevertheless, he carried on to Kingussie. On the way he espied a tinker's encampment. They were Stewart tinkers and, of course, were bound to have pipes of a sort. He greeted the tinkers and told them his tale of woe. Out of one of the tents there was brought an old, ragged set. Malcolm took up the pipes and tuned them to his satisfaction and away he went. The pibroch competition began, and Cluny was certain that his piper would be unable to compete, and unable to explain the reason why when he returned home that evening. Malcolm's name was finally called, and to the utter amazement of Cluny he strode into the arena with his pipes. He played as he had never done before, and when the result was announced Malcolm Macpherson had completely swept the boards — with the tinkers' pipes. That evening it was the chief, and not his piper, who returned crestfallen to Cluny. The redoubtable piper was just too smart for him.

In Newtonmore I was the guest of Mrs Catannach of the Glen Hotel, a grand-daughter of the late Malcolm Macpherson. I arrived at the height of the busy tourist season and it seemed impossible to get accommodation in the whole of Badenoch. As soon as Mrs Catannach learned that the object of my visit was to collect the lore of the district, room was found for me. I stayed there for two months and was very loath to leave in the end to move to another area. The hotel guests were charming and the English guests were most interested in the work I was doing; some of them even went as far as to drive me and my recording machines from one parish to another. Most of them had come to the Glen Hotel summer after summer. Badenoch is full of hotels and draws a large number of summer visitors. I do not think there is any place in Scotland where the climate is so invigorating. There I could be up every morning before seven o'clock — something I accomplished neither before nor since. That was the season that pony-trekking was started at

Newtonmore by the enterprising local hotelier, Ewan Ormiston. The last time I was in Newton-more the pony-trekkers had gone over the hills to the Braemar Gathering. Other centres have now followed the lead given by Newtonmore.

It was in the Glen Hotel I had one of the greatest pleasures that has come my way in recent years. On the evening of the Kingussie Highland Games I met Angus Macpherson of Inveran, son of the late Malcolm, King of the Pipers. Angus had adjudicated the dancing events at Kingussie that day and had come to spend the week-end with his niece. For over sixty years Angus Macpherson has attended Highland Games, first as a competitor and latterly as an adjudicator of piping and dancing. As a piper he won the highest honours, while his son, Malcolm, was said to have at times equalled the late Pipe-Major John Macdonald of Inverness. In an age so dedicated to materialism and its standard of values, it was an experience to have met Angus Macpherson, for he is about the most refined idealist I have ever met. In his veins there flows the blood of generations of artists from the sixteenth century onwards, and to him only the beautiful things in life mattered. I spoke to him about the stories and legends about his father and hoped that they would not be forgotten. By that time Angus had made up his mind to write down his memories of his father and his methods of teaching. He has since done so in his delightful book, *A Highlander Looks Back*. A great deal of the material about his father he has recorded *viva voce* for the Edinburgh University School of Scottish Studies. The problem was to have permanent recordings of his father's style of playing made by pipers whom his father taught. Angus himself was then too old to play the pipes again, and the late Pipe-Major John Macdonald was bedridden. There remained only Pipe-Major William Maclean of Kilcreggan who received his tuition along with Angus himself. Pipe-Major Maclean was then seventy-six years of age but still active. The following winter Pipe-Major Maclean began the recording and played almost fifty pibrochs as he was taught to play them by old Malcolm Macpherson. Six months ago I arrived in Lairg, Sutherlandshire, one fine summer evening. I telephoned Angus almost as soon as I got to Lairg. "Have you got your recording machine?" asked he. I told him I had. "The pipes are going well," said he. I knew that there was something in the wind. I went to see him the following evening, and in the gathering darkness he tuned up and we recorded the "Prince's Salute" — a lovely pibroch composed in honour of the Old Chevalier in 1715. When we finished, I had it played back for him. He was not quite satisfied with his performance. I decided to come back to see him the following morning. The pipes were going really well by the time I reached him. We re-recorded the "Prince's Salute". This time he was satisfied, and went on to play the ground or theme of three other pibrochs. He played them all as he was taught to do by his father. A few days previously he had gone into his seventy-ninth year. He had made up his mind that he would play his pipes again. I am sorry to say, however, that there are few pipers in Badenoch now, although the village of Kingussie has a pipe-band and one of the noted performers of the present day is William Macdonald who lives in Inverness but is really a native of Kingussie. William Macdonald has also the distinction of being one of the best shinty-players in the Highlands.

The villages of Newtonmore and Kingussie have long been nurseries of shinty teams and noted players. The Newtonmore club has won the Scottish shinty trophy more often than any other club. The last time I was in Newtonmore the Scottish Cup and several other trophies were displayed in a shop window on the main street. In many homes there, pictures of noted teams of the past were proudly shown, in many cases teams dating back to the years 1905 and 1906 and the years immediately preceding the First World War, when the late Dr John Cattanach, subsequently killed on active service, was a member of the team. Over forty years have gone since Dr John Cattanach played for Newtonmore, but he is still remembered and will

ABANDONED VILLAGE, LONBAIN, WESTER ROSS

be as long as shinty is played in Badenoch. Shinty will be played in Badenoch for a long while yet, as I observed during my stay at Newtonmore. Although it is principally a winter game, I noticed youngsters who had hardly reached school age going about with their *camain* (clubs) during the long summer evenings. Matches between the rival adjacent villages of Kingussie and Newtonmore are attended with great enthusiasm.

I think that the most enchanting part of Badenoch is on the southern bank of the Spey from Ruthven opposite Kingussie down to Abernethy and the Braes of Tulloch. The ruins of the barracks at Ruthven are still imposing. It was here that the Highland army reassembled after Culloden and was told to disband, amid wailing and lamentation. There are only a couple of farm-houses at Ruthven now, but old Mrs MacGregor at Tromie Hill remembers the time when fires were kindled daily on thirteen hearths in the township of Ruthven. The whole district is well wooded and there was considerable timber trade in this part of the Spey Valley over a century ago. The timber went down the river under the direction of "floaters" who used long iron-shod poles known as floater's cleeks to ensure that the consignment of logs in their charge did not get caught in the river banks and fail to reach Garmouth. A great deal of the Spey-side timber was used as sleepers for the rapidly expanding railroad system during the last century. Mr Joseph Lobban, one of the few surviving Gaelic-speakers in the Abernethy district, told me that his father was a floater. He used to float his timber down the river, deliver and sell it in Garmouth and then walk home again — quite a long distance. I had seen floaters at work on the rivers and lakes of Norway and Sweden, but did not think that they could have been seen here less than a century ago.

A mile or so east of Ruthven there is a fine stone bridge across the River Tromie which runs down to join the Spey. Lower down the Tromie there still stands the old Tromie mill, the last watermill in operation in the Badenoch district, or rather the last that was in use, for to all intents and purposes milling ceased here about 1921. I used to cycle twice or thrice a week from Newtonmore to visit Mrs MacGregor whose husband was the last miller at Tromie and whose people had been millers there for over a century. There is quite a sprinkling of Gaelic-speakers in this part of Badenoch, on the side of the river not affected by the railway-line, and Mrs MacGregor is one of them. I was quite moved by the welcome she and all other ageing Gaelic-speakers of Badenoch gave me when it was discovered I could talk Gaelic. To them all it was a delight to speak Gaelic and hear it spoken, and it was a delight all the more because it was so rare an occurrence. That there is widespread devotion to the language throughout the Highlands is beyond all doubt, but it is not the enthusiasm of zealots whipped up by propaganda, for there is no effective propaganda; it is the spontaneous devotion of a disinterested but unfortunately inarticulate mass to something they feel is a very vital part of their spiritual lives. That there has been no dynamic urge to rehabilitate the Gaelic language is not due to lack of devotion but to the lack of leadership, inspiring leadership similar to that of the late Dr Douglas Hyde and the Gaelic League in Ireland.

At Tromie Bridge there is a road leading to the right past Killihuntly up the valley of the river. A sign-post at the bridge indicates that the track goes over the hills to Blair Atholl in Perthshire. Farther up, the track to Blair Atholl branches off the main road to Loch an t-Seilich and Gaick Lodge, a shooting-lodge, of course. The Forest of Gaick has long been a spot noted for hunting. It was here that "the Gaick catastrophe" occurred over a century-and-a-half ago, an event that is still spoken of with awe. There are two histories of every land and people, the written history that tells what it is considered politic to tell and the unwritten history that tells everything. It is very interesting to observe how "the Gaick catastrophe" is treated by the two histories. On page fifty of the guide-book, *Romantic Badenoch*, we read as follows:

It was at this spot, now marked by a commemorative cairn, erected principally through the influence of the late Mr Alexander Macpherson, banker, Kingussie, that the tragic event known as "the Gaick catastrophe" occurred. On the Monday preceding Christmas (old style), in the year 1800, Captain John Macpherson of Ballachroan, usually called, on account of his dark complexion, the "Black Officer", accompanied by a party of Badenoch men, arrived here for the purpose of providing himself and his friends with Christmas fare from among the wild denizens of "Gaick's stern sombrous solitude". At that time only one building existed in the glen, a substantial stone structure, occupied in the summer and autumn months by herdsmen and sportsmen, and this was to form the headquarters of Macpherson and his party during their expedition. Two days after their arrival a storm of unparalleled fury broke out, and when Christmas came and the hunters did not return, their friends became uneasy regarding their safety. A messenger was accordingly dispatched to Gaick to investigate the cause of their delay, and this individual, when he arrived at the spot where he conceived the house to have stood, was astonished and terrified at not being able to distinguish any mark of the building. Nothing appeared to his view but an unbroken wreath of snow. After some exploration he picked up a cap and a powder-flask, which he recognised as having belonged to some of the party. With these he returned to Kingussie, and on the following day a number of men accompanied him to the lonely spot. This party, after several hours of eager exertion, discovered the foundations of the cottage, which had evidently been swept away by an avalanche of snow from the adjacent hillside. The bruised bodies of the victims were found and carried to their respective homes.

Let us now draw aside the curtain and let us see the Badenoch people who neither write nor read guide books and let us hear what they have to say. Almost all old tradition-bearers had something to say about the catastrophe at Gaick, and what is more, all their accounts of the event tallied. The mere mention of Gaick seemed to inspire terror and all accounts were given in awe-stricken tones. The same story was told not only in Badenoch but also in Lochaber, Glenurquhart, Moidart and even in the islands of Skye, South Uist and Benbecula. People in places distant from each other and who could never have seen and met one another told exactly the same thing. Probably the "Black Officer" was dark-haired and dark-skinned but it was not so much because of any physical attributes that he got his name but because black connotes evil. Capt. John Macpherson of Ballachroan was a very zealous recruiting-agent on behalf of the British Government then in the throes of war with France. His aim was to obtain as many recruits as possible by means fair or foul. His favourite method was to invite the young men of Badenoch into the local inns to drink. The unsuspecting victim accepted the captain's hospitality and went in to drink with him. The wily captain awaited his chance and furtively slipped a shilling into the young man's pocket. In those days shillings were not so plentiful in Badenoch. When the poor man's wits were sufficiently dulled by the effects of drink, he was suddenly confronted by the captain who told him that he had to go into the army. "Why?" the young man would ask. "You have taken the shilling." He had not; he had no shilling. "Try your pockets then," the captain would say. He would search in his pockets and sure enough the shilling was there. The recruit was thus gaffed and whisked off to join the colours. Writers of the histories of Highland regiments may say what they will, but a very, very large proportion of the valiant men who distinguished themselves in the same regiments were either fooled by sleek recruiting-agents or bludgeoned into service by the press-gang. The "Black Officer" of Ballachroan was no exception although his methods were despicable enough. Many of the young men recruited by the wily captain never returned again, and it was the "Black Officer" and not the French who incurred the hatred of the sorrowing mothers of Badenoch. To them the "Black Officer" was wicked enough to be in league with the Evil One, and subsequent events were to prove that they were not far wrong. Whatever success, affluence or power the Captain of Ballachroan had achieved was nothing more than his recompense for having sold himself to a master who would eventually come to claim him, when the stipulated time expired. Exactly a year before the Gaick catastrophe, the "Black Officer" and some companions went to Gaick and were spending the evening in that self-same bothy in which they later met their doom. Towards midnight a sudden knock came to the door. In haste the Captain of Ballachroan went out and closed the door behind him. A strange voice outside greeted him, and above the sounds of the night outside those listening within caught only snatches of the conversation.

"Tonight is the night," said the strange voice.

"It is not tonight," said the "Black Officer" in reply, "but a year from tonight."

The rest of the conversation was drowned in the wind. After a time the stranger was heard to go and the "Black Officer" returned to join his comrades.

The Glenurquhart storyteller had a slightly different rendering of the incident. The Captain of Ballachroan was in Inverness some days before Christmas that same year and was seen talking to a stranger on horseback. Part of their conversation was overheard and it was almost exactly as above. The "Black Officer" returned home to Ballachroan. He had still a year left. As the last Christmas of the century drew near, the Captain of Ballachroan invited some of his friends to join him in the expedition to Gaick. The invitation was accepted by five, but only four went to their doom. The fifth had left his home to join them when his dog rushed out after him and leapt up in front of him and placed his fore-paws on his chest. He tried to shake the dog off but again it did the same and again a third time. All of a sudden the man stopped dead, for the strange behaviour of the animal seemed to suggest some premonition of evil. He went no farther.

What actually transpired at Gaick on that fateful night will never be known. The party from Kingussie arrived eventually and the bodies of the "Black Officer" and his comrades were found. It is said that one corpse was found behind a dyke quite a distance away from where the bothy stood and where the other remains were found. What horrified the searchers most of all was that the gun-barrels of the dead hunters were twisted like corkscrews and there was a terrorised look in the lifeless eyes of the snarling, grimacing dogs. The corpses were placed on stretchers and the party prepared to start on its sad journey homewards.

"Let us go in God's name!" said one man.

The men assigned to the corpse of the "Black Officer" went forward and proceeded to lift their burden but it stayed as if rivetted to the very earth. No strength, no power on earth would raise the corpse of the "Black Officer". In vain they tried, again and again.

"That will not do us any good," said the oldest and wisest member of the party. "Let us go in the name of the One whom he served."

"Let us go then in the name of the Devil," said they all.

The corpse was raised and the party proceeded towards home, bearing the mortal remains of the "Black Officer" at the head of the cortège. They had not gone more than a mile or so when the sky darkened and a terrific blizzard drove in their faces and forced them to a dead halt. In such a storm it was quite impossible to make any headway. The oldest and wisest member of the party spoke up again.

"Put the corpse of the 'Black Officer' behind instead of in front of the others, and perhaps then we can be able to go on."

The remains of the captain were carried back and those who bore him took their place at the end of the procession. Slowly but surely the storm died down and the party was enabled to go on its way. Thus came home the soulless body of the Captain of Ballachroan, a faithful servant of two principalities, the British Empire and the Powers of Darkness.

Chapter Five

URQUHART AND GLENMORISTON

THE Caledonian Canal basin, which runs in a south-westerly direction from Inverness on the east to Fort William on the west, cuts the Highlands in two. Along the valley three lochs, Ness, Oich, and Lochy, lie in line and are joined by the canal. The importance of the Caledonian Canal as a waterway has diminished greatly with the intensification of road transport, but it is still used by smaller craft, especially fishing-boats from the east coast on their way to and from the western coasts. A passenger boat once plied between Fort William and Inverness, but now the little piers and jetties on the lochs lie derelict.

The parish of Urquhart and Glenmoriston lies on the northern shore of Loch Ness, the northernmost of the three lochs in the canal basin. Glen Urquhart and Glenmoriston are both really beautiful glens but the contrast between them is most striking; Urquhart is smiling and prosperous, but beautiful Glenmoriston is slowly and surely on its way to death. The Forestry Commission has acquired and planted a good deal of land in both glens but in Glen Urquhart there has been less planting on land that was and could still be used for cultivation. In upper Glen Urquhart the population has fallen but the decrease is nothing like what it has been in Glenmoriston. In Urquhart too most of the crofters have brought their land outright and the pride of ownership has resulted in a greater desire to farm the land properly. Glen Urquhart is about the most prosperous glen in the whole Highlands and there, crofts and farms have been worked by the same families for generations. The sides of the glen are steep but there are tilled fields all the way up on both sides. In the ploughing season the teams have to move sideways across the hill-faces. Horses could not pull against the incline and it is doubtful if modern tractors can do so either.

In summer, streams of motorists, hikers, and trippers pass by Glen Urquhart. I first went there in late summer and found it most difficult to get any accommodation because I wanted to stay for some weeks. At most houses I was turned away mainly because it was more profitable to accommodate passing trippers who required only bed and breakfast. There were "Bed and Breakfast" signs everywhere. The tourist traffic in the Highlands has been condemned by some on the grounds that it has ruined the traditional standards of hospitality, but in this materialistic age the Highlanders could simply not afford to maintain the old standards. It is certainly my impression that they would like to do so and in certain remote places, where few strangers are seen, the old hospitality remains still. I stayed for six weeks at Milton, a mile or so above Drumnadrochit, and my landlady, Mrs Sinclair, frequently complained that I paid her not too little but too much. She was a widow and had been left to bring up a large family, but no amount of money could have brought the kindness and attention I received under her roof. Had I stayed in the glen only for one night, as most tourists do, I would have left it with a completely wrong impression.

Glen Urquhart is one of the strongholds of the Free Church of Scotland, the sect disparagingly referred to as the "Wee Frees". This body broke away from the parent church in 1843 over the question of lay patronage — the right of the estate-owner to choose a minister for his tenants. Even before 1843 the Puritan evangelical movement which first made itself felt in Sutherlandshire and Easter Ross in the previous century had come to Glen Urquhart. Lay-preachers known as the "Men" made it their business to further the Kingdom of God in parishes where the ministers of the church were lax. Their sole inspiration was the Bible and they preached with a zeal and enthusiasm equalled only by the Covenanters of Lowland Scotland at an earlier period. In actual fact they were the spiritual heritors of the Covenanters and had had little or no influence over the Highlands until after the disaster of the "Forty-five". Many Highland writers today extol the virtues of the traditional religious life of their people, with its strict observance of the Sabbath, its long and tedious services, its aversion to frivolities such as music, singing, and dancing and its assiduous Scripture-reading, but what they really do extol is a relic of Cromwellian England. Puritanism was imported into Scotland by the followers of Cromwell, the spiritual fathers of the Scottish Covenanters. I need only quote a native of Glen Urquhart, the late William MacKay, author of the excellent history of the parish of Urquhart and Glenmoriston and about the best and most impartial of all Scottish historians. In dealing with the religious history of the parish he says:

> The religion of the old Highlander lay lightly on his shoulders, and, like his brother Celt in Ireland, he freely mixed his business and amusements with it. His Sabbath — which till the eleventh century he observed on Saturday and not on the Lord's Day — was not entirely a day of rest. He attended church or chapel in the morning with more or less regularity; but the remainder of the day was given up to pleasures, sports, and his worldly avocations. On that day, as the church records show, he, for generations after the Reformation, drove his cattle to market, brought home his fuel, baked his bread, fished, played shinty, and put the stone. On that day, too, he married, christened, and buried. The Sunday christenings and penny-weddings were made the occasions of such boisterous mirth that during the seventeenth and the early years of the eighteenth centuries, numerous warnings appear on the pages of the Presbytery books against piping, fiddling and dancing at them. The lykewakes were even more uproarious, the chamber of death being filled night after night with jest, song, and tale, the music of the violin and the pipe, and the shout and clatter of the Highland reel. Everywhere the native buoyancy of the Celt asserted itself — in season and out of season. A change was, however, to come over his spirit. Puritanism, which was introduced into Scotland by the English sectaries of the Commonwealth, took deep root after the Restoration among the persecuted Covenanters of the Lowlands. It did not reach the people of Urquhart till old barriers were removed by the events of the Forty-five; but, if it was late in coming, its progress among them was amazingly rapid, and before the end of the century it held them in its coils with a tightness which has not yet appreciably relaxed. To it we owe our rigid sabbatarianism, the sacramental preaching week, our crowded communions, and long communion services. It has done much for religion in the Highlands, but it has not been an unmixed blessing. It has to a great extent destroyed the songs and tales which were the wonderfully pure intellectual pastime of our fathers; it has suppressed innocent customs and recreations whose origin was to be found in remote antiquity; it has in many cases engrafted self-rightousness on the character of religious professors; and it has with its iron hand crushed merriment and good fellowship out of the souls of the people, and in their place planted an unhealthy gloominess and dread of the future entirely foreign to the nature of the Celt.

The Free Church of Scotland today has about 50,000 adherents in Scotland and the main body of them belong to the Highland areas; there is another sect called the Free Presbyterian Church, a body numbering about 11,000 that broke off from the Free Church in 1893. The Free Presbyterians generally go by the name of "Seceders". Even to this very day there is extreme bitterness and hatred between the Free Presbyterians and the Free Church. The effect that such sectarianism can have on the life of small communities can sometimes be disastrous. Recently a Free Presbyterian minister refused to offer up a prayer at a funeral for the simple reason that the dead person was an adherent of the Free Church. Even death cannot put an end to sectarian differences, and, I suppose, some writers on Highland affairs will laud the sectaries for their devotion to principle, but no amount of loyalty to any sectarian principles can outweigh a deplorable lack of Christian charity. One can picture a funeral in a small and moribund Highland community: the bier, the bereaved and only a handful of mourners, barely enough to carry the mortal remains to the grave.

I attended one funeral at Glen Urquhart; an adherent of the Free Church was being buried but I noticed that both the Church of Scotland and Free Church minister were present and both took part in the funeral service. As far as I know, there are no "Seceders" in Glen Urquhart, and their absence may have led to a better understanding between the adherents of the Free Church and the Church of Scotland. In Glenmoriston there are Catholics as well as adherents of the Free Church and Church of Scotland, but I doubt very much if there is any sectarian bitterness in that glen either. In Glen Urquhart there was certainly none at all. The staunchest adherents of the Free Church there are extremely tolerant and courteous even to Roman Catholics, even although one of the two times when the Free Churchman and "Seceders" join forces is when they choose to warn the Scottish nation of the menace of "ever-increasing, idolatrous Popery". The other time is when they decide to knock hell out of royalty for breaking the Sabbath. At times their courage in doing so is quite heroic. One of the really outstanding ministers of the Free Presbyterian Church, the late Rev. Ewen MacQueen of Inverness, while conducting divine service at the time of the Jubilee of King George V, rebuked the reigning monarch in no uncertain terms when commending him to the mercy of the Almighty:

"O Lord, have mercy on King George, for we know he is a bad man and he desecrates Thine Holy Day by going to races, to concerts and to balls."

Except when worshippers go to or from church, there is no sign of human life in Glen Urquhart on Sundays and the whole place is filled with an almost unearthly stillness. Visitors are not encouraged and in many cases "Bed and Breakfast" signs are removed or covered over on Saturday nights. Frequently tourists and visitors refrain from offending the susceptibilities of the local people and do not break the peace of their quiet Sabbath and any regard for local feeling is appreciated. I chanced to be in Glen Urquhart during the weeks that the late John Cobb came to Drumnadrochit to attempt to break the world water-speed record. Cobb very courteously decided that there were to be no trials on Sundays. When he met his death on Loch Ness the whole of Glen Urquhart went into mourning and very genuine grief was felt by all. Today a simple stone cairn by the roadside opposite the spot where he was killed, a cairn raised by the people of Glen Urquhart, honours his memory.

The same strict Sabbatarianism obtains all over the Highlands wherever the Free Church and Free Presbyterians can exercise any influence, although to a lesser extent the adherents of the Church of Scotland are Sabbatarians too. Even the Catholics in Highland areas have been influenced by their Calvinist neighbours. The Highland Catholics never had weddings and dances on Sundays although such are common occurrences in the west of Ireland. However, I watched a football match one Sunday afternoon in Benbecula in the Outer Hebrides. Benbecula is half-Catholic and half-Church of Scotland and members of both denominations took part in the game I witnessed. The adherents of the Free and Free Presbyterian churches, almost within sight across the Ford in North Uist, would have been horrified if they had known of what was happening in Benbecula that Sunday afternoon. There is little doubt that shinty was played on Sundays in Glen Urquhart over a century ago. James Macdonald of Balnain remembers that an older generation in the glen often spoke of a goodly minister who used to hold services in a church up the glen on Sunday afternoons. Whenever he arrived he found the young men and boys playing shinty in a field near the church. He caught hold of a club, rounded up the players and drove them into church. The young men whiled away the time playing shinty until the minister arrived. They had all come there to attend the service.

The communion is the chief event in the ecclesiastical year of the Free and Free Presbyterian churches. The diet of services begins on Thursday and ends the following Monday. In fine weather the services are held in the open when the churches cannot accommodate the crowds that come long distances to worship. An open-air communion service can be an impressive scene. Some sheltered dell is chosen and a wooden kiosk serves as a pulpit from which the preacher addresses a congregation seated on stone ledges, rocks or improvised seats of planking, places on stones, or merely squatting on the grass or heather. The fervent worshippers are near the pulpit and they sit upright or with heads slightly bowed, while on the outskirts of the crowd the less fervent may rest lazily on their elbows. The silence is broken only by the voice of the preacher or the congregation joining in the singing of psalms. No hymns, incidentally, are permitted by the "Wee Frees" and "Seceders", only the metrical versions of the psalms. The metrical versions first appeared in Gaelic in 1659 and are sung to tunes which are evidently influenced by the Gregorian chant of the Catholic Church. By many, the Gaelic psalm-tunes are considered to be very beautiful, but I consider that the melodies of the "vain and worldly" songs of the Gael are immeasurably superior to them. The preachers, of course, have roundly denounced secular songs and music, but it has been impossible to wean all their adherents from them. In certain areas secular songs and tunes have survived almost a century-and-a-half of sectarian thundering. In almost all communities there were strong and independent characters who defied the ministers and the "Men" alike. The Gaelic bard, Duncan Ban MacIntyre, composed a lovely song in praise of Ben Dobhrain on the Perth-Argyllshire border, a song of several hundred lines that was sung all over the old Highlands. One day a lay-preacher came to remonstrate with an old fiddler.

"Do you know the Lord's Prayer?" asked the preacher.

"I do not," replied the fiddler, "but I know 'Ben Dobhrain' from beginning to end."

There was another old lady who knew and loved the songs of the bard, William Ross. This particular morning she spent singing William Ross' songs behind closed doors. A pious neighbour overheard her beautiful singing but not clearly enough to know what was being sung. She came in later and said: "Yours was the beautiful singing this morning. Surely it must have been the Psalms of David that you sang!"

"David, the excremental blackguard!" replied the other. "What good was he compared with William Ross?"

Probably there were people in Glen Urquhart also who considered that the "vain and worldly" songs were worth a great deal and equally as good, if not better, than the religious songs and hymns. The finest song connected with the district is, of course, that composed in honour of Brae Ruiskich (Braigh Rùsgaich) south of the glen by Iain Mac Dhughaill (John the son of Dugald). A hauntingly beautiful melody is wedded to words that reveal a mind of extreme sensibility. The poet has gone to Edinburgh where he is now awakened every morning by the din of the streets and the bell of the five hours and not by the melodious warbling of the birds of Brae Ruiskich. No longer can he hear the bellowing of the antlered stag, on the eve of the Feast of Saint John of the Rood, as he calls to his mate. Stag and hind may lie with one another, but the clergy do not trouble them; they do not go to a kirk session and they are not seen at court.

The kirk sessions that meted out punishment to moral offenders are now a thing of the past. Adulterers were made to sit on a high stool or stand in a prominent place in church while the

SHIEL RIVER, MOIDART: "I WAS QUITE ASTOUNDED BY THE BEAUTY OF MOIDART, ESPECIALLY THE COUNTRY ROUND THE LOWER
END OF LOCH SHIEL ... A STONE BRIDGE SPANS THE SHIEL RIVER WHICH FLOWS OUT OF THE LOCH TO THE WEST."

minister or preacher vilified them for all he was worth before the whole congregation. However, this method of punishment was not peculiarly Highland and it was at one time common to all Presbyterian communities in Scotland.

There is one feature of the communion week services that is Highland and that is the "Question Day" service. At that service, which usually takes place on Friday forenoon, the preacher chooses a text from the Scriptures and calls on the leading elders and lay-preachers to give their interpretation of it. I remember being at one such service in a Free Presbyterian church. It was a lovely summer's day with brilliant sunshine but the service dragged on for four solid hours. One after another the elders of the congregation rose to speak. At that time An Comunn Gaidhealach, the Highland Society that interests itself in the preservation of the Gaelic language and culture, had started holding mods at different centres throughout the Highlands, and one of the holy elders decided to tell what he thought about the mod and An Comunn Gaidhealach. "The Comunn Gaidhealach had a mod in Skye this week. It is supposed to further the Gaelic but in reality it is nothing other than the work of the Devil."

For once my sympathies were entirely with the Devil, but the sad fact was that the holy elder could hardly speak two words of English properly and was addressing hearers whose command of that language was not one whit better. Of course, ministers of the Church of Scotland attended mods and identified themselves with the aims of the Comunn Gaidhealach, but it was not quite for that reason that mods are an evil thing. They are evil because they encourage the singing of "worldly songs" and the playing of equally worldly music on the fiddle and bagpipes — the black sticks of the Evil One.

It is always fairly easy to recognise the "Wee Frees" and "Seceders" by the term that they use for the day the pagan English and the unregenerate adherents of the Church of Scotland call "Sunday". In their church notices it is always "Sabbath" and the same is true whenever they mention the day. Owing to the influence of the press, radio, printed calendars and such things the "Sabbath" is fighting a losing battle. More interesting still is the fate of the Gaelic name. The general name in Gaelic is *Sàbaid* or preceded by the definite article, *an t-Sàbaid* or *La na Sàbaid* (The Day of Sabbath). The term *Di-Domhnuich* (Dies Domini), which in Gaelic is truly beautiful, has been completely driven out of common speech in all Presbyterian areas. I do not think I ever heard a Highland Presbyterian refer to Sunday as *Di-Domhnuich*, but I have heard one Lochaber Catholic say "*Sàbaid*", although Catholics generally use the old Gaelic name, or more correctly the Latin loan-word, instead of the later term borrowed through English from Hebrew. I heard a Presbyterian native of the predominantly Catholic Isle of Barra use *Sàbaid* instead of *Di-Domhnuich*. In the strongholds of Scottish Episcopalianism, such as Glencoe, Ballachulish and Appin, however, the term *Di-Domhnuich* is used even by Presbyterians.

The Sunday service is, of course, the highlight of the communion week of the "Wee Frees" and "Seceders", for it is when they dispense the Sacrament of the Lord's Supper. Anyone who has attended their Sunday Communion services will observe that the actual number of communicants is very small. Invariably they are elderly or well advanced into middle age, and only on very rare occasions are they young. Those who have dedicated themselves to the Kingdom of God and are numbered among the "chosen" are well past the stage of enjoying life in any case. The paucity of the communicants or members and the large number of adherents is a very important fact that tends to be overlooked by writers who talk about the stern and rigid Calvinism of certain Highland communities. The religious feelings of the large number of adherents may vary from devout piety to an indifference that puts them almost beyond the pale. The ministers may indicate what their attitude regarding questions of faith and morals ought to be, but there never is any unanimity in the rank and file of the adherents. Nor can it be said that there is any general standard of behaviour or conduct. They may all seem to be strict Sabbatarians because they do not go out to play games on Sunday, but who is to know what they do behind closed doors. Regular attendance at church services may be due to the fact that there is no other way of spending a long and tiresome day.

Before the minister calls the devout to communicate, he proceeds to indicate the categories that are to be debarred from partaking of the Lord's Supper. Relevant passages from the Bible are read, passages denouncing idolaters, adulterers, usurers, murderers, pilferers and so forth. Before he finishes he has practically succeeded in debarring the whole congregation. The sheep are then separated from the goats and the goats are very numerous. But among the goats there are people who tell stories about Fionn and Oisean, people who sing lovely songs like "*Braigh Rùsgaich*", those who love a pibroch like "MacCrimmon's Sweetheart", those who can dance the "Highland Schottische" all night long and still go on, those who love to watch a good game of shinty and those who will continue to get gloriously drunk at weddings and at New Year. And they remain unrepentant.

Much has been said and written about the part that evangelical Calvinism played in the destruction of Gaelic folktales, folk-music, beliefs and customs and said even by such reliable authorities as the late William MacKay, author of *Urquhart and Glenmoriston*, but the fact remains that at most it can only be said to be one of several contributory factors. It is by no means the most important factor, and it can now be doubted if it is an important factor at all. Writing in the *Scotsman* in the autumn of 1951, John Lorne Campbell of Canna stated that he and other collaborators recorded 200 songs from natives of the Catholic isles of Barra and Eriskay alone. The population of these two islands is over 2,500. In the winter of 1945-6, I recorded 199 songs from two households in the completely "Seceder" island of Raasay, which has a population of less than 300. During a short summer vacation in 1949, Miss Elizabeth Allan, a Glasgow schoolteacher, recorded 250 songs in the half-Catholic, half-Church of Scotland island of Benbecula, while my friend, Fred MacAulay, recorded 280 songs in the strongly "Seceder" and "Wee Free" Isle of Harris. Recently hundreds of songs have been recorded in Lewis as well as in the whole western seaboard from Lorn northwards to Durness in Sutherlandshire, and I have noticed that the contribution of adherents of the Free Church is very large indeed. One of the finest storytellers I have ever met, John Finlayson of Drumbuie, Lochalsh, is an adherent of the Free Church. A Presbyterian, Gaelic-speaking tinker at Muir of Ord, Ross-shire told me more international folktales in two days than I had heard in Catholic Barra in six months. In his recent and rather vituperative book on the Outer Isles, the noted writer Alasdair Alpin MacGregor maintains that folklore has survived to any extent only in Catholic isles because the people there are more superstitious than their Presbyterian neighbours. His main contention, as well as the reason adduced for it, is pure nonsense. I have met dozens of "Seceders" and "Wee Frees" as well as Catholics who swear that they have seen fairies, not to speak of apparitions and omens, who still go in dread of the "Evil Eye", who still resort to "water of silver" to protect their cattle and who still have an intense dislike for going out in boats along with ministers, red-haired women and hens. The tolerant Catholic clergy smiled benignly at their flock when they told stories, sang songs, danced and played the bagpipes and fiddle. They even went so far as to encourage them to uphold their rich cultural heritage, and they and their people deserve much credit for the fact that so much of it remains with us today. Far greater credit is due, however, to the noble tradition-bearers in the Presbyterian areas who clung to that same rich heritage despite decades of evangelical thundering and the threat of eternal damnation.

In Glen Urquhart there are still people who tell stories in Gaelic, sing songs, dance the old

FISHING BOAT, ULLAPOOL

Highland dances, and play the pipes. While I was staying at Milton, I had a visit from my dear friend, the late Robert Persson of Chicago. Robert was a very brilliant and promising social anthropologist and had just returned from Lapland where he was engaged in a study of a nomad community. He came to the glen late one afternoon and that same evening he suddenly decided that he must hear a piper play before leaving the following morning. A piper had to be found at very short notice. I had been informed by Miss Annie MacKenzie of Tornashee that there was a piper living next door to her. We called on Miss MacKenzie and she accompanied us to the piper's house, where we were told that his set was out of order. By this time it was ten o'clock, but Miss MacKenzie remembered that there was a piper up the glen at a forestry unit but it was eight miles away. The three of us decided to hire a car and reach the piper before he retired for the night. It was well past eleven o'clock when we did reach Piper Matheson's house and he had gone off to sleep. In answer to Miss MacKenzie's knocking, he got out of bed and admitted her. She told him our errand and out he came to welcome Robert and myself to the house. Mrs Matheson then appeared and proceeded to make tea for us all. Robert had never heard the pipes in his life, and I could see excitement written all over his face as he watched Mr Matheson take out his pipes, test his reed and drones, and proceed to blow up the bag. The pipes were tuned, and for twenty minutes Mr Matheson played marches, strathspeys and reels. He then stopped.

"Gee!" said Robert. "That was great! Thanks!"

We left some time before dawn. Next day Robert left Glen Urquhart to visit the reindeer reservation at Rothiemurchus. The following Saturday he went to the Abernethy Highland Games and spent the whole day listening to the piping competitions. He wrote to me saying that he was going to buy a set of bagpipes to take home to Chicago. In all his travels in Europe he had heard absolutely nothing to equal the music of the Highland bagpipes. I did not see Robert again, for his promising young life came to a sudden end out in distant Pakistan.

I had hardly been a week in Glen Urquhart when Miss MacKenzie asked me up to Tornashee to meet Andrew Fraser of Blarbeg, "The Brickie", as he is affectionately called. He got his name because of his skill as a bricklayer. "The Brickie" was then over seventy years of age and was a veteran of the Boer War. His physique and vigour completely belied his years and his mental powers were as alert and keen as those of a man in the prime of life. In his younger days he had been a great athlete and shinty-player, and the spring in his step made me suspect that he was a dancer too. Of course, he was a dancer and still is. At the age of seventy he still gave exhibitions of Highland dancing at concerts and gatherings in the glen. Out in South Africa he danced the Highland dances and played shinty there too, as he himself imagined.

"But whenever I raised the stick to strike the ball as I used to do at home, the referee shouted 'Foul!'."

It finally dawned on the poor "Brickie" that he was expected to play a tame, effeminate game called hockey and was not allowed to raise his stick above his shoulder. "The Brickie" must have been quite disgusted with hockey.

Nine months after my visit to Glen Urquhart I was in Oban one cold, thundery day watching the final tie of the Scottish Camanachd competition. The Kyles of Bute team were struggling hard to keep the intrepid men of Lovat, the Fraser country, at bay. I was quite engrossed in the game, when, suddenly, I got a resounding thump on the back. I looked round and there was the indomitable and exuberant "Brickie" himself. He had come all the way from Glen Urquhart to cheer his clansmen to victory.

I do not think there is less gaiety or less social life in Glen Urquhart than anywhere else in rural Scotland. The adherents of the Free Church are not dour, solemn and serious-minded, as many depict them; on the contrary they have as good a sense of fun, gaiety and humour as anyone else. They have a far greater capacity for creating their own entertainment and enjoying themselves thoroughly than the residents of Morningside Drive or Tottenham Court Road. They have a good deal more talent as well. A few nights before leaving the glen I decided to let the young people in the house where I was staying, hear their own voices, for tape-recording machines were a novelty at that time. They in turn asked their friends to join in, and we had a gay and extremely pleasant party. The local postman brought his guitar and a young minister of the Free Church joined us too. He could not sing, but he was very charming and entered completely into the spirit of the party. The life and soul of the company was Mrs Grant of Milton. She was a woman who had braved tragedy after tragedy until the war finally robbed her of the last of her nearest and dearest. Yet she was so full of wit, humour, and laughter that I marvelled at her magnificent bravery. It was evident that her courage and fortitude was an inspiration to the whole parish, for the young people simply adored her. There were no alcoholic refreshments and in any case the majority of the company were too young. It is said that Highlanders find it difficult to enjoy themselves without the help of alcoholic stimulants, yet these young people had no difficulty whatsoever. The kind lady of the house made tea for the whole company at least twice. The young people all sang and sang beautifully in Gaelic, in Scots, and in English, while one young girl sang a French song. A few days before that I had been across in Strathglass and had recorded that lovely Catholic hymn, "The Lullaby for the Christ Child", from Catherine MacNeill of Barra, who was then district nurse at Cannich. I played it back for them and they thought it was beautiful. There was no bigotry among them. Even if there had been the slightest vestige of it, they were far to courteous and well-mannered to offend the stranger.

The Free Church of Glen Urquhart was burnt to the ground since I was there, but I sincerely hope they have had little difficulty in collecting funds to rebuild it, for the loss of their church must have been a cruel blow to those generous, courteous, and sincere people.

Adherence to a certain denominational group is an important determinative factor in the social grading of Highland communities. Members of the Scottish Episcopal Church — which is in communion with the Church of England — are on the highest social plane. There are two main reasons for this: the old county families have inter-married with English families and, in cases where that has happened, the tendency is to move upwards from Presbyterianism to Episcopalianism; and no less important is the fact that the children of so many country families are now educated in England and come under the influence of the Church of England. The Scottish Episcopal Church has come to be the church of the people of quality in the Highlands, and it is to that church that the non-native gentry, who come to shoot grouse and deer, go also.

Next to the Episcopalians come the members of the Church of Scotland. This was the established church of Scotland and its ministers were better paid than the ministers of the sects that broke away from it. They also had extensive glebes, and in cases added to them during the wholesale eviction of crofters. Last century the crofting class could not afford to educate children for the ministry and consequently the Highland ministers belonged to the class of large farmers or "tacksmen", the class that benefited at the expense of the crofters. The "tacksmen" class remained faithful to the Church of Scotland, while a very large body of the crofting class went over to the Free Church. The Church of Scotland remained the church of the middle and professional class. The estate factor, the procurator-fiscal, the bank manager, the doctor, the headmaster and the higher grade Government official are likely to be non-native to a Highland community and consequently non-Gaelic. If he attends church at all, it is likely to be the Church of Scotland, and because of his presence the language from the pulpit has to be intelligible to him. The reason why the Church of Scotland has come to be less Gaelic than the

NEAR ACHNAHA, ARDNAMURCHAN

Free Church is purely social.

The Free Church is more Gaelic than the Church of Scotland for the simple reason that a greater percentage of its adherents will understand Gaelic preaching, and one of the reasons why it is on a lower social level is that very same fact. Whether we like it or not, English is still the hallmark of a higher social standing.

The Free Presbyterians and the Roman Catholics constitute the lowest strata; the former because they have less tradition behind them than the Free Church and are numerous in the poorest and most barren areas, and the latter because they have had less time to overcome the disabilities of the Penal Laws which barred them from the professions and rendered social mobility impossible, and also because Roman Catholicism in Scotland has come to be associated with the Irish immigrants brought to this country to supply the demand for cheap labour.

I must now turn from religion to the less serious subject of the Loch Ness monster. I, however, am not quite so certain that the monster ought not to be taken seriously. When this remarkable creature first hit the headlines, its reported presence in Loch Ness was thought to be nothing more than a clever publicity stunt on part of the hoteliers of Inverness, a stunt calculated to encourage the tourist traffic. I doubt very much if the hoteliers of Inverness could have enough imagination to invent a monster which never did exist. Local opinion supports the belief that the monster is really there and that it has been there for a very long time. Adamnan, who became Abbot of Iona in the year 579, first reported the monster in his *Life of Saint Columba*. Adamnan tells that the saint on one occasion wanted to cross the Ness, and, on coming to the bank of the river, found a group of men burying a man who had been killed by a water monster (*aqualis bestia*). Columba asked his companion, Lugne Mocumin, to swim across the river and bring him a boat that lay on the opposite bank. When Lugne was halfway across, the monster appeared and giving one hideous roar, made after him.

> Then the blessed man (Columba) observing this, raised his holy hand, while all the rest, brethren as well as strangers, were stupified with terror, and, invoking the name of God, formed the saving sign of the cross in the air, and commanded the ferocious monster, saying, "Thou shalt go no further nor touch the man; go back with all speed." Then at the voice of the Saint the monster was terrified, and fled more quickly than if it had been pulled back with ropes, though it had just got so near to Lugne as he swam that there was not more than the length of a spear staff between the man and the beast. Then the brethren, seeing that the monster had gone back, and that their comrade Lugne returned to them in the boat safe and sound, were struck with admiration, and gave glory to God in the blessed man. And even the barbarous heathens who were present were forced by the greatness of this miracle, which they themselves had seen, to magnify the God of the Christians.

The monster, if it is the same one, has been putting in periodic appearances for a very long time and certainly as long as living memory can go back. My old friend, William MacKenzie of Cannich, Strathglass, whose father was a native of Urquhart, told of a man who was digging by the shores of Loch Ness over eighty years ago. It was a warm day in the spring, and when the day's work was done the man went down to the water's edge, took off his boots and stockings and started washing his feet. Suddenly the head of the monster rose above the surface of the shore about twenty yards away from him. The man sprang up and fled in terror, leaving his boots and stockings behind him.

There were a number of similar stories about the monster and his appearances on Loch Ness. The general public first learned of the existence of the monster in the 30s mainly through the efforts of a journalist, John Herries, but the monster was no stranger to the local people. At that time the Glen Albyn road, from Fort Augustus to Inverness, was under construction and a great number of trees which had formerly screened the loch from the old roadway were cut down and, as Mr MacKell, the extremely able and popular headmaster of Glen Urquhart Secondary School, pointed out to me, large parties of workmen spent long days by the lochside and thus the monster had less chance of remaining undetected.

The ancient Castle of Urquhart stands on the headland of Strone to the south of Urquhart Bay and remains an imposing landmark despite its long and stormy history. The castle dates from the twelfth century and figured in the War of Scottish Independence, for it was taken by the forces of Edward I of England and recaptured later by Bruce. For long it was the property of the Scottish Crown, but when the Lords of the Isles rose against central authority it fell into their hands and different custodians held it for them until it became the property of the Grants at the beginning of the sixteenth century. After the battle of Killiecrankie the castle was besieged by the Jacobites, but the Whig garrison held out. In 1692, however, the Whig garrison vacated the castle and they blew up the keep and entrance towers, thus preventing its use as a stronghold by the adherents of King James. Urquhart Castle was never again occupied.

The road southwards from Urquhart to Glenmoriston keeps fairly close to the loch all the way, for the hills rise steeply from the water's edge. The crofters in the little townships of Lenie and Bunloit have to do a fair amount of tilling without the aid of tractor or plough because of the steep slope, but I did notice that there were more goats grazing around these townships than any place I have seen in the Highlands. The cliffs and steep hillsides are ideal for goats, and old records show that they played a very important part in the economy of the district of Urquhart and Glenmoriston for centuries. In April 1545 the men of Glengarry and Locheil raided Glen Urquhart and among other things brought off with them 1,410 goats. It must be admitted, however, that in that raid the district was cleared of all moveable property in a very thorough fashion.

On the way to Glenmoriston one passes Alltsaigh, and here there are only a couple of dwellings, a post office and a youth hostel, but the place is of great interest because of its association with a noted character, the famed reiver-songster, Donald Donn of Bohuntine. It was at Alltsaigh that Donald Donn was captured and his colourful career was brought to an end. He was one of the most famous cattle reivers of the seventeenth century and his activities brought him as far afield from Lochaber as Caithness and Sutherland. On one occasion he captured a pretty young girl in Sutherlandshire and was bringing her home to Lochaber. On the way they rested at a house where a party of women were waulking cloth. The women sang as they worked and Donald Donn composed an impromptu ditty in honour of the fair young maid he had captured. In the course of the song Donald boasted proudly, "I'd raise a *creach* — a spoil of cattle — from the Laird of Grant and drink a dram in the passing."

The women took up the refrain as they worked and the men drank and became more and more hilarious, but the young girl, helped by the waulking women, meanwhile stole out of the house and escaped.

Donald Donn was as good as his word and did despoil the lands of the Laird of Grant, but, as luck would have it, he met Mary, the laird's daughter and fell in love with her and she returned his love. Donald Donn was a nobleman, a scion of the Macdonells of Keppoch, and a reiver of culture and refinement. Mary composed a very beautiful love song to Donald Donn, a song that is still sung and that will continue to delight the Gaelic people as long as their language lasts. To Donald Donn reiving was a noble profession and while he despoiled the rich farmers and lairds, he protected and gave generously to those whose lot was poor. It was not surprising that the

Laird of Grant should refuse to have Donald for a son-in-law and forbade her meeting him at all. But the sweethearts still met furtively on the wooded banks of Loch Ness. On one occasion Donald Donn was returning from Ross-shire with a herd of cattle he had lifted. He left his companions with the cattle on the farm of Borlum not far away from the Castle of Urquhart and went to meet his beloved Mary. While he was away the owners of the cattle appeared and claimed them, for there was among the herd one white cow which they immediately identified. They called on the Laird of Grant to find out why reivers should have found shelter so near his castle. The irate laird swore: "May the Devil take me out of my shoes, if Donald Donn is not hanged!"

Soldiers from the castle went in pursuit of Donald Donn, but he wanted to be near beloved Mary and went into hiding in an almost inaccessible cave on the Ruiskich side of Alltsaigh, a cave that is still called Donald Donn's Cave. There he went on composing songs to his Mary and songs in praise of the wood and cave that sheltered him from his enemies. He whiled away his time in the company of the shepherds of Glenmoriston from across the burn of Alltsaigh. Eventually his pursuers discovered his retreat, but unable to reach him in the cave they sent him a letter, as if from Mary, asking him to meet her at Alltsaigh in the house of one who was represented as being in her confidence. At the appointed hour Donald Donn went to the house of Mary's supposed friend. He received him hospitably and told him that Mary would soon arrive. While they waited Donald Donn was regaled with liquor until he drank almost more than enough. At a given signal the treacherous host admitted sixty-three of Donald's enemies. They closed in on him and tried to seize him but he sprang up and grasped his gun. Unfortunately the gun misfired, but Donald Donn held them off with the butt-end and made his way out of the house. His pursuers made after him through a wood of young saplings and finally caught and overpowered him. Bitterly did Donald Donn regret that his good sword was not by his side in the hour of need. "Though I were to get for myself a full fold of cattle, dearer to me at that hour would have been a sword and shield."

Donald was taken to the dungeon of Urquhart Castle and convicted for stealing cattle. Before the dread sentence of death was pronounced he begged that he should be beheaded like a gentleman and not hanged. His wish was granted. As he awaited death, he sang to his Mary.

"Tomorrow I shall be headless on a hill and no one will feel pity on me. Do you not pity my sad maiden, my Mary, lovely and winsome-eyed?"

As Donald Donn's head rolled off the block, his tongue appealed to his beloved.

"Mary, lift the head! The Laird of Grant has belied his oath."

Today the Forestry Commission has large units under trees in Glenmoriston and in certain places land that was once under cultivation has been taken over. The glen was long famed for its timber, and, as the Gaelic saying went, it was the "smooth Glenmoriston where the dogs do not eat the candles". In the glen, fir torches were used instead of tallow candles for lighting. A famous chief of the Grants of Glenmoriston, Great John of the Castle, who lived towards the end of the sixteenth century, was in London on one occasion when a disparaging reference was made to the fir candles of his native glen. John assured the scoffer that he could produce a finer torch and more brilliant lighting than anything available in London. A wager was set and on the appointed day the Englishman appeared with a splendid candelabrum and the most expensive candles of wax. Meanwhile Great John of the Castle sent word home for John the son of Ewen the Fair, a man of great personal beauty. When the magnificent clansman entered bearing a burning torch of pine from the woods of Glenmoriston, John of the Castle was immediately declared winner of the wager.

Glenmoriston is one of the saddening glens of the Highlands not only because of its

ARDNAMURCHAN LIGHTHOUSE: "ARDNAMURCHAN JUTS OUT INTO THE ATLANTIC AND ARDNAMURCHAN POINT WAS A NOTED
LANDMARK AND DANGER-SPOT FOR SHIPPING IN THE DAYS OF SAIL AND SEAMANSHIP."

associations with the "Forty-five" but more so because of its dwindling population. At Dalchreichart in the upper part of the glen there is a small school and it is one of the many Highland schools that will be closed before long. Here and there derelict crofts can be seen, and although a number of new houses have been erected near Dalchreichart to house forestry workers, they may be the only inhabited dwellings in the area before many years are past. I had long conversations with a couple of crofters in upper Glenmoriston. They were both well on in years and both were convinced that the struggle to wrest a livelihood from the soil would not go on much longer.

Despite the fact that Ludovick Grant, the young chieftain of Urquhart and Glenmoriston, sat warily on the fence until he saw the way things were going, the men of the two glens were heart and soul in favour of the Stuarts and many joined the Prince's army and fought at Culloden. When the Hanoverian forces triumphed, Ludovick Grant was off the fence and was extremely zealous in rounding up the men who had been out with the Prince. The men who had been in the Prince's army were induced to surrender themselves on the understanding that they would be given a free pardon. They did surrender, at least a good number of them, and were shipped off to the Barbadoes and into slavery. Ludovick Grant was never forgiven for the enormity of his offence against humanity and honour.

"O young Laird of Grant, may yours be the dire requital on high; may the cry of fatherless children shut you out from the Heaven of Christ!"

Seven men of Glenmoriston did not surrender. They saw the betrayal of their friends and swore an oath to stand by each other to the very last and never surrender their persons or their arms to the English. They made their home in the Cave of Roderick the Hunter in a small corrie called Corrie Sgrainge, an offshoot of the larger Corrie Dhoe. From their retreat they waged an unrelenting war against the Hanoverians and especially against the Highlanders who served the English soldiers as guides and informers. One informer they shot through the heart at a place called Rob's Marsh. They cut off his head and placed it on a tree close by the high road at Blairie and the skull remained there until well into the last century. The Seven Men were Hugh, Alexander, and Donald Chisholm, three brothers; Alexander Macdonald; John Macdonald or Campbell; Grigor MacGregor and Patrick Grant of Craskie. They were courageous and resolute men who never hesitated in attaking large bodies of Hanoverian troops and depriving them of their stores and the cattle that they pillaged from the lands of Urquhart and Glenmoriston. They become known to the Hanoverian garrison at Fort Augustus and a party of soldiers was sent to capture them. The Seven Men, however, routed the soldiers and continued to remain at large. They had not yet fulfilled their mission. Prince Charles escaped from Benbecula with the help of Flora Macdonald and landed at Morar on 5 July 1746. French ships were said to be in Pool Ewe and Charles was anxious to make his way there, and the Seven Men of Glenmoriston were suggested as guides for the royal fugitive. On the morning of 29 July, Macdonald of Glen-aladale brought the Prince to Glenmoriston where he was received with loyalty and enthusiasm by the Seven Men and conducted to their retreat. For three weeks they were hosts to Prince Charles and entertained him royally. In parting with them the Prince shook hands with each of the Seven in turn. After that Hugh Chisholm never again gave his right hand to any living soul. For their services the Prince gave the Seven Men three guineas each. Any of the Seven could easily have acquired £30,000 by betraying the Prince, but treachery to their royal charge was completely out of the question as far as the Seven Men were concerned.

The saddest and noblest figure in the history of Glenmoriston during the "Forty-five" was the travelling merchant Roderick MacKenzie. He had been out and wandered over the Highlands after Culloden. He was a very handsome man and bore a very close resemblance to Prince

Charles. According to the tradition of Glenmoriston and Lochaber, the merchant's resemblance to the Prince was used to set the Hanoverians on the wrong trail and while they pursued MacKenzie in one direction the Prince went off in the other. Roderick MacKenzie was in Glenmoriston when it was heard that Prince Charles had made his escape from Benbecula and was among the mountains of the western mainland. A party of Hanoverian soldiers came upon MacKenzie on the highway at Ceannacroc in the glen, and, thinking he was the Prince, they tried to capture him. MacKenzie drew his sword and defended himself. The soldiers then riddled his body with bullets. MacKenzie fell and in his dying breath exclaimed:

"You have killed your Prince at last!"

The head was severed from the dead body and brought to Cumberland at Fort Augustus. The Duke brought the head to London but it was beyond recognition before reliable witnesses arrived on the spot to identify it. In the meantime the Prince was safe and sound, but the self-sacrifice of Roderick MacKenzie had saved his life quite as truly as the efforts of Flora Macdonald and others. MacKenzie's headless body was buried near the roadway beside a little stream that to this day bears the name of Caochan a' Cheannaich — the Merchant's Stream. A cairn marked the spot where he fell.

The behaviour of Cumberland's troops in Glenmoriston in that fateful summer that followed Culloden was abominable. Old men were shot in cold blood, pregnant women were ravished by whole parties of soldiers and left naked where the foul deed was perpetrated, houses were given to the flames and all moveable property was pillaged. Almost at that very time the General Assembly of the Church of Scotland was in progress in Edinburgh. The Assembly presented an address to the Duke of Cumberland:

> The Church of Scotland is under peculiar obligations to offer their most thankful acknowledgment to Almighty God, who has raised you up to be our brave defender … (and) guardian of all our sacred and civil interests … since this part of Great Britain has been blessed with your presence…

Glenmoriston suffered not only at the hands of Cumberland's English troops; it suffered also at the hands of Highlanders from whom better behaviour would have been expected. After Culloden, the Earl of Loudon, accompanied by Macdonald of Sleat and Macleod of Dunvegan with the militia of Skye, marched through the glen. The conduct of the men of Skye hardly did them credit although they stopped short before descending to rape and murder. But then it must be remembered that only the very dregs of Skye would have followed Macdonald and Macleod of Dunvegan in a fight against the rightful heir to the throne.

Glenmoriston is a glen of wonders and most of the wonders were associated with its patron saint, Merchard. Merchard was a disciple of Saint Ternan, a follower of Saint Ninian. The story goes that at one time Merchard and two missionary companions were in Strathglass, and while they were there their attention was drawn to a white cow that stood daily and gazed at a certain tree and, though it did not appear to graze at all, returned home each evening quite as satiated as the other cows. Merchard dug at the foot of the tree and there found three new and shining bells. He took one bell himself and gave one each to his companions and told them to go forth and build a church on the spot where the bells rang of their own accord for the third time. His two companions went on their way and Merchard came southwards to Glenmoriston. When he reached the top of a hill now called Merchard's Seat the bell rang for the first time. He went on and the bell rang for a second time at Merchard's Spring at Balintombuie. The bell rang for the third time at a spot beside the River Moriston where the old burial-ground of the glen now is, and there Merchard decided to build his church. The bell continued to be miraculous long, long after the saint's death, and, if it was taken from the ruined church buildings, it always found its way back in a mysterious manner. The sick and aged were cured if they touched it with full faith in its powers, and it used to ring on the approach of a burial. It was preserved among the ruins of Merchard's church until almost the end of last century, when some sacrilegious person removed it and cast it into the river. In the ruins of the old church there is also a baptismal font that never dries up even during the most prolonged drought. The font is still there and bears witness to the powers of Merchard.

No less mysterious but of a later date are the "Miraculous Footprints" of Glenmoriston. It was towards the end of last century that a noted lay-preacher of the Free Church was conducting an open-air service one Sunday at Torgyle. His name, I am told, was Finlay Munro. He was a huge and powerful man. In the course of his preaching he noticed that a couple of his listeners appeared to scoff at his teaching. He turned angrily to them and predicted that they would come to a violent and untimely end, an end such as all scoffers merited. As a testimony to the truth of his prediction he said that the print of his two feet would remain forever in the ground on which he stood. The footprints are still there, deeply imprinted in the black soil. They are to be seen about fifty yards north of the roadway as it turns to the west nearing Torgyle. I went to see them one morning in early September. They are huge footprints, three or four inches into the dark soil, and all around them there was lush, green grass. The footprints are miraculous without the slightest doubt.

Chapter Six

STRATHGLASS, EASTER ROSS AND INVERNESS

IT WAS by that lovely road that winds up through Glen Urquhart that I first approached Strathglass, for the strath lies to the west and almost at right angles to the glen. Flanking the strath to the east there is an almost unbroken ridge of high ground that stretches down to the Aird country of Lovat, while three lovely glens, Glen Affric, Glen Cannich and Glen Farrar, run parallel into it from the west.

In the minds of all Highlanders, Strathglass will never cease to be associated with the valiant and noble Chisholm clan, a clan that was finally overtaken by dire tragedy. One of the very finest songs that was thrown up by the "Forty-five" was the lament for young William Chisholm of Strathglass who was mortally wounded on the field of Culloden. In her grief his young widow sang:

"O young Charles Stuart, it is your cause that has grieved me; you have bereft me of everything I had, in a war on your behalf. Not cattle, not sheep do I mourn but my spouse, even if I were alone with nothing in the world save a shirt."

The widow, of course, spoke for hundreds of other women to whom the cause of young Charles Stuart had brought some deep personal loss, for like her their lot had changed utterly. From being objects of envy they were now to be pitied for what they had lost. There are passages of great intensity and beauty in the widow's song as she sings of the matchless nobility and comeliness of her dead husband, a complete absence of rancour, for she spares one fleeting thought for the Prince when she asks who will now wield the sword or fill the throne, but that can hardly have much place in her thoughts now that her first love is no more, while any thought of the Hanoverians and their conduct is quite beneath her notice. Naturally enough the song has always had a great appeal in the Gaelic areas, but I doubt very much if any of the younger generation in Strathglass today have ever heard of it, but there are hardly any Chisholms left there now in any case.

The real tragedy came not at Culloden but over fifty years later when the "Clearances" began, and Strathglass was one of the places that suffered most of all. There is a very close link between the Strathglass and Glengarry "Clearances" slightly earlier, for a mother and daughter were mainly responsible for both. Ironically enough both Strathglass and Glengarry remained faithful to Catholicism, and those responsible for the evicting of the Macdonells and Chisholms were themselves at least nominal Catholics. That the Highland "Clearances" should have begun in Catholic areas may have been quite accidental, but on the other hand the beginning might have been greatly facilitated by the assumption that there would be less public outcry if Catholics were evicted *en masse* from their ancient homes, and the success the perpetrators of the Glengarry "Clearances" met with may have emboldened others to embark on the eviction of Protestant communities. The Sutherland "Clearances" followed soon afterwards and were carried out in a manner calculated to disgrace any civilised country.

One of the most hated names in the Highlands was that of Marsailidh Bhinneach, Light-headed Marjory, the widow of Duncan Macdonell of Glengarry, who died in 1788. It was she who gave the whole of Glenquoich to a sheep farmer and in doing so evicted over 500 people from their homes. In 1795 her daughter, Elizabeth, married William Chisholm of Strathglass. Chisholm was often in poor health with the result that the management of the estate came into the hands of his wife, a woman of the same stamp as her hard-hearted mother. The Strathglass evictions began in 1801 and before thirty years had gone only two of the ancient stock remained in possession of an inch of land on the Chisholm estate. Most of the dispossessed found their way to Nova Scotia and Upper Canada, while a few were given land on the neighbouring estate of the Frasers of Lovat. Later in the century another Chisholm, a descendant of a collateral branch of the family, came into possession of the estate, and, on his return from Canada, found few, if any, of his name to receive him. He brought back a few Chisholms from the Lovat estate and settled them on his own land. But then it was too late to undo the evil of earlier days, and now the estate has finally passed out of the hands of the Chisholm family and there are very few of the name in Strathglass at the present day.

This uprooting of the natives of Strathglass was one of the major tragedies of the Highlands, for, undoubtedly, they were a very fine race. One Sunday I went to chapel at Cannich and saw some of the few that remain. The men were exceptionally fine specimens physically and were all well above average stature. Others of the Chisholm clan I have met in different parts of the Highlands. There seem to be more Chisholm families in Stratherrick, east of Loch Ness, than there are in Strathglass — Stratherrick, of course, was part of the Lovat lands. One wet September evening I crossed Strome Ferry and was on my way to Lochalsh. I had heard about a Chisholm living in the neighbourhood and wished to contact him. I found his house eventually but his wife told me that he was not at home. I went some distance farther on and noticed a very tall man kneeling by a hay-rick in a field close to the road. I hailed him and he rose up and came over to talk to me. He was the man I wanted to meet. He came originally from Strathglass, and certainly he looked a credit to the name he bore. He was a truly magnificent figure of a man and wore a deer-stalker's cap and a kilt of dark green tartan. That was the first and only time I have ever seen a Highland crofter wearing the kilt while engaged in his daily work. There seemed to be nothing incongruous about it, but his kilt was drenched with rain. It was only when I left him that it occurred to me that I had seen something I had never seen before.

Every time I visited Strathglass I made a point of going to see William and Sandy MacKenzie at Cannich. They were stalwart, splendid old fellows with white, flowing beards. They had spent most of their lives as ghillies and gamekeepers and lived in retirement in a neat little cottage by the roadside about a mile to the west of Cannich. They lived alone but their little house was always clean and tidy, although I found it difficult to imagine two such enormous men doing their household chores. They were natives of the strath although their parents were from Glen Urquhart and Gairloch to the west. Gaelic had always been and still was the only language they spoke when together, and both were excellent tradition-bearers. The last time I saw them was on a dark, wet November evening. There were a couple of workmen visiting them and they were engaged in filling in football coupons by the light of the fire. On a deal table in the centre of the room a small candle flickered but it afforded less light than the fire. William turned his head slowly round and, with an almost supercilious smile on his face, said to me in English: "I am a football fan." I knew that in his heart William thought that football was no game compared with shinty, but that was his way of saying so. The candle finally burnt itself out and we sat by fire-light for the rest of the evening. Within a few days His Royal Highness the Duke of Edinburgh was due to arrive at Cannich to open the new hydro-electric power station there. Electric current was so necessary for centres of population like Inverness, the industrial Lowlands, and England, but William and Sandy MacKenzie, living within a stone's throw of the new, immense power station, seemed to have been forgotten. His Royal Highness came and went, but William and Sandy MacKenzie saw the winter through with only the light of the fire. Anyhow, I don't think they cared very much.

Farther down the strath at Crelevan near Struy lived Peter Macdonald and his son Charles — the latter named in honour of Prince Charles Edward Stuart. Peter was a native of Glenmoriston and had first come to the strath as a gamekeeper but rose to the position of estate-manager. All the schooling he ever had was in the little primary school at Dalchreichart, Glenmoriston, but that could not deter a man of his ability. He was a veteran of the Boer War and had been decorated for valour. Peter had a lovely speaking-voice and spoke the purest Gaelic and sang well too. He was full of the traditions of his native Glenmoriston and from his mother had inherited a good deal of the traditions of the now desolate Glenquoich, for she was born there. He was one of a large family. He gave me a most interesting account of dancing-schools and masters and their activities in Glenmoriston seventy years ago. The dancing-masters were itinerant and when they came to Glenmoriston and held classes during the winter evenings in the local school, the youngsters over a certain age all wished to avail themselves of the tuition. The fee for a dozen or so lessons amounted to something like thirty shillings, which in those days was a very considerable sum, and for members of large families it often meant that they had to do without footwear for the winter, if the tuition fees were to be paid. Of course, Peter, like so many of the other youngsters in Glenmoriston at that time, would go barefoot all winter rather than miss the dancing classes. The fees were paid and Peter went to the classes in his bare feet. They were there taught the Highland solo dances and other country dances popular at the time, but the dancing-master was as equally insistent on a high standard of deportment as on graceful and correct dancing. No dancer could rush across the room to grab a partner, no dancer could enter or leave the company without conforming to the rules laid down by the master, but in those humble surroundings the master had the barefoot youngsters of Glenmoriston bowing like so many Spanish grandees.

No one can ever visit Glen Affric and forget it and almost the same can be said for Glen Cannich and Glen Farrar. I shall long remember that autumn morning when I first travelled by bus down from Cannich to Beauly. The leaves were just beginning to show the change of colour and the river on our right twisted and turned in its leisurely course down the strath. On all sides the wooded hills rose steeply. The bus was full of school-children of the age of twelve and over and they were on their way to the Junior Secondary School at Beauly. Under the new system children from primary schools in the remote glens are sent to technical and junior secondary schools in the larger centres of population when they reach the age of twelve. Such a policy of centralisation may have its advantages but I doubt if the results are always beneficial to the children concerned. That morning, of course, the very same thing was happening in scores of other glens and landward areas throughout the Highlands. In the first place, the drift from the glens, the remote and sparsely populated areas, and from the home, even although it lasts only for eight or nine hours each day, starts at a very early age. Whatever influence the environment of the home, the way of life in the glen with its background, history, and traditions, may have on the spiritual and mental life of the child and the formation of character, it ceases when the child is suddenly uprooted, as it were, and daily transplanted to a new and almost alien environment where not only the way of life but the language spoken may differ from that of the home. Whatever may be said in favour of the new system, one thing at least is certain: it is going to hurry the Gaelic language to extinction. As I went down through Strathglass that autumn morning I could not help thinking that it had already done so.

Inverness proudly calls itself the capital of the Highlands. The population of the town has increased enormously during the last two or three decades. To a large extent it has increased at the expense of the surrounding countryside, although too there has been a large influx of people from the south. Racially the majority of Invernessians are of Gaelic stock, but I am not so sure that they are conscious or even proud of what ought to be their heritage. For one thing they pride themselves on speaking the best English in the British Isles — which, of course, is pure nonsense. That "best English" is still full of Gaelic words and idiom. If the citizens of the town prided themselves in speaking the best Gaelic, their claim would be much stronger. Personally I would recognise Oban and not Inverness as the capital of the Highlands.

East of Inverness is Culloden Moor. One look at the surroundings is quite enough to make one wonder why on earth Prince Charles chose that bleak moor as the site on which to give battle to the Hanoverian forces with their superiority both in numbers and artillery. The only reason seems to be that Prince Charles had complete faith in the invincibility of his Highlanders under any conditions. Every year the Gaelic Society of Inverness, a society that has a long and distinguished history, holds its pilgrimage to the scene of the battle. As a rule the speakers who address the gatherings on the occasion of the annual pilgrimage are anxious to point out that, although they honour the memory of the dead Jacobites, their loyalty to the present dynasty and régime must not be questioned.

The Jacobites went down at Culloden, but in defeat there was no disgrace: many Jacobites, such as Major John MacGillvary and Gillies MacBain, both of whom accounted for over a dozen redcoats before they fell, distinguished themselves with heroism that has never been forgotten. For the Hanoverian régime Culloden may have been a military triumph but morally it was an overwhelming defeat. Throughout the whole campaign the Jacobite forces conducted themselves with a restraint that was remarkable: prisoners were treated humanely and so also were the enemy wounded. It was the express wish of Charles himself that the captured or wounded Hanoverians were to suffer no harm at the hands of his men, for, as he said himself, they were "my father's deluded subjects". Even the bitterest of enemies of the Jacobites could not furnish any records of sadism and brutality on the part of the Highlanders. Despite that, terms such as "wild and barbaric" were applied to the Highlanders for two centuries after Culloden, and not even yet have they been completely erased from the official history textbooks used in Scottish schools. What must amaze one now is not the magnitude of the lie but the thoroughness with which it has been perpetuated. A couple of years ago my scholarly friend, Dr Iorwerth Peate of Cardiff, was warned against the dangers of undertaking a journey to the Western Isles by a douce Scottish Lowlander who believed in all sincerity that the Highlands were and still are thoroughly treacherous and dangerous.

The conduct of the Hanoverian troops on the field of Culloden is one of the very black chapters in the history of Britain. In the account of the "Forty-five" written in Gaelic by John MacKenzie there is a fairly detailed description of one of the grimmest episodes. About forty wounded Highlanders were huddled into a barn near Culloden House, the doors were securely locked and, despite the piteous entreats of the unfortunate men, the building was given to the flames and all within perished. MacKenzie goes on to state that the excesses of the Hanoverian troops were so enormous that only the timely intervention of Cumberland himself prevented a very serious clash between some Scottish and English detachments under his command. The Jacobites executed for their part in the Rebellion went to their deaths firmly convinced of the justice and righteousness of the cause they espoused, and nothing could have strengthened their conviction more than the conduct of Cumberland and his minions on the field of Culloden and after.

The low-lying, rich, agricultural lands on the shores of the Moray Firth present a striking

184

contrast to the mountains and glens inland. Here is a land of large and prosperous farms. The peninsula of the Black Isle due north of Inverness is particularly rich. The Black Isle is in Easter Ross for the county march is between the villages of Beauly and Muir of Ord. At Muir of Ord I had the pleasure of coming into close contact with one of the most interesting and colourful communities in the Highlands, the Stewart tinker clan. The Stewarts are the largest and most numerous of the Highland tinker clans, although there are others such as the Macdonalds, MacPhees, and MacAllisters. In the main they are nomadic, although within recent years they have tended to settle down in one place. They are not gypsies in the strict sense but the descendants of itinerant craftsmen and fugitives, especially fugitives as a result of the upheavals following the "Forty-five". The territory of the Stewart tinkers extends from Perthshire northwards to Inverness, Ross and Cromarty, and Sutherland, and out to the Western Isles. The necessity of having to send their children to school now limits their freedom of movement, but they still wander over a wide area and generally keep to the same itinerary year after year. Certain families of them have a winter encampment and flit to another district where they operate during the summer months. The traditional craft that they practised was mainly that of the tinsmith but they could also be rag-and-bone merchants or the makers of horn spoons. In some cases they supported themselves by huckstering or mere beggary. How long the tinker community will survive the advent of the Welfare State still remains a difficult question to answer.

The day of the small local craftsman is gone, not to speak of the itinerant tinsmith who now has to compete against the chain store and ubiquitous delivery van. The older members of the Stewart tinker clan still make tin utensils and find a limited market for them but it is a market that shrinks from year to year. Other ways will have to be found to support life, and in rich agricultural areas such as Easter Ross the tinkers become farm-labourers and are employed by the local farmers in the harvest time. In Perthshire the Stewart tinkers find employment as berry-pickers on the fruit-farms. They hardly take kindly to this type of work. They always regarded their own tinker's craft as a noble one and any other kind of work was beneath their dignity. Some tinkers were horse-dealers and today a certain class of tinkers deal in second-hand cars. The more opulent tinker-clans now use motor transport, but the Stewarts always use horse-drawn vehicles, gigs or light drays but hardly ever the horse-drawn, gaily-painted caravans of the gypsies. I should imagine that the Stewarts would find it quite as difficult to sleep in caravans as in houses. Their tents are of canvas drawn taut over a framework of pliant willow saplings pointed at each end and stuck into the ground. The tents are mostly oblong and structurally they are very like the roofs of the old-type thatched houses. There are no gables, no corners to catch the wind.

My colleague Hamish Henderson, in his indefatigable quest for singers of songs and ballads, had found the Stewart family late one Saturday evening in the month of June and had given me directions as to where they were to be found when I went to Easter Ross a couple of weeks later. I could not have noted his directions very carefully for I had to trudge the six miles from Muir of Ord to Beauly and three miles back again in heat and brilliant sunshine before I found them. Their encampment lay a little way back from the main road and the top of one of their tents was barely visible above a green ridge in a field. As I approached the camp, which was in a corner fenced off from the rest of the field, there was no sign of life except that one shaggy, dun pony grazed leisurely not far away from the largest of the tents. A dog appeared and barked — rather timidly, I thought — and then a barefoot child sprang out of the nearest tent followed by a young woman carrying a smaller child. She came up to the fence with a strange and intent look on her face. It was still fairly early in the morning and she must have wondered what brought me along. The look on her face almost unnerved me, for I had never gone on such an errand to a tinker's encampment before, but I managed to stammer through the purpose of my visit. The mention of Hamish Henderson's name eased the tension considerably.

"He's a nice man," said she, "and a fine singer."

Questions then followed fast. Did I sing? Did I have a recording machine? I told her I was mainly interested in tales and legends and wished to speak to the old gentleman. She seemed slightly puzzled and, realising that there might be more than one old man in the camp, I asked for Alexander Stewart. She gave a call in the direction of the farthest off tent, and out of it came an elderly man in his bare feet, wearing a very tattered shirt and equally ragged pair of trousers. His eyes were heavy with sleep, but in them I could detect open hostility. I spoke to him in Gaelic and he immediately asked to which island of the Hebrides I belonged. I said that I was born in the Island of Raasay. He turned round angrily and asked if I was the son of the shoemaker there. I told him that my father had been a tailor but was now dead. For a moment he became quiet and thoughtful but said nothing. I then asked him if he did ever hear old tales or could remember any, for I was interested in collecting them.

"The old stories must pay you well," said he, "or else you would not be looking for them."

I tried to parry him by saying that I was often out of pocket on account of the same tales, but I could see that he was not entirely satisfied. I asked him if he knew the tale of Conall Gulban, a long heroic tale. He did, of course. I then began to show definite interest and excitement and asked him if I could come back at three o'clock that afternoon so that I could hear him tell it.

"All right!" said he gruffly.

As I left him I could not help thinking that I had seen him before, but where or when I could not think. There was something strangely familiar about him.

I returned to the camp at three in the afternoon. On my way there I met the women folk as they went to the village of Muir of Ord to do their weekend shopping. They were accompanied by four or five children ranging from the ages of five to twelve. The woman I had met in the morning returned with me to the camp and the smaller children came also. I was ushered into the largest of the tents. It seemed large and roomy inside, about thirty feet in length by ten at its broadest in the centre. A large opening in the canvas on one side served as a doorway and also admitted light. In the very centre there was an iron stove with a vent leading from it out through the top of the tent. In the stove a fire of wood burned, and on the top of it there was a kettle boiling. At each end there were two iron bedsteads up against the side of the tent with a narrow passage between them. Right opposite the doorway there was a small couch draped with a faded tartan plaid. There were cups, plates, knives, spoons, and tins lying about. All the same, the place was not unduly untidy: the beds were neatly made but there was not an abundance of bedclothes. It was the height of summer anyhow.

I sat down on the couch and awaited the arrival of Alexander Stewart. There was no sign of him. The young children made a dive for a package I had placed on the floor. There was a half-bottle of whisky, some bottles of beer and sweets in it. They divided the sweets equally among them, but the young woman immediately took the bottle of whisky and hid it. She said that old Grace, Alexander's mother, would come soon. She knew a lot of songs.

Old Grace did come. She was accompanied by a little man whom I learned later was her brother. She was tall and dignified although stooping slightly. He red hair was streaked with grey. Her features were still very fine and she must have been a beautiful woman over sixty years ago. She was well over eighty. She sat down beside me. The children seated themselves on the floor and on the beds and were very quiet and attentive as the old woman questioned me about origins and relatives. There were two red-haired youths in also, and they and one little girl

PINE TREES, GLENFINNAN

especially had inherited the old lady's good looks.

"Your grandfather and I," said Grace, "were neighbours for many years in Braes in the Isle of Skye."

When I was a little boy I used to live in my grandfather's house in Braes, Skye, and, of course, I remembered the tinkers' encampment in a sheltered gorge not far distant from where we lived. The Stewart tinkers know everybody in the Highlands, their family history and relationships. Eighty years of wandering must have given Grace an immense knowledge of the Highland people. She told me that she was planning to go to Gairloch in Wester Ross the following week. In recent years she had gone there every summer. In her the wander lust was still strong. The people of Gairloch are remarkably kind and good to the tinker fraternity. It has been said, somewhat unkindly, that the reason is that they fear the power of the tinker's curse and will do their utmost not to incur their displeasure. Grace, however, did not believe that was the reason for their kindness. They were by nature a kindly folk.

The bottle of whisky was given back to me and old Grace drank my health. She then got down to singing and it was evident that she knew a great number of songs. Women are usually the bearers of the song tradition rather than the tales and legends, and I was right in the assumption that she would prefer songs. She sang one seventeenth-century Gaelic lament to Sir James Macdonald of Sleat, the lament composed by the Bard of Keppoch, Iain Lom. The air of the song was new to me. I questioned her about songs I had heard in the isles and elsewhere throughout the Highlands. There was one very beautiful song that was sung to me by Mrs Patrick MacCormick of Benbecula, and no one else seemed to know it except her alone. It was the song of a woman who "paid dearly for the fishing of her menfolk and for the stoup that was on the table in the house by the shore. That was the year that bereaved her, and she was without her foster-son whose bed was now on the floor of the ocean and whose fine, lovely shirt was being torn asunder by the seals." Grace was deeply moved by the sad and simple beauty of its theme, and although she did not know the song, it reminded her of the lament for John Garve Macleod of Raasay, the famed chieftain who was drowned on his way home from Lewis in the year 1671. Grace then sang the lament for John Garve, and in her rendering of the song there were a couple of quatrains that I have not seen in print. Grace then decided that the youngsters should have a chance of being heard. One pretty little girl of five, with light brown hair and eyes matching exactly in colour, then sang a love song in Gaelic. The child knew Gaelic perfectly. Then the thin, delicate woman I met in the morning sang in English. Grace did not approve of English songs and did not hesitate to say so. Just then another pretty girl of about twelve entered the tent and this one was fair-haired and blue-eyed. She was asked to sing and immediately started to sing the Gaelic song sung earlier by the girl of five. Old Grace intervened to say that that song had been sung already, and without a moments hesitation the fair-haired girl started anew with:

"Early one morning as I rode o'er the ranches..."

I was quite stunned. She sang the American folksong beautifully, but it was such a contrast to what she had first intended to sing. The meeting of the two cultures was almost amazing.

When the song was finished, the thin, delicate woman ran out and returned immediately, rushed for the whisky-bottle and hid it. The men were on the way. Alexander Stewart arrived, accompanied by two younger men. They were flushed with drink and in a mellow and noisy mood. The public-houses in Muir of Ord had closed at three o'clock and the men had to return to the camp. Old Grace seemed displeased. They might spoil her party. The women who had gone shopping returned also; they were Alexander's wife and daughter, also called Grace, and they were accompanied by a young red-haired woman of twenty or so. The young woman was betrothed to the elder of the red-headed youths and they were to be married the following Saturday. I wished them well and they came over and shook hands with me.

Old Grace still tried bravely to continue singing but there were many interruptions — too many in fact to make recording worth the while. There was a younger Grace and she was dark-haired and very striking. She sang too, in Gaelic, and she had a lovely but very high-pitched voice. For a while her singing quietened the men, but they started again as soon as she finished. The grandmother then spoke of the song I had heard in Benbecula. They wanted to hear it, and, when they did, one of the young men came over and implored me to send him a copy of the words. Before that afternoon I should not have thought that one of the tinker clan would value a song so highly, but I had a lot to learn.

The men then started singing but their voices were not nearly as good as those of the women and girls. They were still very noisy and the women repeatedly apologised for the noise they made and told me to come back again another day, when the men would be sober and quiet. One of the young men, a stalwart, strapping fellow sat down on a bed and started shaving with the help of a very small mirror held in one hand. He cut himself badly.

By this time the hidden bottle reappeared and Alexander Stewart sat down beside me.

"Do you know the Police Sergeant in Beauly?" asked he.

"I do," said I. "He and I were at school together."

"He is the shoemaker's son from Raasay. I thought you were his brother when I first saw you this morning. He is a nice man, but do you know that he locked me up in the cells at Beauly a fortnight ago?"

That I did not know, but I quite understood why the mention of my native isle had made Alexander Stewart see red that morning. His next statement, however, took me quite by surprise, but it solved the mystery that had engaged my thoughts from the moment I set eyes on him in the morning.

"The wife and I spent three weeks in your father's barn when we were married."

I had seen him before, and my mind went back to one stormy winter's day over thirty years ago. That very day a young tinker couple were seen going past our township to a post, sheltered by high ledges of rock, which was a favourite encampment of tinkers when they came to our island. They were not seen returning and it was assumed they would spend the night there. The short day darkened and the storm increased in violence. During the night the fury of the wind and rain awakened my father and mother, and they thought of the tinkers, out in such a night. As soon as the first signs of dawn appeared, my father got up and went to look for them. He found them sheltering behind a rock, cold and drenched to the skin. Their tent had been blown into the darkness of night. Two days before that, the parish minister at Portree had pronounced them man and wife, and that was the second night of their honeymoon. My father brought them home, and when they got dry clothes and food, he sent them to a barn which was half-empty. They spent three weeks there. Every morning they disappeared but returned towards evening, lit a fire on the earthen floor of the barn and settled down for the night. All the young men in the township went to visit them night after night. I was then too young to be allowed there, but I did learn that the tinker in our barn had great stories.

After a lapse of thirty years I had come face to face with him again. I asked him if he could tell me a tale. He wanted to sing a song, but told me to come back again on Monday. I had to leave for Sutherlandshire on Monday afternoon but, if he came down to the Ord Arms Hotel at eleven o'clock on Monday morning, I would see him there. Of course, he would come down. He sang his song but I forgot what it was about, for I was much more interested to hear his story-telling. Outside there was brilliant sunshine and it was stifling in the tent; apart from the heat of the day there were so many people crowded into such a small space. It seemed to be a very large family unit; there was the old grandmother and her brother; Alexander Stewart, his wife and his brother; Alexander's large family of sons and daughters, ranging from the ages of thirty to ten, and a daughter-in-law with her children. Certainly there were four generations of them, but I am not certain as to the actual relationship of all of them. The girl who was to be married the following week did not, of course, live there. As I was about to leave, Alexander told me that I would be most welcome at the wedding. This was something almost too good to be missed and it was with great regret that I told him that I would be up in Sutherlandshire for a whole month. They all stood up and shook hands with me as I was leaving. Their manners were most charming.

The following Monday morning there was no sign of Alexander at eleven o'clock. Noon came and went and there was still no sign of him. At half-past two in the afternoon he appeared as if he were dead on time. By sheer good luck I succeeded in not showing any annoyance, and it was a good thing too, for it was crass stupidity on my part to have imagined that the tinkers' day would be broken up into so many hours. I ought to have known that the Stewart tinkers would have little sense of time. I doubt very much if they ever have possessed clocks and watches. I was too preoccupied with time in any case, but, unfortunately, the train to the north was due to pass by in an hour's time. We went into the public bar of the hotel and drinks were ordered. I got the recording machine fixed up and Alexander started to tell a long heroic tale. He was a wonderful storyteller, and the silence of the bar was broken only by the clinking of the cash-till. Apart from Alexander's storytelling, the machine picked up no other sounds. He told two tales, and I had to rush for the train.

A month later I returned from Sutherlandshire to Muir of Ord. It had been a glorious month of sunshine, but the fields around Muir of Ord were parched and burnt brown and the farmers were faced with the total loss of their hay-crop. I went to look for Alexander Stewart. I found him sitting cross-legged in front of one of his tents. Before him there was a T-shaped anvil of steel about an inch in thickness. The base was driven into the ground and it stood a foot and a half in height. I had never seen a tinsmith's anvil until then, and Alexander was busy beating a sheet of tin into shape on it. He set down his tools immediately, and we returned to Muir of Ord. Old Grace had gone away westwards to Gairloch and some of the young men and girls had gone with her. I might see them there as they would not be back until September.

I spent four solid hours recording tales from him that evening. When we finished, I walked part of the way with him to his tent, and, on parting, told him I would go for him the following morning. I did so, but on arriving at the encampment, I was told that he had set out for Muir of Ord about an hour earlier. I must have missed him on the way. There was nothing for it but to return to the Ord Arms Hotel. There I found Alexander waiting patiently in the public bar.

He again told stories for hours, and the stories were wonderful. Not only did he tell legends about the famed MacCrimmon pipers of Skye, about Ossian the son of Fingal, but also the tales that are as old as the Megalithic Age and which have spread from country to country and nation to nation. Folktale scholars in practically all European and American countries now use a system of folk-narrative classification first devised by a Finn, Antti Aarne, and later perfected by Professor Stith Thompson of Bloomington, Indiana, and now called the Aarne-Thompson system. It is, in fact, a register of all the folktales that are known almost all over the world. No matter what tale I choose to think of, Alexander had it and told it right away. Sometimes he depicted his characters with such clarity and intimacy that I could almost swear he had seen and known them. He did not believe that fairies exist, but he had no doubt about the *bean nighe*, the washerwoman or, as she is called sometimes in English, the banshee, who washes the clothes of

THE RIVER COE IN GLEN COE

those who are about to die. One night many years ago he heard her pounding on the wet clothes of the doomed in a stream in the Isle of Mull. He listened to her for a long time, and she was there right enough.

It was from his grandmother, Clementina Stewart, that Alexander heard most of his stories and that was about forty years ago. Clementina was, of course, so named in honour of Clementina Sobieski, the daughter of the valiant John of Poland and mother of the Prince — and to the Stewart tinkers there is only one Prince.

The late Dr Alexander Carmichael in his monumental work *Carmina Gadelica*, the prayers, charms, runes, incantations, and legends of the Gael, tells how it was that the tinkers came to be:

> When Christ was being taken to the tree of crucifixion, in the hurry the black Jews forgot to provide themselves with nails. They went to the blacksmith and asked him to make nails to nail the hands and the feet of the Saviour to the cross. But the blacksmith refused to make nails for such a purpose. The Jews went to the whitesmith (tinsmith, tinker) and asked him to make nails to nail the hands and the feet of the Saviour to the cross. The whitesmith did the work as the Jews asked of him, and the hands and the feet of Christ the Blessed Saviour were nailed to the tree of crucifixion. This is why the blacksmith is esteemed and honoured among men, while the whitesmith is contemned and despised, and this is why the race of the whitesmith is spread and scattered here and there throughout the great world.

Chapter Seven

SUTHERLAND AND WESTER ROSS

THE county of Sutherland is in the north-west corner of the Highlands, but there is a good stretch of its coastline on the east as well from Ord of Caithness southwards to the Dornoch Firth. It hems Caithness in the north-eastern corner and the Atlantic washes its western shores and on the east it is bounded by the quieter waters of the North Sea. Sutherland is a wide, desolate, and beautiful county, certainly the most desolate if not the most beautiful of all Scottish countries. I can only say that I saw it under ideal conditions, during a whole month of brilliant sunshine and cloudless skies. But what struck me most of all was the terrible emptiness of great stretches of the country. In the year 1801 the population of Sutherlandshire was 23,117; it rose to 25,793 in 1851, but when the preliminary reports of the census of 1951 were published the figure had fallen to 13,664. According to the same census reports the number of persons able to speak Gaelic was 3,324 for the whole county, while there was one solitary soul whose only language was Gaelic. I am quite convinced that a visit to Sutherland would make any thinking Highlanders feel murderous and that was exactly the way I felt. But it was also like visiting a vast necropolis, but a necropolis where no tombs, headstones, or graves were visible. The people of Sutherland that the casual visitor meets are the same slightly reserved but courteous and pleasant Highlanders that you find in any other county. There is a strange dignity about them, but deep down in their hearts there is an under-current of bitterness and resentment, but that undercurrent will never be laid bare to anyone except a fellow-Highlander and fellow-Gael who speaks to them in their own language. The Highlander will discover that, no matter how it starts, the conversation will sooner or later veer round to the "Clearances", and he will learn that in Sutherlandshire the "Clearances" will neither be forgotten nor forgiven.

It was that sunny afternoon that I left Alexander Stewart at his storytelling in a public-house in Muir of Ord and rushed to catch the north-bound train that I first saw Sutherlandshire. It was not the loveliness of hills, fields, woods, and blue inlets of sea that first caught my attention, but a massive pillar on a hill-top overlooking the sea about twenty miles or so to the north. I must have seen it first after the train left Fearn in Easter Ross. I lost sight of it again as we ran along the southern shore of the Dornoch Firth, but it was to reappear later over the village of Golspie, completely dominating the whole countryside. Next day I learned that it was a statue of the first Duke of Sutherland. From the very first I resented that immense monument and that was even before I got to know in whose honour it had been raised. Perhaps it would be fair to say that the noble duke was not entirely responsible for the atrocities committed by his factors and agents, but if he had been less motivated by self-interest and had taken the trouble to find out what was really happening on his estates, there might have been some slight reason for a monument to his memory.

The approach to Sutherland by way of the Dornoch Firth was very beautiful that summer's afternoon. Low green headlands jutted into the blue waters at almost regular intervals and the hills rose gently on either side. We passed the Kyle of Sutherland and followed the course of the River Shin. To the left lay the loveliest strath in the north, Strath Oykell. I caught only a fleeting glimpse of it the first day, but I was to see it again on my way to Lochinver and the western seaboard. We then passed the village of Lairg, which seems to be the hub of the county. All roads in Sutherland seem to converge on it; I always seemed to find my way back there during the course of the month's visit. On leaving Lairg the railway-line turns eastwards again down Strath Fleet and past the district of Rogart, one of the few districts where there are a fair number of crofters and smallholders. The most distinguished son of this area was Sir John Macdonald, the first Premier of Canada. The local people are still very proud of him.

I stopped at Brora that night and stayed at the Links Hotel, a lovely hotel overlooking a glorious stretch of sand. I was much too late for dinner, and apologised to a very charming lady, who turned out to be the proprietrix.

"Oh, but we have kept something for you," said she.

It was the height of the tourist season and the hotel was full. I was impressed by such consideration for a guest who was to remain for one solitary night.

Brora was once a prosperous fishing village, but the fishing has more or less gone. The little houses still lie huddled by the shore, but there was no sign of boats anywhere. Brora, however, boasts of a huge woollen mill and distillery. I was given a half-bottle of the produce of the latter and it was truly fine stuff.

Next morning I called on Mr T. E. M. Landsborough, the Director of Education for the county. My attention was drawn to a huge map of the county on which the location of the schools was pin-pointed. There were several around the edge of the map and one right in the very centre. It must have been miles and miles away from any other district. The map gave a very good indication of the distribution of Sutherland's population. During the "Clearances" the people were hounded from the rich inland straths and forced either into the emigrant ships or to eke out a precarious livelihood on the barren, crowded coasts. The school distribution map showed how very thoroughly the job had been done. All this was brought home to me while we were discussing something entirely different. Mr Landsborough knew the county and its people well. He has learned Gaelic, but, unfortunately, his subsequent transfer to Clackmannan has been a great loss to Sutherland. He gave me a list of contacts throughout the county and all of them proved valuable and helpful.

My first night in Sutherlandshire was spent in Brora and so also was my last. As a village it was pretty enough but there is a sameness about all the villages along the eastern coast of Sutherland and Ross-shire. The really attractive places are inland. It was, however, the few people I met on my first visit that induced me to go back again a month later. During my short visits I learned a great deal about the place, its traditions and history, but I was very fortunate in the informants I met.

Hector Sutherland and his son Cairn have a tailors and outfitters business in Brora. They are well established and thrive despite the competition of larger firms and combines. They specialise in the making of kilts and make them very well indeed. Before I finally left them I placed an order for a kilt. I was more than satisfied with it when I received it. All over the Highlands tailors and clothiers are being forced to shut up shop and theirs is a lot common to all other local craftsmen. I could have purchased a kilt in Edinburgh or Glasgow, but in Brora I had the pleasure of being able to contribute something to a small local concern.

The first day I met Hector Sutherland he was perfectly willing to give me any information I sought but most reluctant to allow his voice to be recorded. I do not think he liked the idea of having it made permanent. It may have been that he did not want his voice to survive him, but in any case I had a very persuasive ally in his son and we succeeded in overcoming his objections. Hector Sutherland is one of the few surviving Gaelic-speakers in the district and a most intelligent and discerning old gentleman. In his younger and more active days he was prominent in the activities of the Radical Liberal Party during the time of the crofter and Land League agitation. He was full of memories of that period. He once heard Gladstone address a meeting.

The best and most truthful accounts of the Sutherland Clearances are to be found in the writings of two ministers, the Rev. D. Sage who wrote *Memorabilia Domestica*, and the Rev. Donald Macleod, author of *Gloomy Memories*. Both were, I am almost certain, ministers of the Free Church. The sad fact was that at that time only ministers could have sufficient education and a good enough knowledge of English to champion the cause of the crofters and bring their oppressors to the bar of public opinion. The Gaelic-speaking crofters could not put their case before the English-speaking public of Britain. They were not so very unfortunate despite that, for they were also championed by a fine Highlander, General Stewart of Garth, and the noted writer and geologist Hugh Miller, a native of Sutherland. The Sutherland estates had to enlist the help of Mrs Harriet Beecher Stowe, the writer of *Uncle Tom's Cabin*, who travelled to Sutherland and wrote a defence of the estate policy, a defence based on *An Account of the Improvements on the Estates of the Marquis of Stafford* written by the notorious Sutherland factor, James Loch. The Rev. Donald Macleod went into exile in Canada with his evicted parishioners, and from there replied to Mrs Beecher Stowe:

> I have read from speeches delivered by Mr Loch at public dinners among his own party, [that he would] never be satisfied until the Gaelic language and the Gaelic people would be extirpated root and branch from the Sutherland estate; yes, from the Highlands of Scotland. He published a book, where he stated as a positive fact, that when he got the management of the Sutherland estate he found 408 families on the estate who had never heard the name of Jesus — whereas I could make oath that there were not at that time, and for ages prior to it, above two families within the limits of the country who did not worship that Name and holy Being every morning and evening. I know there are hundreds in the Canadas who will bear me out in this assertion. I was at the pulling down and burning of the house of William Chisholm. I got my hands burnt taking out the poor old woman from amidst the flames of her once-comfortable though humble dwelling, and a more horrifying and lamentable scene could scarcely be witnessed.... . If you took the information and evidence upon which you founded your *Uncle Tom's Cabin* from such unreliable sources (viz. Loch's Account), who can believe one-tenth of your novel? I cannot.

Loch's predecessor in office was the notorious Patrick Sellar. The clearing of whole tracts of country and the burning of people out of their homes was largely initiated and directed by him. The unfortunate victims were suddenly deprived of shelter and many died as a result of alarm, fatigue, and cold. Some old men were driven insane and took to wandering among woods and rocks until death mercifully intervened. Pregnant women were taken in premature labour and several children did not long survive their sufferings.

> To these scenes [says the Rev. Donald Macleod in his *Gloomy Memories*] I was an eye-witness, and am ready to substantiate the truth of my statements, not only by my own testimony, but by that of many others who were present at the time. In such a scene of general devastation, it is almost useless to particularise the cases of individuals; the suffering was great and universal. I shall, however, notice a very few of the extreme cases of which I was myself an eye-witness. John Mackay's wife, Ravigill, in attempting to pull down her house, in the absence of her husband, to preserve the timber, fell through the roof. She was in consequence taken in premature labour, and in that state was exposed to the open air and to the view of all the by-standers. Donald Munro, Garvott, lying in a fever, was turned out of his house and exposed to the elements. Donald Macbeath, an infirm and bed-ridden old man, had the house unroofed

over him, and was in that, state exposed to the wind and rain until death put a period to his sufferings. I was present at the pulling down and burning of the house of William Chisholm, Badinloskin, in which was lying his wife's mother, an old bed-ridden woman of nearly 100 years of age, none of the family being present. I informed the persons about to set fire to the house of this circumstance, and prevailed on them to wait until Mr Sellar came. On his arrival, I told him of the poor old woman, being in a condition unfit for removal, when he replied, "Damn her, the old witch, she has lived too long — let her burn." Fire was immediately set to the house, and the blankets in which she was carried out were in flames before she could be got out. She was placed in a little shed and it was with great difficulty they were prevented from firing it also. The old woman's daughter arrived while the house was on fire, and assisted the neighbours in removing her mother out of the flames and smoke, presenting a picture of horror of which I shall never forget, but cannot attempt to describe.

Patrick Sellar was subsequently charged with culpable homicide before the Court of Justiciary at Inverness. Several "tacksmen" or large farmers, merchants, and some local gentlemen constituted the jury and, not surprisingly, the accused was "honourably" acquitted. But the "Clearances" continued. In one month parts of the parishes of Golspie, Rogart, Farr and the whole of Kildonan were ruthlessly consigned to the flames.

> The consternation and confusion [wrote the Rev. Donald Macleod] were extreme; little or no time was given for the removal of persons or property; the people striving to remove the sick and the helpless before the fire should reach them; next struggling to save the most valuable of their effects. The cries of the women and children, the roaring of the affrighted cattle, hunted at the same time by the yelling dogs of the shepherds amid the smoke and fire, altogether presented a scene that completely baffles description — it required to be seen to be believed. A dense cloud of smoke enveloped the whole country by day, and even extended far out to sea; at night an awfully grand but terrific scene presented itself — all the houses in an extensive district in flames at once. I myself ascended a height about eleven o'clock in the evening and counted two hundred and fifty blazing houses, many of the owners of which were my relations, and all of whom I knew personally, but whose present condition — whether in or out of the flames — I could not tell. The conflagration lasted six days, till the whole of the dwellings were reduced to ashes or smoking ruins. During one of these days a boat actually lost her way in the dense smoke as she approached the shore, but at night was enabled to reach a landing-place by the lurid light of the flames.

The inhabitants of the parish of Kildonan, a beautiful strath, numbered nearly 2,000 souls and were, with the exception of three families, utterly rooted and burnt out, and what had been the *petite patrie* of themselves and generations of their people before them was turned into a lonely wilderness. The resultant physical and mental suffering was so intense that some lost their reason. The Rev. Donald Sage gives a very moving account of his farewell service in Strathnaver on the Sunday before the blow fell there in May 1819.

> In Strathnaver we assembled, for the last time, at the place of Langdale, where I had frequently preached before, on a beautiful green sward overhung by Robert Gordon's antique, romantic little cottage on an eminence close beside us. The still-flowing waters of the Naver swept past us a few yards to the eastward. The Sabbath morning was unusually fine, and mountain, hill, and dale, water and woodland, among which we had so long dwelt, and with which all our associations of "home" and "native land" were so fondly linked, appeared to unite their attractions to bid us farewell. My preparations for the pulpit had always cost me much anxiety, but in view of this sore scene of parting, they caused me pain almost beyond

SALMON NETS DRYING, KILCHOAN, ARDNAMURCHAN: "KILCHOAN IS A PRETTY LITTLE VILLAGE LYING IN THE SHELTER OF THE
HILLS AND LOOKING SOUTH ACROSS THE SEA IS THE LOVELY ISLE OF MULL."

endurance. I selected a text which had a pointed reference to the peculiarity of our circumstances, but my difficulty was how to restrain my feelings till I should illustrate and enforce the great truths which it involved with reference to eternity. The service began. The very aspect of the congregation was of itself a sermon, and a most impressive one. Old Achoul sat right opposite to me. As my eye fell upon his venerable countenance, bearing the impress of eighty-seven winters, I was deeply affected, and could scarcely articulate the psalm. I preached and the people listened, but every sentence uttered and heard was in opposition to the tide of our natural feelings, which, setting in against us, mounted at every step of our progress higher and higher. At last all restraints were compelled to give way. The preacher ceased to speak, the people to listen. All lifted up their voices, and wept, mingling their tears together. It was indeed the place of parting, and the hour. The greater number parted never again to behold each other in the land of the living.

It has been argued that the "Clearances" were necessary because the Highland areas were overcrowded and unable to support the number of people subsisting on poor and barren soil. Between the years 1801 and 1851 the population of Sutherland increased by over two thousand. There was a great deal more overcrowding in 1851 due to the fact that, whereas it was evenly distributed throughout the country in 1801, the native population was crowded around the coasts by the middle of the century. During the same period the population of all the other Highland counties increased also. There was a great deal more poverty in the Highlands in the middle of the century and it was principally due to the fact that the best land was taken from the people and leased to sheep-farmers and tacksmen. The rental of one sheep farm was often greater than the combined rental of fifty small-holdings. The "Clearances" instead of alleviating poverty and hardship increased both. Some of the evicted crofters, as I heard several intelligent Sutherlandmen remark, were in most cases in comfortable circumstances and possessed as many as twenty to forty head of cattle.

The "Clearances" caused such anger and resentment among the native Gaelic population that, on the outbreak of the Crimean War, the War Office was seriously perturbed by the failure of recruiting campaigns in the Highlands. All Highland proprietors were asked to co-operate and raise as many men as they could. During a recruiting drive lasting for six weeks James Loch and a military officer did not succeed in getting one man to enlist on the Sutherland estates. On hearing this the Duke of Sutherland hastily travelled up from London and called a meeting of all the male inhabitants of the parishes of Clyne, Rogart, and Golspie. The meeting was well attended, and his Grace rose to deliver an anti-Russian diatribe and stress the necessity of going to fight for the Queen and her government. He stated that every man who enlisted would receive a bounty of £6. He sat down, but there was no response, no movement among his hearers. The platform party exchanged anxious looks but still no response. The Duke finally got up and asked the reason. For a long time there was complete silence until an old man, leaning on his stick, was seen approaching the Duke. He spoke quietly and deliberately.

"I am sorry," said he, "for the response your Grace's proposals are meeting here today, so near the spot where your maternal grandmother, by giving forty-eight hours' notice, marshalled fifteen hundred men to pick out of them the nine hundred she required, but there is a cause for it, and a grievous cause, and as your Grace demands to know it, I must tell you, as I see no one else in this assembly is inclined to do it. Your Grace's mother and predecessors applied to our fathers for men upon former occasions, and our fathers responded to their call; they have made liberal promises which neither them nor you performed; we are, we think, a little wiser than our fathers, and we estimate your promises of today at the value of theirs, besides you should bear in mind that your predecessors and yourself expelled us in a most cruel and unjust manner from the land which our fathers held in lieu from your family for their sons, brothers, cousins and relations, which were handed over to your parents to keep up their dignity, and to kill the Americans, Turks, French and the Irish; and these lands are devoted now to rear dumb brute animals, which you and your parents consider of far more value than men. I do assure your Grace that it is the prevailing opinion in this country, that should the Czar of Russia take possession of Dunrobin Castle and of Stafford House next term, that we could not expect worse treatment at his hands than we have experienced at the hands of your family for the last fifty years. Your parents, yourself and your commissioners have desolated the glens and straths of Sutherland where you should find hundreds, yea, thousands of men to meet you and respond cheerfully to your call, had your parents and yourself kept faith with them. How could your Grace expect to find men where they are not, and the few of them which are to be found among the rubbish or ruins of the country, have more sense than to be decoyed by chaff to the field of slaughter; but one comfort you have; though you cannot find men to fight, you can supply those who will fight with plenty of mutton, beef and venison."

Innumerable stories are still told of incidents during that unhappy time and, to all appearances, they are being passed on to the younger generation. In Brora I heard that a regiment of Irish soldiers was ordered from Fort George to assist in the eviction of crofters from the district of Col-bheinn. The regiment passed through the village and somehow got wind of what they were expected to do. At a bridge a couple of miles beyond the village they turned back. A woman from Badbea, just across the county march in Caithness, was being forced into an emigrant ship. She had a baby in her arms, and, when she reached the shore, she refused to go into the little boat that was to bring her to the ship. The baby was rudely snatched from her arms and brought aboard the ship. The poor mother then had to follow.

About the most notorious factotum employed by the Sutherland estates was Domhnall Sgrios, Donald Destruction. His was the unsavoury reputation of having set fire to houses in seven different straths. He was in the process of setting fire to houses near Lairg when news came that a body of Crimean veterans of the 93rd Regiment had crossed the Dornoch Firth. Domhnall Sgrios fled for his life. The soldiers pursued and captured him. He was stripped naked and draped in whins.

Even the evictions, however, produced a brand of humour. The small croft of an evicted native of the parish of Clyne was added to the glebe of a minister. Shortly afterwards the reverend gentleman was holding a catechising meeting in the parish. The meetings were usually convened in private houses and ministers tested the scriptural and religious knowledge of their flock. This minister in question asked one of his hearers how many commandments there were. "Nine," came the immediate response. The minister looked surprised and repeated his question. Again the answer was the same.

"Surely you must know that there are ten commandments," said the divine, more in sorrow than anger.

"There are not," replied the other. "You yourself did away with the tenth when you coveted your neighbour's little piece of land."

There was another poor crofter who did not have enough money to pay his friend. The factor informed him that he would have to pay his rent within three weeks or be evicted. The perplexed crofter went to seek the advice of his minister. The minister counselled earnest prayer and the crofter went home. A fortnight later the minister met him again and he was grinning from ear to ear.

"How are you?" asked the minister.

"Ah," said the other, "the Lord's the boy."

"Why do you say that the Lord's the boy?" asked the minister.

"The factor's dead!" replied the crofter.

The effects of the "Clearances" are still painfully evident throughout the whole of Sutherland. One dull Saturday afternoon I went by bus from Lairg westwards to Lochinver. The road was narrow and there were passing places at regular intervals. We went up Strath Oykell. It was really beautiful with lovely stretches of green grassland on both banks of the river. There were quite a number of sheep to be seen but hardly a dwelling, hardly a living soul anywhere. The journey took more than five hours. The few vehicles that met us carried not any of the folk of Sutherland but tourists and anglers. I thought of the kind of land that some of the crofters in the west of Lewis try to cultivate and compared it with what I saw in Strath Oykell. My thoughts need not have gone as far afield as Lewis. We finally reached Lochinver and there were crofters attempting to wrest a livelihood from barren, rocky soil. The following Monday I returned to Lairg. This time the sun shone from a cloudless sky and there was a thin veneer of mist on the slopes of Ben More. The scenery was enchanting. Perhaps on such a day over a century ago people of my race and blood were driven from Strath Oykell.

That same afternoon I had to go from Lairg to Durness on the northern coast of the country. Again the journey took some time and I do not remember passing more than a dozen or so houses. The road went by Loch Shin to the west, and, according to the Ordnance Survey maps, there ought to have been a school beyond Loch Shin by the side of the smaller Loch a Ghriama, but when we got there we discovered that only the gable-end of the school remains. That is one school that will never be reopened. A week later I returned to Lairg, this time from Tongue. We had to climb through lovely winding glens and gorges for the first part of the way and when we finally got to the highest point on the roadway, at the foot of Ben Clibreck, the wide expanse of the county stretched before us, flat, desolate wilderness almost as far as the eye could see. Away to the south-west was Ben More of Assynt. In between there seemed to be nothing but an interminable sea of mountain grass.

Through time I shall forget most of what I saw and heard during the month in Sutherland, but one memory will remain for a very long while. The old gentleman I met at Tongue one sunny morning made a deeper impression on me than almost anyone I have ever met. It was not only his presence that struck me but what he had to say and what he did say gave me more insight into the thoughts and feelings of the generations of Highlanders who suffered through the "Clearances" than anything else. I am sure he is now dead, for he was ninety-three years of age when I met him and even then there was about him an air of indifference to the vanities and frivolities of this life that sometimes distinguishes those on the threshold of Eternity. He was tall and gaunt and spoke in quiet and deliberate tones. I went to his house and he came out in answer to my knocking. After the usual preliminaries I told him in English that I was interested in stories.

"I do not know the story," said he.

I realised my mistake and turned to Gaelic and asked if, by any chance, he had heard the old natives telling stories about Rob Donn MacKay, the noted eighteenth-century Gaelic poet of Sutherlandshire. He was silent for a moment and then answered in the language he knew best and loved most.

"To me it is a cause of great sorrow that the Gaelic is going down. Please come inside."

I followed him in and when he had seen me seated by the window, over he went and brought down from a shelf an old leather-bound volume, a first edition of the Gaelic poems of Rob Donn. He sat down at a table beside me, opened the book and turned over the pages that were brown and discoloured with age and continual thumbing.

COTTAGE ON NORTH SIDE OF LOCH MORAR: "LOCH MORAR IS REPUTED TO BE THE DEEPEST FRESH-WATER LOCH IN THE BRITISH ISLES. THE LOCH IS NOW A NORTH OF SCOTLAND HYDRO-BOARD RESERVOIR, BUT THE BEAUTY OF IT REMAINS UNAFFECTED."

"I shall read the poem Rob Donn made in honour of Prince Charles Edward Stuart for you."

The local chieftains at the time of the "Forty-five", the Earl of Sutherland and Lord Reay, the head of the MacKays, were both Hanoverians, but the common people must have shared the strongly Jacobite sentiments of the poet Rob Donn, sentiments that had not quite gone after the lapse of over two centuries, for the old man entered into the spirit of the song with tremendous gusto and enthusiasm. Strangely enough his own closet connection with the "'Forty-five" was through a great-grandfather who, as one of the Reay militiamen actively engaged on the Hanoverian side, guarded the French sailors from the sloop *Hazard*, which was driven ashore at Tongue by British warships. The French ship was bringing funds to the Jacobites, and when it was driven ashore, the men escaped, one of them carrying with him the box of gold pieces which were thrown into a little loch near Tongue. The men were finally rounded up and a body of Reay militiamen guarded them. Although it was said that one local man became rich in a mysterious way all of a sudden, the gold thrown into the loch was never known to have been recovered. During a period of prolonged drought and when the level of the loch was low, a cow went into it to drink and came out with a gold piece stuck in one of its hooves, but no more was seen of the French money.

The "Clearances" had hardly ceased when the old man was born over ninety-three years ago and memories of the time were still fresh in his mind. He spoke for long in the same quiet, deliberate tones.

"The soldiers came back from the wars," said he, "and found the houses where they were born reduced to ashes and knew not where in the wide world their flesh and blood had gone. If Napoleon had come over, things would not have been as bad as that. Napoleon always had a very great regard for the Gael."

From Lochinver there is a narrow, winding road along the coast southwards into Wester Ross. It is not a good road by any means but one that affords marvellous views of the mountains to the east and south. The road will eventually take one to Achiltibuie, away in a remote and almost forgotten corner of the county. Achiltibuie is about eight miles from the village of Ullapool by sea but by road the distance is well over twenty miles. I commiserated with one local lady that the distance from Ullapool was so great.

"Oh," said she, "that is exactly what we want. We like the isolation."

My friend, Sandy Folkarde, and I arrived in Achiltibuie late one dark Friday evening in autumn. We had never been there before and we knew no one. We left the following Tuesday and in the interval had got to know practically everyone in the place. But what a grand, gay, lovely little community there was there! There were quite a number of young people too, in fact a large number for so remote a district. In Sutherland I had been forced to stay at several hotels that catered mainly for anglers and in them all the atmosphere was dull, dreary, and unfriendly. Although there were a couple of anglers staying at the Summer Isles Hotel at Achiltibuie, the atmosphere there was a complete contrast. The proprietor and his wife were a charming couple and they were most fortunate in their staff. Two of the waitresses were pretty Gaelic-speaking girls from Gairloch and they had a charm of manner that would make their more sophisticated sisters in the south feel envious. I do not remember whether the hotel cook, Mrs Murray, was outstanding as a cook, but she had a most wonderful singing voice and sang Gaelic songs better than anyone I have ever heard at mods throughout the Highlands. She was a natural singer, quite untrained, but it was most enthralling to listen to her. No party, no *célidh* in Achiltibuie could ever be complete without her. Her maiden name was Macleod and she is a close relative of the late Reoderick Macleod, the doyen of all Gaelic singers. Even strangers who had come to live in the district and who had been accustomed to sophisticated, highly trained singers were positive that they had rarely, if ever, heard anything like Mrs Murray's singing. On one occasion she went to compete at the local mod (Gaelic musical festival) held at Ullapool and was not even placed. Of course, the adjudication at some of the Gaelic mods is sometimes farcical, and it must certainly have been so when Mrs Murray went to compete. She is still a young woman and I hope her singing will delight the ears of the people of Achiltibuie for many a long day to come. The outside world may never hear of her.

Mrs Murray was not the only talented person in Achiltibuie. There was John Campbell of Coulnacraig, also a fine Gaelic singer and a perfect example of the native Highland gentleman. There was Kenny John Macleod of Achduart, a really brilliant traditional fiddler. Kenny John is married to an English lady, who now thinks that Achiltibuie is the finest place on earth. In the neighbouring house there was another English lady, married to Kenny John's cousin, and she too loved the way of life in Achiltibuie. Although the scenic attractions of the district were considerable, for the Summer Isles lay out to sea and there was a grand vista of mountains across Loch Broom, the charm of the place was undoubtedly in its people.

Perhaps the most remarkable of all was the late Murdo John Maclean. This man had the whole history of the area at his fingertips. His knowledge of the family history of Achiltibuie, Coigach, as the district is called, was remarkable. He told, for example, that there are twelve Maclean families in the area, families unrelated except through marriage. He could tell the circumstances and the time of the arrival of the twelve progenitors of the families. While we were in his house, the local postman, Duncan Maclean, called to deliver letters. Murdo John told us that the postman was descended from a fugitive who had come to Achiltibuie from the field of Culloden and that the postman was Duncan son of Kenneth son of Duncan son of Kenneth son of Duncan. Murdo John himself could name his antecedents back for nine generations. We spent hours and hours recording information from him, but what we did record was only a tiny drop in the wide ocean of his knowledge. Within a year of our visit he was dead and except the little we got his lore has gone with him to the grave.

It took us the best part of a day to get from Achiltibuie to Poolewe. By sea the distance is less than half that by road but we had to get round Loch Broom and on such a journey one simply could not hurry. We passed through one of the finest and most picturesque tracts of country in the north. Here and there we caught glimpses of the open sea and grand mountains towered above us on all sides. The sun shone brilliantly as we left Achiltibuie but we ran into a torrential shower of rain as we neared Ullapool. The village was cold and wind-swept; no doubt it is a good centre, but hardly the place to attract holiday-makers itself. We did not stay long there but pushed on again, and, as soon as we did, the skies cleared. Loch Broom is long and narrow and Strath More, which leads down to it, is thickly wooded. Just where the wood ends, we branched off to the west again, a narrower road this time but undoubtedly the one to the west and to Gairloch. The ground dropped suddenly and to our right were the magnificent Falls of Measach. We started to climb again, away from the deep gorge, and when we got to the top of a bare moor, the landscape was dominated completely by a very stately mountain to the west, An Teallach. We lost sight of it again as we began to descend to Strath Beg and Little Loch Broom. The strath was very pretty and wooded and I thought that the smaller Loch Broom was lovelier than the larger. It was somewhere along this road that we saw a sign announcing "Super Bed and Breakfast". Happily enough the tourist industry, despite its effect on the traditional hospitality of the Highlanders, has not taught them to spell properly, or else this was a very clever piece of advertising. Away across the loch we could see the township of Scoraig. Some years ago this township figured prominently in the news when a number of young men from Glasgow decided to abandon the city and take up the life of crofters in Scoraig. I have not heard how they fared, but I doubt if the enterprise succeeded. The main road by-passed Scoraig and, according to present trends, it is a doomed community. Unfortunately, too, the tradition of seamanship is not being maintained in those small, remote coastal communities, and in the absence of a proper road the people are now more isolated than ever they were. Before us we could see another township, Badluchrach, right opposite Scoraig, and for some unaccountable reason the main road by-passed it as well. However, a track much poorer and rougher than the main highway did branch off to Badluchrach and it may have a slighter chance of survival than Scoraig.

We were travelling by what is locally known as the "Destitution Road" as it was made as the result of a grant to relieve distress in the leanest years of last century. Those who engineered it may not have worried whether it served the best interests of the communities or not. At one point opposite Gruinard Island the gradient is so very steep that modern engineers have decided not to tar the surface in the interests of safety. The rough gravel surface makes it much easier for motorists to negotiate the incline. It certainly was the steepest gradient I have ever encountered on any Scottish road.

We stopped at Laide School and recorded psalm-singing in Gaelic from the children. Three of the children acted as precentors and gave out the line. Earlier we had visited the school at Achiltibuie and recorded psalm-singing there. Miss Munro, the school mistress at Laide, has done splendid work in the teaching of Gaelic to the children. In this area Gaelic has now ceased to be the language of the home, although the parents mostly know Gaelic. Miss Munro teaches Gaelic to the children almost as soon as they are enrolled. She finds that even the youngest children are very keen to learn. She brought one little girl of seven out to the floor and asked her to read a passage in Gaelic. The child had a perfect Wester Ross accent. Her name was Eileen Walker and her parents had come from Lancashire to Laide and were now living there. The roll of Laide School is small: Miss Munro was the sole teacher and there were only a dozen or so pupils.

At Aultbea the Destitution Road seems to end and give place to a better and wider road, the road that links Aultbea with Achnasheen, the nearest railway station. There is a naval depot at Aultbea and the sheltered waters of Loch Ewe were of immense value to the British Navy. The reason for a better road in this area is, of course, not far to seek. The fairly large crofting community at Inverasdale on the south-western shore of Loch Ewe did not, however, have such a good road, but its plight was much better than some other communities in Wester Ross which have no road at all.

The very fine gardens at Inverewe, once the property of the late Osgood Mackenzie, have now been taken over by the National Trust. Not far from the entrance to Inverewe Gardens there is a simple stone cairn to the memory of the late Alexander Cameron, the Tournaig Bard. We paid a visit to the bard's son, Roderick Cameron, who lives at Achmore, near Poolewe. Roderick is also a songster and some of his songs are known over a wide area of the Highlands. Roderick Cameron enlightened me on a point which hardly seems known at all to Highlanders of the present day. One of the most popular Gaelic toasts still in vogue is *Slainte mhór*, which we take to mean something like "Great Health". What it really means is "The Health of Marion" — *Mór* being the Gaelic form of Marion. Marion was the "kenning" or secret name for Prince Charles Edward Stuart. Thus the Jacobites could toast him without the Hanoverians being any the wiser.

Flora Macdonald dressed the Prince up as a woman and brought him from the Outer Isles to Skye. While in this attire, the Prince was fording a stream somewhere in Skye and in a moment of forgetfulness he lifted his skirt well above the knee. He was being watched by an unseen Hanoverian militiaman, who, on observing this, exclaimed in Gaelic:

"Oh, Marion, haven't you become immodest since last year!"

The Highlanders in the Hanoverian army must have used the "kenning" also.

One afternoon I went to the churchyard of Gairloch to see the grave of the Gaelic poet William Ross. A handsome stone in the centre of the burial-ground marks the spot where he was believed to rest, but earlier that year some grave-diggers discovered an older stone some yards away from the spot that was said to hold his dust. The stone was about three feet high but it had sunk into the ground out of sight. It was examined and on it there was found an inscription carved in rough lettering: "William Ross died 1791 aged 27 years." The stone was set up again in the very spot where it was found. The discovery of the second headstone created quite a sensation in the locality, but it does seem that the exact spot where he was buried had been forgotten. Outside the churchyard there is a memorial to John Mackenzie, the writer of the Gaelic account of the "'Forty-five" and also the author of the most noted of all Gaelic anthologies, *The Beauties of Gaelic Poetry.* John Mackenzie was a native of Gairloch.

We were leaving Poolewe and on our way to Strome Ferry and Lochalsh when two female hikers beckoned to us that they wanted a lift. I had just one fleeting glimpse of one of them as we passed but that was enough to impress on my mind how very fair and attractive she was. Her companion was very charming also. We had come all the way from Edinburgh and down through Wester Ross and had encountered no hitch-hikers until that moment. We decided to stop and ask them how far they were going. They were going to Strome Ferry. They puzzled us at first. They were not Scottish, nor were they English, for we could have recognised their accent. They were not American as far as we could guess, for their voices were low and rather pleasant. We finally asked them. We were then told that we were not very observant, for their rucksacks bore the name, flag, and emblem of their country. It was Canada. They were undoubtedly a credit to their country, but they did not seem to have any Scottish affinities. They had been to London and the Edinburgh International Festival and were on their way to Skye and later to Ireland and the Continent. They were quite certain that they wanted to see Skye but were not quite so sure about Ireland. They seemed to have fallen foul of anti-Irish prejudices in England, but we advised them to go and judge Ireland and the Irish for themselves. I was told later that they did go to Ireland and came completely under its spell. They had not heard so very much about Scotland apart from the Burns suppers, haggis, and Caledonian societies. They had heard about Bonnie Prince Charles and were almost surprised to learn that he was still the Prince to so many hundreds of Highlanders. Most of the time they questioned us about the Gaelic language and its present position in Scottish life and its status in schools. They became genuinely interested in Gaelic and they were not at all happy about the desperate straits in which it now finds itself. There was something Scandinavian about the loveliness of the blonde, Lueny Hurst, but I had seen few, if any, girls in Norway and Sweden quite so attractive. We brought her and Frances Hewton safely to Strome Ferry and did not see them again.

Loch Maree is beautiful with its wooded islands and the magnificent Slioch towering over it, but I still think that it does not quite equal Loch Shiel in Moidart. Loch Maree, however, draws more visitors and there is a very fine hotel on its shores. It attracts a large number of anglers. The village of Kinlochewe lies at the meeting of three glens and there is a very steep climb up through the wide Glen Dochertie on the road to Achnasheen. At Achnasheen we turned westwards again down into Glen Carron. At Strome Ferry the ruins of the old castle are still there to be seen, the castle that figured in much of the fighting between the Macdonalds and their powerful enemies, the Mackenzies. The castle was besieged and blown up by the Mackenzies in the year 1602.

We crossed Strome Ferry into Lochalsh. Lochalsh was once the patrimony of the Macdonalds but later passed into the hands of the Mackenzies. Today Mackenzie is the commonest surname in Wester Ross. Farther inland in Kintail, however, almost every second person you meet is a MacRae. The MacRaes were allied to the Mackenzies and were noted archers and fighting-men in days gone by. Even yet they invariably are a stalwart and handsome folk, immensely proud of their clan and its traditions. I have heard about a MacRae who was averse to wasting time by talking about anyone who did not belong to the clan, and the MacRaes were always regarded by other Highlanders as being a strong and intrepid race. There is a story told about a High-lander who, on his deathbed, asked that parts of the Holy Writ be read to him. The old man had been a warrior in his day and his son, anxious to please him, proceeded to read about Samson and the Philistines. The slaughter of the Philistines by Samson excited the old fellow, and he asked:

"To what clan did Samson belong?"

The son was not without a sense of humour and answered:

"I think he was of the MacRaes of Kintail."

"I thought so," said the father. "If the MacRaes could not do that, no one else could."

I stayed in the village of Plockton, near the mouth of Loch Carron. Plockton is a very pretty little village, and there is here a gay and very lively community. Plockton was a prosperous fishing village, and although the fishing has gone, to a large extent the tradition of seamanship is being maintained. The annual regatta is the event of the year in Plockton. One of my Plockton friends, Kenneth John Mackenzie, distinguished himself in the Middle East in the Second World War and rose to the rank of Lieutenant-Commander and was awarded the Distinguished Service Order. After the war Kenneth John came back home to teach in Plockton Secondary School. He is a very fine seaman indeed. The training that stood him in good stead in the services started when he was a little boy in Plockton. His other main interest is in Gaelic songs, and he is a fine singer also.

Loch Alsh runs in from the west for about eight miles and one arm goes to the north-east and is called Loch Long, while to the south-east Loch Duich stretches to the foot of the splendid mountain ridge dominated by the Five Sisters of Kintail. Two deep valleys approach the head of Loch Duich, Glen Shiel, and Glen Lichd, and the Five Sisters form a massive rampart between them. To the south of Glen Shiel there is an equally high and impressive ridge of mountains and another north of Glen Lichd. Loch Duich is the most beautiful sea loch that I have seen in the Highlands. Whether in rain or sunshine, the loch and its surroundings are impressive. The Castle of Eilean Donnan stands sentinel at the mouth of Loch Duich. This was the ancient stronghold of the MacRaes and was restored by the late Col MacRae-Gilstrap. The castle is actually on a little island and is joined to the mainland by a bridge. In the year 1539 the castle was besieged by the Macdonalds of Sleat under their chieftain, Domhnall Gorm. The garrison defending the castle was small but among them was a noted archer called Duncan the son of Gilchrist MacRae. Donald Gorm of Sleat was clad in mail and his only vulnerable spot was his heel. During the heat of the battle the archer said to the constable in command of the garrison: "You deal with the men and I shall single out the Big Cockerel himself." An arrow from the bow of Duncan Gilchrist MacRae found the heel of Donald Gorm. The wounded chieftain was taken down Loch Alsh to an island near Ardintoul and placed in a hut where he died. The site of the hut where Domhnall Gorm died is still pointed out. In Kintail there is still another and equally interesting variant of the story, as told by Alick Mackenzie of Dornie. When the castle was attacked the garrison consisted of two persons only, an old man and his son. The old man was blind and the son was too weak to draw the bowstring. The son took aim and the old man drew

SCOTS PINE, ARISAIG

the string that sent the fatal arrow into the heel of the doomed chief of Clan Donald. In *The History of the Western Highlands and Isles of Scotland*, published in 1836, Donald Gregory gives a more factual but perhaps less interesting account:

> This fortress was [he writes], at the time, almost destitute of a garrison, and, had the insurgents succeeded in their attempt, a formidable rebellion in the Isles would have been the consequence. But their leader, trusting to the weakness of the garrison, and exposing himself rashly under the walls of the castle, received a wound in the foot from an arrow shot by the constable of the castle, which speedily proved fatal: for, not observing that the arrow was barbed, the enraged chief pulled it out of the wound, by which an artery was severed; and the medical skills of his followers could devise no means of checking the effusion of blood which necessarily followed.

John Finlayson of Driumbuie, Lochalsh was one man who was absolutely steeped in the traditions of Lochalsh and Kintail. It was enchanting to listen to him, for with him the past seemed as living as the present; one could almost see the warriors of long ago, witness their acts of valour and hear the very words they spoke. He told of one time when Macdonell of Glengarry came northwards in an eight-oared galley to despoil Kintail. The wild and beautiful glen to the north-east of the head of Loch Duich is called Crò Chinn t-sàile, the Cattle Fold of Kintail, and there was the burial-ground of the district and heart of the ancestral clan lands. Macdonell came to plunder the Cattle Fold of Kintail, however, and he landed in a place called Loch Beag, Little Loch. The men of Kintail withdrew, probably because they could not muster a force sufficient to resist the reivers. On landing, the Macdonells went to a house, and it was the second house that came their way, and there they found four little boys busily picking the meat off a bone. They slew three of the boys but the fourth escaped. Eventually the reivers returned to their galley and set off for home. The men of Kintail came back and decided to have their revenge. They started building an eight-oared galley in a little dell, which to this day is called Glaic a' bhàta, the Dell of the Boat. When the galley was finished, the Kintail men went southwards to Loch Nevis. As they entered the loch, they saw Macdonell's galley lying at anchor. They approached as quietly and stealthily as they could, and it was a fine, calm day. Macdonell himself sat in the stern of his galley eating bread and cheese. With each mouthful he sang: "I eat this and go on my way to the dark women of the Fold. If we do not get bread, sure it is that we shall get meat."

The Kintail galley drew nearer and nearer, and as soon as it came alongside, four men on the windward side of Macdonell's boat were dead. The stoutest of the Kintail men leapt aboard armed with a battle-axe and surprised the unsuspecting Macdonell.

"Have mercy!" said Macdonell.

"What mercy did you have on my three beardless, yellow-haired little ones whom you did not leave to pick the bone they had in their hands? I will have your head."

Off came Macdonell's head and the men of Kintail brought it home with them and placed it underneath the threshold of the church of Clachan Duich so that all going in and out could trample upon it. Word too was sent to the chieftainess of Kintail, the widow of Mackenzie:

"The head is there and do you come and trample upon it along with us?"

Few places in the Highlands can surpass the district of Loch Alsh and Loch Duich in scenic beauty. The road from Kyle of Lochalsh turns in a semicircle over the hill and emerges on the shores of Loch Alsh at the township of Balmacara. Houses with trim little flower gardens lie along the roadside all the way to Dornie Bridge which spans Loch Long. The road climbs again till one looks down on the Castle of Eilean Donnan. Across Loch Duich is Letterfearn which nestles on the shore of the loch against a green background of wooded slopes. The mountains rise on both sides. The road twists and turns but with every turning one sees the mountains from different angles. At the head of the loch there is a hairpin bend into the Crò of Kintail and then the climb up into Glen Shiel begins. From sea-level there is an ascent of over eight hundred feet. On both sides of the glen there is a series of peaks rising to over three thousand feet. One does not easily forget Glen Shiel.

NATURAL HIGHLAND WOODLAND

LORN AND WEST PERTHSHIRE

LOCH Leven, an arm of Loch Linnhe, serves as the boundary between Nether Lochaber and Lorn, while to the west this enchanting land is washed by the waters of Loch Linnhe and farther south again by the Firth of Lorn between the mainland and the Isle of Mull. North Lorn is a country of magnificent mountains and three beautiful, winding sea lochs, Loch Leven, Loch Creran, and Loch Etive. The main attractions of South Lorn are, of course, the town and environs of Oban.

It is not surprising that Oban has become the most popular holiday resort in the West Highlands and that its population swells to twice the number during the tourist season. Of course, it is the main centre of population in a lovely area and its own situation is most attractive. Oban lies on a beautiful bay sheltered by the island of Kerrera and backed by three steep, wooded hills. Most of the large tourist hotels are on the sea front, while recent housing schemes have extended the boundaries of Oban well into the valleys between the hills. On the central hill above the town stands the noted landmark known as "MacCaig's Folly". MacCaig was an opulent native of Oban, but his project of presenting his birthplace with this huge replica of the Coliseum never reached fruition. From the hill on the which MacCaig's Folly stands there is a glorious view of the hills of Mull to the west and Morvern, Ardgour, and Appin to the north, while away to the east rises the beautiful Ben Cruachan. The view from Pulpit Hill to the south of Oban is equally fine, while the ancient ruins of Dunolly stand guard over the northern entrance to Oban Bay. I have never seen a more beautiful sight than sunset over Morvern as seen from the hills above the town or the sea front itself. On a fine summer evening in the height of the tourist season the Oban sea front is as crowded as Piccadilly Circus. The popular bathing beach, however, is at Ganavan Bay, a sandy shore a couple of miles to the north, and there are few sandy beaches in this part of the coast. Oban is a fishing port and the port for the Hebrides, and hence come farmers and crofters from Uist, Barra, Coll, Tiree, Mull, Lismore and the smaller islands, as well as the whole western mainland, to sell their cattle and sheep at the annual sales. Many young girls from the Hebrides find seasonal work in Oban's tourist hotels. One would imagine that by now there would be little trace of any Highland character about Oban owing to the annual influx of tourists, but strangely enough Oban is much more Gaelic than Inverness or even Stornoway in Lewis, although in recent years the natives of Stornoway have become more alive to their heritage than was formerly the case. There is, however, quite an appreciable difference between Oban in the height of the tourist season and Oban in the dead of winter, even though the place can still be beautiful on clear winter days. Oban has retained a warmth and friendliness which completely belies the contention that tourism is bound to breed a spirit of venal materialism. Strange as it may seem, the friendly and leisurely atmosphere of Oban reminds me of Galway City in the west of Ireland. Oban is much more like Galway than it is like Inverness and it may be because the Gaelic communities are on the west.

The thousands of tourists who visit Iona and Staffa make Oban their centre and heavy traffic is thus assured every year, but there are any amount of other attractive districts within easy reach on the mainland. One of the favourite tours is round by Appin and Glencoe and back by

Loch Etive. One dull August morning I left Oban by train and went to Appin and Glencoe. I travelled with a large party of tourists, for it was the height of the season, and my fellow-travellers were unmistakably English and Cockney industrial workers and their families; within the past few years it can be noticed that very many of those touring the Highlands belong to the working classes as apart from the professional and upper-middle class. No doubt that is due to the higher wages and improved standards of the workers in industry and the like. I did notice that the main topic of interest was not the scenic beauty of the area but the food in the different hotels and boarding-houses in which they stayed. All the way from Oban to Ballachulish they talked and talked about the meals they had had in different places. I doubt very much if they ever looked at Glencoe; they certainly did not care whether they saw Appin or not, and Appin is about the loveliest district in the Highlands. Even the fact that there was a light drizzle of rain could hardly absolve them. However, I must admit in their favour that I did not hear one word about extortionate prices and the filth and slovenliness of Highlanders and Highland guest-houses. That subject was exhausted by writers of travel books in the seventeenth and eighteenth centuries, especially people such as Pennant and MacCulloch. But perhaps the Highlands and Highlanders have changed!

There is a car and pedestrian track over the railway bridge at Connel Ferry but all except rail travellers have to pay toll here. There is no other way of going from Oban to Appin except by sea. There is a wonderful view from the bridge up Loch Etive and to the stately Ben Cruachan and also to the west towards Lismore, Morvern, and Mull. Above Benderloch station there is a vitrified fort known by the very pedantic name "Beregonium". The ancient capital of Scotland was reputed to have been here. Other names in the locality, such as Selma and Lora, are the result of the influence of MacPherson's *Ossian* and can hardly be invested with hoary antiquity. Both road and railway then run along the shores of Loch Creran through Barcaldine, which is rich and heavily wooded with hazel. Loch Creran narrows considerably halfway up and here the ways part. The railway goes over the bridge which spans the narrows, but the road continues round the end of the loch. Going round the head of Loch Creran on an autumn day when the trees are alive with colour is an unforgettable experience. Glen Creran is a beautiful, wooded, lonely glen.

Across the loch is Appin. This area is one of the few strongholds of Scottish Episcopalianism in the west. The Stewarts of Appin were Jacobites all along and must be still. They still tell of the heroism of seven brothers named Livingstone, who rescued the banner of the Stewarts at Culloden and brought it safely back home to Castle Stalker. The walls of the castle are still intact, for it stands on a little island in the bay a short distance from the shore.

The Strath of Appin, which runs westward, from Loch Creran to Loch Laich on Loch Linnhe, is fertile and wooded. It is a well-farmed valley and supports a number of small-holders. There is a famous old inn at Creagan and this place figured during the time of James Stewart of the Glens who was hanged for the killing of Colin Campbell of Glen Ure, an episode now widely known through Robert Louis Stevenson's *Kidnapped*. The unfortunate James Stewart was hanged for a crime he did not commit, while the actual murderer was locked up by his friends and was driven insane by the thought that an innocent man should pay the penalty. The dead body of James Stewart hung on the gallows for a long time at a spot near the present Ballachulish Ferry until, one stormy night, it was taken down and given a Christian burial by those same Livingstone brothers who rescued the banner of the Stewarts on the field of Culloden. After that, the Livingstone brothers had to flee to the Isle of Mull. The interior of the inn at Creagan was attractive and old-fashioned the first time I visited it; the windows were small and the tables and seats narrow and high, while for service one had to ring a massive ship's

LORNE AND WEST PERHSHIRE

bell of burnished brass. At that time it could not have changed much since the days when unfortunate James of the Glens visited it.

The road to the north winds through the woods along the shores of Loch Linnhe till you come to Glen Duror, another lovely, wooded glen. Across the water the hills of Ardgour rise like a serrated rampart against the western sky. Above Duror there is a fine mountain, Beinn a' Bheithir, which sweeps round in the form of a horseshoe and shelters Gleann a' Chaolais, where there is now an extensive forestry plantation, from the storms of the south-west. Here we come to the mouth of Loch Leven and the entrance to the loch is narrow with strong tidal currents. The skill with which the Ballachulish ferrymen pilot their boats to and fro across the channel is almost uncanny. During the tourist season they have their full complement of cars and trucks on every run. The car-ferry saves motorists a journey of several miles around the head of Loch Leven, but for those who have time to spare it is really worth their while to go round by Kinlochleven. The loch is long and narrow, its shores are steep and heavily wooded in places. The village of Kinlochleven was non-existent until the British Aluminium Company established a factory there, utilising water-power from the surrounding hills. I have heard the older genera-tion in Lochaber call the place Kinlochmore, for that was the name of the small township that was there before the arrival of industry. Kinlochleven might be like any other village in the industrial Lowlands except that it is surrounded by wild and high mountains.

But we must return back down the loch to Ballachulish. This is the terminus of the railway line from Connel, and the railway still functions and will until a new, wider, and straighter road is built through Appin. There are slate quarries at Ballachulish, but production has gone down a lot during recent years and the same is true regarding other slate quarries throughout the county of Argyll. Ballachulish, as one might expect, is not a very attractive village, for it is too close to the slate quarries and there are slates everywhere. What one sees at Ballachulish, however, is soon forgotten on reaching Glencoe.

Glencoe is the most famous glen in the Highlands and it is so not only because of its scenery, which is wild and magnificent, but because of its grim history and the memory of a night of dark treachery and bloodshed in February 1692. The Massacre of Glencoe goes down to history as a blot on the name of Campbell and not so much blame is attached to the monarch who signed the order to extripate the luckless Macdonalds. William of Orange was no doubt fully aware of what he was doing when he signed and counter-signed the order to murder old Macdonald and his clan in cold blood, even though the fact that Macdonald had taken the oath of allegiance was concealed from him. The massacre was rather the result of deliberate, planned official policy rather than the outcome of a blood-feud between the Campbells and Macdonalds of Glencoe. The real and unfortunate truth was that the Campbells were no more than tools used by unscrupulous authorities to overawe the Jacobite Highlands. The name of Campbell has been eternally disgraced by the events of that dark February night, not so much because the victims were dispatched without warning but because the time-honoured code of hospitality was outraged. Despite all that, it will surprise many to know that even to this very day in such districts as Keppoch and Moidart, both in the heart of the Macdonald country, popular tradition exonerates the Campbells. In Moidart the story was told that on the night preceding the massacre a Campbell soldier went to visit one of the Macdonald houses. He had been to that same home on several evenings previously, and, as they sat round the fire on the fated night, a greyhound lay sleeping in front of the fire. For a few moments all conversation stopped and the Campbell soldier spoke to the sleeping dog: "O greyhound, if you knew what I know, your bed would be on the heather this night!" No sooner had the visitor gone than the family made for the hills and escaped. Another story had it that a Campbell soldier told the

BEALACH NA BA, LOOKING DOWN TOWARDS LOCH KISHORN

terrible secret to a grey stone. Many of the Macdonalds did escape on the night of the massacre.

I first saw Glencoe on a darkening November evening some years ago. Even if I had not known that it was Glencoe, I would have been awe-stricken, for under such conditions it was exactly the sort of place where terrible things could happen. The mountains on both sides were covered with a dark mist almost half-way down the slopes, and the wind soughed right down the glen. It was desolate, dismal, and frighteningly gloomy, in every respect the scene of a terrible tragedy where one could almost hear the spirits of the dead cry to high heaven for vengeance. I was glad I was not a Campbell but one of their traditional enemies. I next saw Glencoe in the sunlight of an August day. It was awe-inspiring but vivid with light and colour. There was an almost imperceptible sheen of purple and blue on the higher slopes of heather, green stretches of grass alternating with grey tarns down to the very banks of the river, which was fed by numerous streams that cascaded like silver down the steep sides of the mountains. Here and there were the ruins of former dwellings, and I wondered how those who did live there managed to overcome the fear of landslides. To the left towered three fine peaks, Bidan nam Bian and the lesser and greater Buachaille Etive, while the long, high ridge of the Aonach Eagach rose sharply on the right. The road up the glen climbs to a height of over a thousand feet and once we got to the top, the bleak Moor of Rannoch stretched before us. We soon branched off to the left down the winding road that follows the bed of the Etive River. Below us there was a deep gully all the way. At one point the bus-driver took one hand off the wheel and, pointing up to his right, said: "That is Buachaille Etive Mór up there," in his soft western voice, but even the softness of his voice did not prevent a shudder running through the spine of his frightened passengers as they looked at the depth of the gorge on the left of the road. We finally got down to Dalness; this is now a small township of a few houses, although it was a populous hamlet at one time. Apart from a few large houses, mostly shooting-lodges, there are not many signs of habitation in this beautiful glen. It is now too far away from busy thoroughfares and too difficult to access. The road came to an abrupt end at the head of Loch Etive, and we alighted from the bus and boarded a launch which brought us down the loch. By this time it had started to rain again. Along the shores there were some houses but most were derelict and in ruins. There was no trace of a road on either side. We did pass a motor-launch, presumably on its way to one of the lonely farm-houses by the lochside. Nearer and nearer the shapely shoulders of Ben Cruachan loomed through the greyness of the afternoon. We were approaching the turn of the loch and the narrows at Bonawe.

It was here I discovered that all the passengers on the boat were not English. As I stood peering over the railings through the rain and mist, the boat suddenly gave a lurch and a young lady standing next to me was thrown against my shoulder. She begged to be excused, but it was her voice that caught my attention. It was a soft, lilting western one, but not Highland. It was a voice from Kerry and its possessor, a charming young school-teacher, had come to Oban with her friend a couple of days previously. Both of them were school-teachers and had never been to the Highlands before. They had come to Oban in the height of the tourist season and without any advance booking, and accommodation was found for them by the first stranger to whom they had spoken as soon as they stepped off the train. Glencoe and the whole area around Oban had impressed them tremendously, but they were even more impressed by the courtesy and kindliness of the folk of Argyll. Both of them knew Irish-Gaelic well and taught through the medium of that language, and, more interesting still, both were firmly convinced that the Irish language rehabilitation policy would succeed. A great many Irishmen have a very discreditable tendency to pour scorn and ridicule on all efforts to restore Gaelic to its rightful position as the national official language of the Republic. Strangely enough the very worst offenders are the Irish Celtic scholars who are solely interested in the dead bones of Old and Medieval Irish, and are, with few exceptions, shamelessly cynical in their attitude to the living language. Some Irish scholars in their attempt to ridicule the rehabilitation of the language have ventured to assert — without either adequate study or authority — that there is more Gaelic and purer Gaelic in Scotland than in Ireland despite all the efforts of the Irish authorities. That is arrant nonsense. According to recent census figures there were over 500,000 Irish-Gaelic-speakers as opposed to 93,000 Scottish, and anyone who knows the Gaelic-speaking communities in both countries must admit that the Gaelic spoken by the young and middle-aged in a great part of South Galway is purer and better than that of any of the Scottish communities, and the reason is that less English is spoken in Galway and there Gaelic is an obligatory subject in all schools. While the main aim of primary education in the Highlands is the teaching of English and arithmetic, the Gaelic language will have little or no chance unless it becomes a compulsory subject in the curriculum of all schools.

One of the most important events in the Oban year is the Argyllshire Gathering. This function lasts for two days and takes place in the middle of September, when the county families and their guests are on holiday, either grouse-shooting or deer-stalking. Pibroch competitions take place in one of the local halls on the first day and these competitions are generally poorly attended, although a small number of the "country" folk grace them with their presence. The pipers themselves are engineers, mechanics, apprentices or even school-teachers, with an occasional army piper or gentleman's gardener-cum-piper or stalker-cum-piper thrown in. On the second day piping, dancing, and athletic competitions are held in the open-air, in a field specially reserved for the Argyllshire Gathering and used for no other purpose. A special covered enclosure is reserved for "members", namely county families and their friends, and the general public is not admitted. The stand is usually full of sophisticated, painted, and ungainly women with their husbands masquerading in their kilts and plaids and their young sons, home on vacation from school in England, replete with impeccable non-Scottish accents and kilts and shepherd's crooks twice their own size. The county gentlemen invariably act as stewards and officials at the Gathering. On the evening of both days there are Highland Balls for the exclusive enjoyment of the "quality". At a recent gathering I chanced to be in the cocktail-bar of one of the principal Oban hotels when a large party of county folk arrived on their way to the ball. The men were mostly dressed in kilts and some in the regimental evening dress of Highland regiments, and they were, of course, accompanied by their wives and girl-friends. I had the rare opportunity of scrutinising them at close range, and what struck me most was how utterly English they were both in mannerisms and speech. The sober truth is that there is no longer any Scottish or Highland aristocracy and there has not been for a very long time. The real Scotland, however, is to be met with in the Oban pubs on the evenings of the Gathering or in the hotels where the pipers stay, especially the Commercial Hotel which has been the resort of pipers at Oban Games for many long years. Quite exquisite piping may be heard there all night and there also may be seen such well-known figures as Dr John MacInnes of Glenelg, who rose to the very top of his profession and was one of the most distinguished psychiatrists in the industrial midlands of England. There too may be seen the convivial Hebridean gentleman, Donald MacPhee of Nunton, Benbecula, former athlete, dancer, and fiddler, who for the last fifty years has crossed the Minch to attend the Argyllshire Gathering.

Only two main roads lead out of Oban, the one to Connel and Tyndrum and the other to Ardrishaig and Kintyre. The road to Kintyre climbs over the ridge south of the town and ascends again to Kilbride and Kilmore and along the shore of Loch Feochan. This is now a countryside of sea-lochs, hills, and woods and the mountains fall gently away, as Cruachan is really the most southerly of the high peaks of Argyll. All the way to Ardrishaig there is rich, sheltered and very attractive country, a contrast to the wilds of Wester Ross and Sutherland. Kilmelfort and Kilmartin are each at the end of arms of the sea. East of Kilmartin is the southern end of Loch Awe. The loch stretches in a north-easterly direction across the country and maintains an equal breadth almost the whole way, except when an arm runs off to the north-west and, narrowing through the Pass of Brander, brings the waters of Loch Awe into Loch Etive. There was an ancient burial-ground on Inishail, the largest island on the loch, and these burial grounds on islands are commonly met with in the Highlands. There is another on Eilean Munda on Loch Leven.

An old story is associated with the little island of Fraoch Eilean on Loch Awe, but it is a story associated with other districts as well. Fraoch was the most handsome of the whole Gaelic warrior band and Maeve, the Queen, loved him, but that love was not returned for Fraoch loved Maeve's golden-haired daughter. Maeve vowed that, if she could not have Fraoch, no other woman would, not even her own daughter. Maeve feigned illness and said that there was no cure for her unless Fraoch brought her a handful of the red berries that grew on the rowan tree on Fraoch Eilean, and this tree was guarded by a fearsome dragon. Fraoch swam across to the island and while the monster was asleep, plucked the handful of berries and brought them to Maeve. Maeve, however, was not satisfied with that and asked Fraoch to return to the island, uproot the whole tree and bring it to her. Fraoch returned to the island and tore the tree out by the roots but, on his return, the dragon overtook him just on the shore of the loch. There a dire struggle began and although the "young maiden of the white palms" came and gave Fraoch a knife of gold to defend himself, he and the dragon fell side by side on the strand. The central motif is very old and belongs to other nations as well. The same story is also told about an island on Loch Laich in the Ross of Mull and about an island on Loch Freuchie near Amulree in Perthshire. The story of Fraoch appears in an Irish manuscript of the tenth century.

The magnificent ruins of Kilchurn Castle stand right on the water's edge at the northern end of the loch. The castle is said to have been built by Black Duncan Campbell, Knight of Lochow, who took part in the Crusades. The stonework is remarkably well preserved and the whole structure is imposing to this very day. Tradition has it that the castle was last occupied by Hanoverian troops during the "Forty-five".

Both road and rail run from Loch Etiveside through the narrow Pass of Brander. The arm of the loch gradually narrows until it becomes a swift steam flowing westwards into Loch Etive. The steep defile is one of the most impressive in Argyll. Ben Cruachan rises to the north and the ground rises rapidly all the way until one enters Glen Strae. A couple of miles onwards is the entrance to Glen Orchy, but before you reach Dalmally there is a road branching to the south-west along the side of Loch Awe. It then veers to the south and rises over the brow of the hill and descends again into Glen Aray. The glen is wooded and deserted and there are few dwellings to be seen until one passes the castle of Inveraray, the seat of the Duke of Argyll. The village of Inveraray cannot have changed very much for the last century. It is quiet and pretty. Both sides of Loch Fyne are green, rich, and wooded. One hardly gets the impression that here is an arm of the sea. A couple of miles north of Inveraray is the old castle of Dundarave. It is still inhabited but it looks like a relic from the seventeenth century. It was once the seat of the Macnaughtons, a powerful clan away back in the time of Robert the Bruce. The road to the south winds round the head of the loch and up Glen Kinglas and over the Rest and be Thankful to Loch Long and Arrochar and takes us out of the Highlands proper.

Let us retrace out steps to Dalmally and notice a monument on a hill to our right before we

CROFT AT TALMINE, SUTHERLAND

come to the village. The monument was erected to the memory of the Gaelic poet Duncan Ban MacIntyre. Duncan Ban was born in Glen Orchy and fought on the Hanoverian side at the battle of Falkirk. He composed two songs about the battle and does not disguise his glee in having been on the losing side. One of his songs especially left no doubt as to where his sympathies lay, for he deplores the fact that all the Highland clans did not band together as there is no longer any respect for the sons of Scotia now that Charles Edward is gone, nothing but the triumphant crowning of the Prince will give him solace. A couple of miles east of Dalmally a narrow road branches off the main highway which continues through Glen Lochy and into Perthshire and Tyndrum. This narrow road goes into Glen Orchy and winds its way for miles along the course of the River Orchy. The glen is beautiful, but I have seen it only once, in the sunshine of a short December day. It is a much richer and more colourful glen than the bleak Glen Lochy which, unfortunately, many more tourists and travellers see now. Even in December there was still a vestige of green along the banks of the river and the higher ground was a profusion of browns, ranging from light to deep russet. There was only a thin veneer of snow on the mountain-tops, but the waters of the river and the myriad of streams that joined it were silvery and sparkling in the winter's sunshine. Bright winter days in the Highlands can be lovely, and that morning in Glen Orchy will long remain fixed in my memory. We passed one or two very lonely farms, no doubt they were prosperous sheep farms, but a great deal of the glen must have been cultivated at one time and have supported a much larger population than now. At length we got to the top of the glen and came within sight of Ben Dobhrain with its smooth slopes towering to the height of over three thousand five hundred feet. To some Highlanders there may be mountains more beautiful than Ben Dobhrain, but to the vast majority it is the most renowned, renowned because of Duncan Ban MacIntyre's song in praise of it. Duncan was unlettered but composed some delightful poetry in praise of the beauties of nature and the joys of the chase. His latter days were spent in Edinburgh, but before his death he returned to climb Ben Dobhrain for the last time. On that occasion he composed a touching song bidding a last farewell to the mountains. I have seen Ben Dobhrain with a deep coating of winter snow and I have seen it in the mist and rain of an autumn afternoon; I have seen it in the sunshine of an early June morning and have seen it also lit by the rays of a setting July sun, and it is always the same majestic Ben Dobhrain. The winter's sunshine had gone and given place to the greyness of twilight that last day I saw it. Close to the foot of the ben we joined the Glencoe road and turned southwards to Tyndrum and the county of Perth.

Perthshire is Scotland's most central county and is on the southern fringe of the Highlands. Stirling is known as the "gateway to the Highlands", but I should imagine that there are two gateways, one at Callander and the other at Dunkeld in Perthshire. Much more seems to have been written about Perthshire than any of the other Highland counties. In any case it was more accessible than the more northerly and westerly counties in the days when travel was not as easy as it is now. Loch Katrine and the Trossachs are within easy reach of the industrial midlands and draw thousands of tourists and trippers during the holiday season. Sir Walter Scott's value as publicity agent will be felt for a long time yet. I saw Loch Katrine and the Trossachs once and only once, but it was not in the height of the tourist season but on a cold day towards the end of December. I got as far as the pier at the eastern end of Loch Katrine. There was a little pleasure steamer tied up at the pier. It seemed so rain-drenched and forlorn. There was not a soul to be seen. I looked out towards Ellen's Isle but saw neither the Lady of the Lake nor any other lady. All I did see was the rain dropping on the still waters of the loch. Ben An to the right and Ben Venue to the left were both very impressive and seemed to hide the greater part of the sky. There seemed to be so much of wood, loch, and mountain within a small area. In summer it must be lovely, but its grandeur is on a much smaller scale than that of Glencoe or Glenshiel. Loch Achray and Loch Vennachar are almost a continuation eastwards of Loch Katrine. At the eastern end of Loch Vennachar is Coilantogle and there one can still see the ford that has been made immortal by Scott's "Lady of the Lake".

A couple of miles west of Callander is the Pass of Leny and it is here one really enters the Highlands. The defile is narrow, steep, and heavily wooded and there is a lovely waterfall just beside the roadway. There is just enough breadth in the Pass of Leny to allow the road and railway to go through side by side. Once through the pass, road and railway part, the road along the eastern shore and railway along the western shore of lovely Loch Lubnaig. Loch Lubnaig is one of the most beautiful lochs in Perthshire. It is set in a deeply wooded glen and in its calm, dark waters there always seems to be the reflection of the hills on both sides. It is a favourite spot for trippers in summer. At the northern end of the loch is Strathyre and a bonnie strath it it too. Most Scots, even if they have never seen the strath, have heard about its beauty because of the popular song "Bonnie Strathyre". A couple of miles to the north and on our left is Balquhidder and Loch Voil beyond it. There is a stretch of very low ground between the end of the loch and the railway line. In periods of heavy rain and flooding it can be completely submerged. In the churchyard of Balquhidder there is the grave of Rob Roy MacGregor. Gaelic is still spoken on the Braes of Balquhidder and this must be about the most southerly outpost of the language now. There is a profusion of beautiful place-names around Loch Voil, and even in their anglicized form they sound well: Lochlarig, Ardcarnaig, Monachylemore, Craigruie, Murlagan, Stronvar, Achleskine, and Stronslaney. I am sure that only very few people in Balquhidder now know what all these names mean. No doubt Rob Roy knew the meaning of them all.

A little to the north of Balquhidder, Loch Earn comes into view. It is a long and almost of uniform breadth all the way. There is a very popular hotel at Lochearnhead, owned by Ewan Cameron, a noted Highland athlete and massive figure of a man. Within recent years his hotel has become a centre for pony-trekking and water-skiing. From Lochearnhead there is a steep climb up Glen Ogle, which is a bare and uninteresting glen. Glen Dochart, however, is pretty in places, especially towards the western end around Loch Dochart and Loch Iubhair. There are ruins of a castle on a little island on Loch Dochart. A mile west of Luib station there still stands the solitary gable-end of a house occupied at one time by Rob Roy MacGregor. The eastern half of the glen is richer and there are good farms all along the valley till one reaches the long and winding Loch Tay.

We are now in the lands of Breadalbane, which stretch from Tyndrum in the west along the Tay valley eastwards to beyond Aberfeldy. This is now Campbell country, but it was once the land of the MacGregors, MacNabs, Maclarens and other smaller clans elbowed out by the shrewd, grasping, and unscrupulous seed of Diarmid, the most Gaelic and — strangely enough — the most opportunist and fortunate of all Highland clans. The Campbells always contrived to be on the winning side, although in fairness to the first Campbell Earl of Breadalbane it must be said that he departed from tradition by joining the Jacobites in the "Fifteen". During the last century there were particularly ruthless and brutal "Clearances" on the Breadalbane estates. But dispossession was no new thing in this area; from as early as the middle of the sixteenth century the MacGregors were driven from their lands in Glenorchy. Of all Highland clans the MacGregors have the most tragic history.

Strathtay really begins at Kenmore at the eastern end of the loch and runs east until the Tay is joined by the Tummel, where the river then runs south to Dunkeld. Not far east of Kenmore the Tay is joined by the Lyon. Aberfeldy is the largest centre of population in this area and the village lies on a green expanse where the river flows round almost in a semi-circle. There is a road to the south that climbs up the ridge of hills to Glen Cochill and Amulree and then drives down the Sma Glen to Crieff. This road is well worth following, as it passes through a wild but lovely district. Glen Almond is particularly beautiful. The road from Aberfeldy to Logierait passes through the rich and fertile Grandtully and at Logierait the Tay meets the Tummel and turns south. The whole river-valley to Dunkeld is very lovely. The ground on the banks of the river is low and rich and on both sides the slopes rise gently and are heavily wooded in places. The valley narrows as one approaches Dunkeld and the slopes rise more steeply. Dunkeld itself is in an idyllic situation. Here there is a very fine old cathedral. Dunkeld was a very important ecclesiastical centre in early Scotland. The railway line to Badenoch and Inverness passes through Dunkeld and we may follow it northwards for a space. The valley of the Tummel is of much the same pattern as the lower Tay valley. Pitlochry is again, like Dunkeld, in an ideal situation and it attracts a large number of visitors during the season. Here there is a very flourishing theatre. North of Pitlochry the Tummel is joined by the Garry, which comes down through the Pass of Killiecrankie. To the west is Loch Tummel, reputed by travellers of the last century to be the most beautiful loch in the Highlands. Loch Rannoch and Loch Tummel are in one straight line. The southern shore of Loch Rannoch is very heavily wooded. From Queen's View, not far from Fincastle, one can see how lovely Loch Tummel really is. The wooded slopes rise gently on both sides and away to the west is Schiehallion with its shoulders rising gradually and symmetrically to the summit. At all times of the year, but especially in late spring and autumn, the prospect from the Queen's View is thrilling. Nevertheless, I consider that Loch Tummel lacks the grandeur of Loch Shiel.

Two miles north of the junction of the Tummel and Garry is the Pass of Killiecrankie. It was here that the Highlanders under "Bonnie" Dundee completely routed the Williamite army under the command of the Gaelic-speaking General Hugh MacKay of Scourie, a soldier of Continental experience. It was late in the evening of 27 July 1689, that Dundee made his advance, but the battle was over in a few minutes and Dundee himself fell mortally wounded in the hour of victory. To the Highlanders Dundee was known as Iain Dubh nan Cath, Black John of the Battles, and it was his personality and good looks as well as the espousal of the cause of the old Scottish dynasty that brought the Macdonalds, the Camerons, and the Stewarts to his standard. Cameron of Lochiel led his clansmen to Dundee's colours, while his own second son was a captain in MacKay's army. Dundee's campaign was the first of the series of armed attempts to put the Stuarts back on the throne and it is a strange coincidence that the leaders of the first and last attempt should have had a common attribute, "Bonnie" Dundee and "Bonnie" Prince Charles.

From Killiecrankie northwards the valley of the Garry is narrower and less fertile than that of the Tummel until one reaches Blair Atholl. A little beyond the village of Blair Atholl can be seen the stately ducal seat, partially hidden by trees. Since I wrote the earlier chapters of this book, James Stewart Murray, the Gaelic-speaking Duke of Atholl, has passed away. I doubt if his young successor speaks Gaelic. Montrose is now Scotland's only Gaelic-speaking duke. From Blair Atholl northwards the country is wilder and higher until one reaches Drumochter and crosses into Badenoch.

I now return to Aberfeldy and cross the River Tay and bear to the left towards Fortingal. The most remarkable feature of Fortingal is the very ancient yew tree of immense girth that still stands and which must be almost two thousand years old. My old and revered teacher, the late Professor W. J. Watson, maintained that the tree was a sacred one and the scene of pagan ceremonies and, as soon as Christianity came, a church was built beside the yew to convert the pagan site into a Christian one. Just beside the road at Fortingal there are very picturesque thatched houses. They are large and two-storeyed and appear closer to the English than West Highland type. They have a heavy covering of thatch. A short distance west of the village is the pass leading into Glen Lyon.

It was on Christmas Day a year or two ago that I first saw Glen Lyon and, although I have not seen the glen at its best, I must confess that there is hardly any glen in all the Highlands to equal it. The leafless trees and swift waters of the river were lit by rays of winter sunshine as we came through the Pass of Lyon and the summits of Cairn Mairg and Cairn Gorm were covered with a heavy pall of white and motionless mist. The road winds up the glen as it has to follow the course of the river. At intervals along the way there were farms, but sheep farms mostly as the soil here is vastly different from what it is lower down in Strathtay. We stopped for a short time at Bridge of Balgie. Here there is a road to the left over the river and across the hills down to the side of Loch Tay. We were not going that way, for we had decided to go as far up the glen as the road would permit. At Bridge of Balgie we called to see the district nurse, Nurse Sutherland from Unst, whom I had met in Shetland the previous summer. Like all Shetlanders, Nurse Sutherland was extremely generous and hospitable. My friends and I must have spilt a fair amount of whisky on her carpet, for she had filled our glasses too unsparingly. It was not the least bit lonely in the glen in wintertime, she said, for there was always plenty to do and plenty of social life. Occasionally they went down to Aberfeldy to do their shopping, but delivery-vans always came up the glen when weather and road conditions permitted.

Darkness was falling when we left Bridge of Balgie and we had still many miles to go to Invermeran at the top of the glen. The glen seems to widen out as you go farther west and it became wilder and barer. At one point our car had to ford a stream, for there was no bridge and the surface was such as to make progress rather slow. The Hydro-Electric Board was building a dam near Loch Lyon and there were cranes, crushers, and ramshackle sheds all over the place. We got safely past and reached the house we had intended to visit, the house of a keeper and deer-stalker, who had spent the greater part of his life in Glen Lyon. We were very hospitably received by Mr Maclaren and his family and it was late in the evening when we decided to leave. We were told that the Hydro-Electric Board had made a new road southwards and that it would bring us to Lochearnhead. We found the road and it led us over the hills and down into a deep valley. The night was pitch black and the lights of our car were bad. We had no idea where we were. We were following the course of a river, and when we got well down into the valley, there was a large house by the roadside with lights shining brightly from all its windows. Outside there was a sign telling that it was the Bridge of Lochay Hotel. In I went and the first person I met was little John Maclean from Benbecula, whom I knew well from the Outer Isles. I asked where I was and my astonished clansman told me that I was about a mile from Killin. We had come down Glen Lochay and were now right beside Loch Tay. John Maclean worked as bartender in the hotel. It was Christmas night and the public bar was crowded and noisy.

I had always wanted to see Glen Lyon, for I associated it with Clan Gregor, the "Children of the mist and sorrows". The MacGregors claimed Glenorchy, Glenstrae, and Glen Lyon as their ancestral lands, but as early as the year 1432 Glenorchy had come into the clutches of Campbell of Lochow and a son of the Lochow family became the first Campbell Laird. In the early years of next century Glen Lyon was to become the property of the Glenorchy Campbells by charter, and in 1560 they acquired superiority over Glenstrae. The MacGregors had to scatter far and wide and find land where they could. They still had their chiefs but these chiefs were in reality leaders of landless and broken men. The "broken men" earned a reputation for lawlessness, whether deservedly or otherwise, and by an Act of Parliament the MacGregor chiefs had to produce hostages as a surety for the good conduct of their clansmen and these hostages had to be relieved quarterly. Archibald, seventh Earl of Argyll was granted control over Clan Gregor by the Privy Council because their chief had failed to replace his hostages. On the instigation of Argyll, the MacGregors attacked Colquhoun of Luss and James VI of Scotland commissioned Colquhoun to deal with them. In February 1603 the MacGregors completely routed the Colquhouns at Glen Fruin, not far from Dumbarton. The Government decided to wipe out the Clan Gregor and the crafty Argyll received a commission to carry the decision into effect. Even their very name was proscribed, their chief was executed, eighteen of his principal clansmen drawn and quartered, they were prohibited from carrying weapons except pointless knives, or from meeting together more than four at a time. They became outlaws, the fines amounted to something quite considerable and, incidentally, they found their way into the pockets of Argyll, who generously proposed that a proportion should be paid to the King of Scotland and, by this time, of England. Despite all this the Clan Gregor survived and a considerable body of them took part in the campaign of Montrose and a century later in the army of Charles Edward. It was indeed a strange way of showing their ingratitude to the memory of the first occupant of the throne of the United Kingdom.

A wealth of tradition has sprung up around the unfortunate Clan Gregor. Macdonell of Tirandrish in Lochaber sheltered seven MacGregors for many years. Finally he became so afraid of incurring the ire of the authorities and a ruinous fine that he had them dispatched. In a spot about a mile east of Spean Bridge and right on the banks of the river there are, or were, seven pine trees to mark the graves of the MacGregors. Some of the trees were recently cut down, much to the annoyance of the older people in the area. The pine was the emblem of Clan Gregor. Almost all Highland Gaels know the three lovely songs about Clan Gregor; the poignant lament of the widow of Gregor Roy MacGregor, who was beheaded at Taymouth in 1570; the song of Clan Gregor and the song to MacGregor of Roro in Glen Lyon. In all these songs there is stark intensity and sincerity and burning words have been wedded to wistful and enchanting melodies. To MacGregor of Roro, "whose heritage it was to be in Glen Lyon", the advice is given:

When you go to the tavern, drink only one drink. Drink your dram without sitting and be attentive to your men. Spurn not any vessel but accept even a ladle or baler. Turn winter into autumn and stormy spring into summer. Make your bed among the crags and let your sleep be light. Though rare is the squirrel, a way can be found to capture it. Noble as is the hawk, often it is caught by stealth.